The Image of Australia

The Image of Australia

British Perception of the Australian Economy from the Eighteenth to the Twentieth Century

Craufurd D. W. Goodwin

Number 42 in a series published for the
Duke University Commonwealth-Studies Center
Duke University Press, Durham, N.C.
1974

LCC number 73–81711
ISBN 0–8223–0310–8

Printed in the United States of America by
Kingsport Press, Inc., Kingsport, Tennessee

Preface

My obligations are many to friends, colleagues, and a variety of organizations for assistance with this project. The research was begun while I was a Guggenheim Fellow and Smuts Visiting Fellow at Cambridge University in 1967–1968. I am grateful to the Managers of the Smuts Memorial Fund and to the John Simon Guggenheim Memorial Foundation for their support. Part of the manuscript was prepared at the Villa Serbelloni with kind hospitality from the Rockefeller Foundation. The Duke University Research Council has assisted with travel and other support. The bulk of Chapter 2 was published as an article in the *Journal of Economic History* and is reprinted here with permission.

The willing and efficient cooperation of a large number of libraries has made this book possible. In particular, I thank the William R. Perkins Library of Duke University, the University Library and Marshall Library of the University of Cambridge, the Library of the Royal Commonwealth Society, London, and the National Library, Canberra. For identification of contributors to several periodicals, I have used the exceptionally valuable *Wellesley Index to Victorian Periodicals 1824–1900*, ed. W. E. Houghton (Toronto, 1966).

Several persons have kindly read early drafts of this manuscript and have made valuable suggestions. I want especially to thank Messrs. Roger Joyce of the University of Queensland, A. W. Coats of the University of Nottingham, Warren Samuels of Michigan State University, and Neville Cain of the Australian National University. Because I did not follow all of their advice, as well as for other reasons, they are absolved of responsibility. Nancy Hutchinson and Jan Hall, students at Duke University, took on the agonizing task of checking references. Finally, my deep appreciation goes to Mrs. Dorothy Moore who, with supreme good humor, has struggled through the typing of bushels of notes and manuscript.

C. D. W. G.

Contents

Introduction

This book grew out of several earlier research projects. Studies I have carried out on the development of economic thought in Canada, Australia, the British West Indies, and British West Africa indicated to me that economists in these "developing" countries were deeply influenced by economic analysis and opinion in the imperial metropolis of Great Britain.[1] Consequently, my curiosity was raised about how British writers actually saw and understood economic institutions and events in the countries of the Empire-Commonwealth. A preliminary survey showed that the relevant literature was enormous. For example, the volume of writings in Britain about economic affairs in either India or the West Indies alone was daunting. A pilot project of manageable proportions seemed in order, and a combination of factors led to the selection of "the British image of the Australian economy."

Perhaps of greatest importance was the circumstance that relative to the literature on some other colonies, British writings on Australia were manageable in size and could be conveniently defined both in time and space. Moreover, the relationship between these two countries in comparison to that between many other metropolitan and colonial regions was relatively unencumbered by complexities of sharp linguistic, religious, or cultural difference. British interest in the Australian economy (rather than

1. *Canadian Economic Thought* (Durham, 1961); *Economic Enquiry in Australia* (Durham, 1966); "Economic Analysis and Development in British West Africa," *Economic Development and Cultural Change*, XV (1967), 438–51; "Economic Ideas in the Development of Jamaica," in C. D. Goodwin and I. B. Holley, eds., *The Transfer of Ideas* (Durham, 1968), pp. 138–69; and "The Transfer of Economic Ideas in the Commonwealth," in R. S. Smith and F. T. de Vyver, eds., *Economic Systems and Public Policy: Essays in Honor of Calvin Bryce Hoover* (Durham, 1966), pp. 252–74.

in the possibility of an Australian economy—manifested by the early explorers) began late in the eighteenth century and has continued to the present time. Britain has been Australia's only colonizing power, and even after full Australian political autonomy, economic links remain close. Of particular significance for the content of British thought about Australia was the extended period over which British writers perceived great economic value in the new land. Moreover, a number of dramatic features of the continent's development, including convicts, gold, and advanced democratic institutions, sustained a high degree of interest.

The objective of the book stated in the most simple terms is to understand how literate Britons perceived the form and operation of the Australian economic system and activity within it. Emphasis is placed upon the *general* perception; numerous examples may be cited of departures from the norm. Individuals, and even entire categories of persons, held special views; for example, select groups of civil servants often were exceptional cases, as were colonial agents. Moreover, specialists on particular aspects of the economy—merchants, bankers, brokers, sea captains, etc.—had bodies of knowledge on particular industries or events which are not dealt with in this study. It is hoped that a perspective on such exceptional persons may be gained from an appreciation of the wider picture.

This examination was carried out with certain questions firmly in mind, and it may be helpful for the reader to know these at the outset. They include the following: How was information about the Australian economy brought to Great Britain? What were the stimuli for inquiry? How was information given form and meaning by the interpreters? and, What were the bodies of social and economic theory which were brought to bear on the subject? What did observers see or think they saw in Australian society, and what did they convey to their audience? Related work in several other disciplines was helpful in pointing out where answers to these questions might lie.

If terminology from psychology is used, much of the material examined in this book may be placed in two categories. In the first, description of the Australian economy by travelers and by Australian natives themselves can be said to reflect direct "perception" of conditions and events. To the extent that authors reproduced faithfully their reactions to stimuli this literature is evidence of direct sensory "percepts." In the second category, discussion of the Australian economy by persons who had no direct or current experience with it can be described as reflecting "mental imagery."[2] The distinction between percept and image is, of course, neither simple nor unambiguous. Psychological studies reveal how easy it is, even in simple controlled experiments, for a subject to mistake an image for a percept, while the authors dealt with in this study worked in real-life complexity.

The psychology of mental imagery is concerned mainly with understanding sensual reactions to relatively simple stimuli by individual human beings, for example, a person seeing or imagining a single object or scene. The material of this study is far less rigorous than is the evidence of such straightforward experiences. It consists of reports by many persons of percepts and images of all or part of an economic system expressed in literary terms under uncontrolled conditions. Psychological concepts applied to this material have only analogical significance. Nevertheless, psychological theory is useful to suggest information which should receive close attention, and possible relationships which might be explored. For example, the reports of visitors to Australia which were prepared on the voyage home or shortly thereafter may reflect a phenomenon quite analogous to the afterimage, which follows directly upon a percept.[3]

The state of psychological research on "memory imagery" and "imagination imagery" is still relatively primitive, but it holds out hope of being even more suggestive for historical inquiries of this type. Imagination imagery appears to be least subject to self-control and most dependent on external stimuli. "It is of central origin but it is possible that some of its vividness and lack of con-

2. Allan Richardson, *Mental Imagery* (New York, 1969), pp. 2–3. For information about the psychological literature concerning mental imagery I depend heavily upon this work.

3. Richardson, pp. 15–16.

trollability is due to the spontaneous and ambiguous events occurring in the sense organs themselves."[4] The memory image, on the other hand, "involves a process of *reconstruction* and not the *reviving* or 're-excitation of innumerable fixed, lifeless and fragmentary traces.'" What external conditions affect the reconstruction of memory fragments to produce images is one general question underlying this study. In general it appears that the human mind depends on formulae and various similar devices to remember and make sense of stored information, such as for example numerical rules with respect to dates and times. The evidence below suggests that social theory, as one element in the cognitive process, may perform a similar function by aiding in the sorting and retrieval of material concerning an economic system.

In the relationship of images to problem solving, the evidence of the psychologists seems to be of most direct relevance. As Professor Allan Richardson reports: "Imageless thought most often accompanies the solution of routine tasks. As in perception and memory we utilize familiar knowledge for familiar purposes in familiar situations without being aware of it. Images of a concrete quasi-sensory type or of a verbal auditory-motor type are more likely to form when some barrier to further thought is encountered and the solution is not immediately available."[5] The situation of observers in one country watching and attempting to understand the economy of another, often with urgent policy problems before them, would seem to contain the twin conditions for image building—unfamiliar situation and barriers to further thought.

The conditions which affect perception appear to be almost as complicated as those which affect imagery; they include "our transitory moods, expectations, and needs and other motivational states" as well as education and national origin. "We know that in learning to perceive and to recognize objects and events in the outside world (and the inside world) we build up categories and schemes that systematically bias our experience of the real

4. Richardson, p. 128.
5. Richardson, p. 81.

world."[6] Inkblot tests reveal situations where imagery and perception virtually come together. Subjects are found to refer blots to a variety of mental images until they find one which "fits," and the hitherto formless mass then takes on shape and significance not only for themselves but for their audience. In some cases where certain images have been especially strong, sufficiently high expectational levels are generated to cause subjects to perceive parts of a scene which are consistent with the image but are not in fact there at all. In such cases the image has clearly determined perception itself.

Social scientists as well as psychologists have attempted to develop the theory of images. Professor Kenneth Boulding has suggested helpful terminological advances in the field, and he has speculated about the fundamental role of images throughout society. He thinks of humans as possessing an "inventory" of images which are constantly being replaced and supplemented. Messages may either add to, clarify, or introduce doubt and uncertainty into an image. In some cataclysmic cases a message may bring about the radical "reorganization" of an image: "a message hits some sort of nucleus or supporting structure in the image, and the whole thing changes in a quite radical way."[7] Usually receivers simply reject messages which conflict with prevailing images; "then one day we receive a message which overthrows our previous image and we revise it completely." The message senders in such cases are crucial and unusual: "To a very large extent change in the image comes about through the impact on society of unusually creative, charismatic, or prophetic individuals."[8] Among the conditions which will affect an image's stability and resistance to change, Professor Boulding stresses internal consistency; at the same time he concludes that "image reorganization" may be a process which is as inscrutable as genetic mutation.

In the study of international relations political scientists have explored the significance of images for national behavior, espe-

6. Richardson, p. 142.
7. Kenneth Boulding, *The Image* (Ann Arbor, 1961), p. 8.
8. Ibid., p. 75.

cially at times of crisis. This literature refers to senders and receivers of messages, and it distinguishes between on the one hand "signals" which are "statements or actions the meanings of which are established by tacit or explicit understandings among the actors" and "are issued mainly to influence the receiver's image of the sender," and on the other hand "indices" which are "statements or actions that carry some inherent evidence that the image projected is correct because they are believed to be inextricably linked to the actor's capabilities or intentions." Indices, in contrast to signals, are "beyond the ability of the actor to contrive for the purpose of projecting a misleading image." Looked at in another way, "behavior that is felt to be too important or costly in its own right to be used for other ends [i.e., as a signal] is an index, and such behavior tends to make the greatest impact on observers."[9] The study of international economic images viewed in this way would appear to be concerned mainly with the perception and interpretation of indices, such as aggregate economic performance—but not entirely. Enunciation of an image may lead to the broadcast of signals, as in the defensive reaction of a country which believes it has been maligned. Moreover, a country dependent on close relations with another will send image-affecting signals in the form of pronouncements from political leaders or messages via diplomatic channels.

Historians such as Daniel Boorstin and Philip Curtin have done important work on international image formation, but have not developed any distinctive body of theory or methodology comparable to that of the psychologists and political scientists through which to deal with the topic systematically.[10]

The various strands of aggregate international image formation cannot be isolated easily. Social, political, religious, strategic, and even biological images are important and are usually bound up with economic elements. An important factor in determining relative weights among the several images seems to be the signifi-

9. See Robert Jervis, *The Logic of Images in International Relations* (Princeton, 1970), pp. 18–40.
10. Daniel J. Boorstin, *America and the Image of Europe* (New York, 1960); *idem*, *The Image; or What Happened to the American Dream* (New York, 1962); Philip D. Curtin, *The Image of Africa* (Madison, 1964).

cance a society attaches to various aspects of its own affairs and affairs of others, what Professor Boulding calls "value scales." In Africa today, to take a current example, racial questions have a premier place in the consciousness both of the intellectuals and the mass of the people; consequently, the overall image of other nations among Africans is affected significantly by the condition of race relations in these countries—or rather the appearance of these relations. Economic affairs are distinctly secondary. In Britain, on the other hand, since the time of Adam Smith economic affairs have had correspondingly great prominence as a criterion for judging both domestic affairs and the performance of societies abroad. As a result, economic images have been of exceptional importance.

The social scientist, the economist in particular, has affected the formation of international economic images in at least three ways. First, he has identified what information is important either directly or vicariously for the receiver of the image. The economist informs both the layman and his own professional colleagues that different variables are worth watching carefully; these may be levels of output, employment and trade, marriage age, land tax rates, price changes, or almost anything else. By formulating a body of theory which need not be understood outside the profession, the economist defines the elements in society which should be significant for any viewer—lay or professional—for explaining and predicting behavior. By defining self-interest the economist also effectively directs attention toward some matters rather than others and in this way shapes the parameters of perception.

Second, the economist through the construction of models establishes performance norms for particular economic systems. He prescribes how an economy could operate given certain conditions and implicitly thereby establishes how it should behave and the background conditions it should attempt to introduce. He shows how a "healthy" economy will have, say(full employment, price stability, a growing export trade, advanced technology, or whatever, and his reader is quick to reach the conclusion that economies without these characteristics are unhealthy, decadent, or backward. Very much in the manner of a cybernetic control device, humans refer messages received to the behavior norms which have been established, and then strive to attain consistency by use of outgoing messages. Incoming messages inconsistent with a prevailing image are liable to bring about change either in the circumstances which gave rise to them or in the image itself. The most stable images and circumstances are those which do not have feedback messages with which to cope.

The third way in which economists have influenced image formation is by arranging for the collection and presentation of certain types of data rather than others. At least since the eighteenth century, economists have prescribed what information is important about an economic system and have effectively persuaded governments and private agencies to collect and make this information available. Inevitably, images must be constructed of what material is at hand. In situations where there has been a metropolitan relationship among nations, as between Britain and its colonies, social scientists at the center have usually established the standards and criteria for data collection at the periphery and therefore have determined what raw material will be gathered for constructing images of the colonies. This third channel of influence is related to but distinct from the first, which involves identifying *what* information is important. Here the consideration is *making available* certain types of information rather than others.

The relationship between economic science and international images takes effect at several levels and is reflected in different bodies of written material. The highest level is the plane of scientific inquiry where the implication of contemporary economic theory for international appraisals is expressed directly or indirectly in the professional literature. The second level is the open comment of professional economists about other nations, which may or may not follow directly from the corpus of theory. This level is observed usually in semiprofessional literature such as the generalist monthlies and weeklies. The third level is nonprofessional social commentary which draws to some extent upon professional economics but is expressed in non-technical terms in books, magazines, the newspapers and other mass media. Finally, there is a reverse or feedback effect from the formalized images of foreign areas upon the development of economic theory—the doctrine from which these images in part sprang. In this study three types of data are found to be most useful in understanding British perception of the Australian economy: first, the views of economists who wrote directly about the country and were read in Britain; second, discussion of Australian economic events by non-economists—observers and general commentators; and third, examples of the impact of the first two types of literature upon the ideas of the average educated man. I have examined economic discussion wherever it could be found: in books, pamphlets, periodicals, professional and learned societies, and government publications. More attention was paid to serious analytical discussion than to random comment, but both were taken into account. Items which seemed likely to yield the highest returns in terms of economic comment received most attention. These included, in particular, the organs of professional economists, such as the publications of the British Association, the Royal Statistical Society, and the Royal Economic Society; the semiprofessional London *Economist*; and the principal generalist periodicals in which economists and their followers presented interpretations for policy of theoretical doctrines. Newspapers were consulted only selectively for specific purposes. "Second," "third," "fourth," and even "fifth" levels of research material which were not examined systematically include the daily and weekly press (of smaller centers as well as London); debates in Parliament; the private comments of observers found in manuscript form; and discussions of Australia in professional groups made up of bankers, merchants, insurance agents, and trade unionists.

Since one major purpose of this study is to understand the views of persons familiar with economic principles, the type of literature examined changes over time as these principles became more complex. Toward the end of the nineteenth century, concentration upon generalist periodicals gives way to a focus on professional journals, where, increasingly, formal economic opinion found expression.

Even though the coverage of this book is *British* perception of the Australian economy, not all the authors examined are British; non-British writers are included if their works were influential in Britain. In fact a significant proportion of the relevant writers were Australian residents or natives; these together with such men as Paul Blouet, a Frenchman, and Baron Hübner, an Austrian, are presented as molders of British perception rather than as representatives of it.

This book contains a bias towards middle-class views, both because these more than those of the "lower classes" were reflected in relatively well-reasoned and disciplined discussion, and also because they have been preserved most effectively in the literature. In a sense, then, this is a study of the image and perception of a subculture rather than the totality of British society. Moreover, with its focus principally on economic affairs, the work may suggest attitudes toward Australia by such writers as Dilke or Trollope which did not apply in all matters. The emphasis here is steadily on economic thought, and if a writer tempered a criticism of tariffs or land policy with a favorable comment on cricket or flowers, the two are not given equal time. A wide range of special studies either with broader focus on public opinion or concentration on a single man should be consulted by the reader.[11]

The attention given to different time spans in the study is uneven; in particular the last half of the nineteenth century receives disproportionate space. The main reason for this allocation of effort is that over time the literature under examination fluctuated widely in volume and in significance. Certain periods, such as the 1850's and the 1890's, which were major turning points in the formation of British perception receive more detailed analyses than decades in which views were firmly established and the pace of change was slow. As raw material for illumination of human images and perception, the literature is often far from perfect; but it is all we have.

No direct attempt has been made in this work to assess the

11. E.g., Werner P. Friederich, *Australia in Western Imaginative Prose Writings, 1600–1960* (Chapel Hill, 1967); Joseph Jones, ed., *Image of Australia*, issue of *Texas Quarterly*, V (1962); S. B. Lijegren, *Aspects of Australia in Contemporary Literature* (Upsala and Copenhagen, 1962); Anthony Trollope, *Australia*, ed. P. D. Edwards and R. B. Joyce (Brisbane, 1967).

significance of British attitudes for the course of Australian history. However, it is at least plausible to speculate that the effects were substantial. For example, the image of Australia may have affected outward flows from Britain of capital and labor both in volume and in type. To mention only one probable direct effect, the dark pictures painted by many respectable middle-class interpreters at certain times must have discouraged some emigration from the professions and some conservative investment. On the other hand, this same picture may also have stimulated emigration of discontented individuals, and it may have attracted high-risk investment. In Australia itself there is evidence that, at least at times, consciousness of a poor or undeserved reputation in Britain was a factor in the development of national feeling. An external image became a source of self-image.

The state of opinion about the Australian economy within British government offices (especially the Colonial Office and the Treasury) is a subject which has already attracted the careful attention of historians in Australia and elsewhere;[12] it is considered here only incidentally, as at such times when important reports or policy statements about Australia were published by government. The effects of public opinion upon these offices and upon Parliament itself should be topics for future historians.

It is always a question when writing in the history of ideas how much social, political, doctrinal, biographical, and economic history to introduce as background. The danger in leaving this material out is that the ideas under examination may take on an unreal and disembodied appearance. The problems of including the material are several: first, the account may become undesirably extended; second, the limited background material must assume a superficial and dogmatic character; and third, there is real danger of implying a necessary causal relationship between ideas and events. An example will illustrate the third problem. The dark view in Britain of government activity in Australia may have been strongly influenced by depressions in Australia or by stock-market

12. E.g., A. G. L. Shaw, *Convicts and Colonies* (London, 1966); J. J. Eddy, *Britain and the Australian Colonies, 1818–1831* (Oxford, 1969); P. Burroughs, *Britain and Australia, 1831–55* (Oxford, 1967); S. J. Butlin, *The Foundations of the Australian Monetary System, 1788–1851* (Melbourne, 1953).

crashes in London. But, on the contrary, it may not have been so influenced and may have reflected merely the power of laissez-faire doctrine. To describe the depressions or the crashes in very great detail would assert causal connections which have yet to be proved or even investigated seriously.

The problem of appreciating the total context of British perception of the Australian economy is, of course, doubled because the ideas were developed in one country about another, and the evolving milieux of both countries are clearly relevant. The approach taken here has been to give minimum attention to the general background and to urge readers to consult standard authorities where necessary.

It should be emphasized that it is not the purpose of this study to endorse or reject the views of Australia which are described. Nor is it a primary objective to assess the accuracy or reasonableness of the British perception to gain thereby a better understanding of Australian economic development. Rather, the goal first and foremost is to discover how the British perceived this development. As the reader moves through the book he will become aware that the distinction between truth and error in an information sense is not crucial for this study. Data which were "wrong" in present-day terms are just as meaningful as those which were "right" so long as they contribute to the perception. The focus is on the knowledge which made up the image. Much of the material examined may look like "rubbish" to the modern reader. It is no less important for this appraisal. The purpose of this exercise is to gain some understanding of how one people sees another; if the perception is distorted and unreasonable, by modern standards, this is significant in itself.

It is hoped that some readers will be stimulated to deal with many of the unanswered questions which are raised throughout this book. Perhaps it may be found, also, that the approach used here will be applicable to further studies of attitudes toward developing countries by the advanced nations of the world.

The Image of Australia

· 1 ·

Convicts and Wool: Cui Bono?

Terra Australis had a shadowy place in the European literature of discovery and imagination as early as the beginning of the seventeenth century, but accurate information was scanty and was for almost two centuries inextricably mixed with fancy.[1] In the eighteenth century and early years of the nineteenth, Australia was still known only in vague outline to most of the British people, including political economists. Interest in the continent increased, but the focus in written works remained mainly on details of exploration and on the exotic flora and fauna. After Cook's voyages in the 1770's and the settlement at Botany Bay in 1788, the excitements of crime and punishment were added to the hopes for discovery of new staple products and the fascination with geography generally. A steady stream of military officers, ship's surgeons, clerics, and even literary convicts provided general accounts of the colonies, while government inquiries dealt with such technical economic matters as administrative costs, land disposal, immigration, the volume of trade, and the impact of transportation on the convicts.[2] However, with the distraction of

1. See Werner P. Friederich, *Australia in Western Imaginative Prose Writings 1600–1960* (Chapel Hill, 1967), Chaps. 1–3; and R. H. Major, *Early Voyages to Terra Australis Now Called Australia* . . . Hakluyt Society Series No. 25 (London, 1859). The reasons for the first settlement of Australia, whether economic, strategic, or evangelical, need not be examined here; until an actual Australian economy came to exist, there could be no perception of it. The strongest case for economic motives behind the settlement is made by K. M. Dallas in *Trading Posts or Penal Colonies: The Commercial Significance of Cook's New Holland Route to the Pacific* (Hobart, 1969). A discussion of the alternative hypotheses is contained in G. J. Abbott and N. B. Nairn, *Economic Growth of Australia* (Melbourne, 1969), pp. 46–56. See also C. M. H. Clark, *A History of Australia,* I (Melbourne, 1962), 1–112.

2. Among the most important early works of description were these: Sir George Young, *The Following Is a Rough Outline of the Many Advantages That May Result to this Nation, from a Settlement Made on the Coast of New South Wales*

the French Revolution and the Napoleonic wars, public scrutiny was not intense, and what may have been a reasonable statement of the picture of Australia held by most educated men in Great Britain as late as the 1820's was provided by Charles Lamb in a

---

(London, n.d. [1785]); George Barrington, *A Voyage to New South Wales* (London, 1795); David Collins, *An Account of the English Colony in New South Wales* (London, 1798); *A Concise History of the English Colony in New South Wales* (London, 1804); G. Paterson, *The History of New South Wales* (Newcastle, 1811); Matthew Flinders, *A Voyage to Terra Australis* (London, 1814); John Oxley, *Journals of Two Expeditions Into the Interior of New South Wales* (London, 1820); Edward Curr, *An Account of the Colony of Van Diemen's Land* (London, 1824); Barron Field, ed., *Geographical Memoirs on New South Wales; by Various Hands* (London, 1825); Peter Cunningham, *Two Years in New South Wales* (London, 1827); Phillip Parker King, *Narrative of a Survey of the Intertropical and Western Coasts of Australia* (London, 1827); James Bischoff, *Sketch of the History of Van Diemen's Land* (London, 1832); Alick Osborne, *Notes on the Present State and Prospects of Society in New South Wales* (London, 1833); Charles Sturt, *Two Expeditions Into the Interior of Southern Australia* (London, 1833); Augustus Prinsep, *The Journal of a Voyage from Calcutta to Van Diemen's Land* (London, 1833); George Bennett, *Wanderings in New South Wales* (London, 1834). In most of these works economic information was secondary to narrative and geographic description. By the late eighteenth century material about Australia began to appear in various geographical and historical compendia: e.g., *A New Moral System of Geography* (London, 1790); Patrick Colquhoun, *A Treatise on the Wealth, Power and Resources of the British Empire* (London, 1814); Alexander M'Konochie, *A Summary View of the Statistics and Existing Commerce of the Principal Shores of the Pacific Ocean* (London, 1818); James Bell, *A System of Geography, Popular and Scientific*, VI (Glasgow, 1832); Robert Montgomery Martin, *History of the British Colonies* (London, 1834). Because of its convicts and Aborigines, Australia was seen as a fertile missionary field. The activities of intrepid missionaries, including their efforts at economic development, were described in church publications and elsewhere. For example, an early discussion of the achievements of Samuel Marsden is contained in "Voyage to Australasia," *Eclectic Review*, V, Part II (1809), 977–96. A notion of the working-class image of the Australian colonies in Britain during the first half of the nineteenth century may be gained from G. C. Ingleton, *True Patriots All, or News from Early Australia,—As Told in a Collection of Broadsides* (Sydney, 1953). The broadsides described how settlers could experience great hardship or make large fortunes. See esp. pp. 196–97 and 210–11. The Royal Geographical Society showed sustained interest in Australian exploration. The first three articles in the first year of the Society's *Journal* in 1831 were on Western Australia, and almost every subsequent volume had Australian reports. As trade increased with the Australian colonies, so did commercial reporting in the regular daily press and in such special periodicals as the *Asiatic Journal* (London, 1816–45), *Oriental Herald and Colonial Review* (London, 1824–29); *Colonial Gazette* (London, 1837–46), and *Simmonds's Colonial Magazine and Foreign Miscellany*, continued as the *Colonial Magazine and East India Review* (London, 1844–52). "New Holland" was given a surprisingly large entry of ten pages in the third (1797) edition of *Encyclopaedia Britannica*, VIII, 612–22. It was concerned mainly with the voyages of discovery and the natives. The mounting interest of the press, the public, Parliament, and various government offices in Australia after the end of the Napoleonic Wars is described in J. J. Eddy, *Britain and the Australian Colonies, 1818–1831* (Oxford, 1969), esp. pp. xiv, 44, 49, 50, 53, 59, 61, 73, 81 f., 143.

well-known letter from "Elia." A recent emigrant to the colonies received the following communication from a friend in the homeland:

I cannot imagine to myself whereabout you are. When I try to fix it, Peter Wilkins's island comes across me. Sometimes you seem to be in the *Hades of Thieves.* I see Diogenes prying among you with his perpetual fruitless lantern. What must you be willing by this time to give for the sight of an honest man! You must almost have forgotten how *we* look. And tell me what your Sydneyites do? are they th—v—ng all day long? Merciful heaven! what property can stand against such a depredation! The kangaroos—your Aborigines—do they keep their primitive simplicity un-Europe-tainted, with those little short fore pads, looking like a lesson framed by nature to the pickpocket! Marry, for diving into fobs they are rather lamely provided *a priori;* but if the hue and cry were once up, they would show as fair a pair of hind-shifters as the expertest loco-motor in the colony.

We hear the most improbable tales at this distance. Pray is it true that the young Spartans among you are born with six fingers, which spoils their scanning? It must look very odd, but use reconciles. For their scansion, it is less to be regretted; for if they take it into their heads to be poets, it is odds but they turn out, the greater part of them, vile plagiarists. Is there much difference to see, too, between the son of a th—f and the grandson? or where does the taint stop? Do you bleach in three or in four generations? I have many questions to put, but ten Delphic voyages can be made in a shorter time than it will take to satisfy my scruples. Do you grow your own hemp? What is your staple trade—exclusive of the national profession, I mean? Your locksmiths, I take it, are some of your great capitalists.[3]

Preliminary Cost-Benefit Analysis

Australia was categorized by most Englishmen under the all-encompassing heading "colony" and therefore came to be judged in terms of the well-known "gains" and "losses" to the mother country from having dependencies. The gains from colonies were thought to be trading advantages, a refuge for "surplus" labor and capital, direct tribute, and strategic services for the fleet. Costs

3. John Mason Brown, ed., *The Portable Charles Lamb* (New York, 1949), pp. 496–97. The letter first appeared in the *London Magazine* in March 1822.

were distortions in a free-market economy and the expenses of administration and defense.[4] After the first few decades of settlement, Australia ranked relatively high among the colonies in the judgment of most observers.[5] It gave little trouble and expense beyond the costs of penal supervision. Unlike Canada, it could not involve the parent in expensive and dangerous controversy with a powerful neighbor; and unlike the West Indies, it did not depend for survival upon subsidies and the distasteful institution of slavery. In addition, it performed a valuable service in providing a home for the most troublesome segments of Britain's redundant population—convicts and the poor. Australia's reputation as a haven for unemployed members of the lower classes

4. A good contemporary statement of the costs and benefits of colonies is Donald Winch, ed., *James Mill: Selected Economic Writings* (Chicago, 1966), pp. 317–22; see also R. N. Ghosh, *Classical Macroeconomics and the Case for Colonies* (Calcutta, 1967). Sir William Molesworth described the low costs of defending Australia relative to those of defending other colonies in *Speech in the House of Commons, on the 10th of April, 1851, for a Reduction of the Colonial Expenditure of the United Kingdoms* [sic] (London, 1851), p. 18. The characteristic preoccupation of the Treasury and of such politicians as Joseph Hume with colonial expenses is discussed in J. J. Eddy, pp. 186 and 206. The costs of any interference with the free market were a special concern of Robert Wilmot Horton. See *ibid.*, p. 217.

5. Before it could be demonstrated with confidence that the colonies could produce wool and other staples such as whale oil at competitive prices, economic assessments tended to be unfavorable. Patrick Colquhoun concluded in 1815 that "the British population at New South Wales may be said to be lost to the nation." He could discern only "slender expectation from the facts which have been disclosed of its ever proving otherwise than a heavy expence to this country, without any hope of remuneration from its trade or any other advantage with respect to the better disposal of criminal offenders which may not be attained under other arrangements, at one tenth part of the expence." *Treatise on the Wealth, Power, and Resources, of the British Empire* (London, 1815), pp. 419 and 420. Similar contemporary views are described by J. J. Eddy, pp. 64–65. In later years some other writers continued to believe that the costs of colonies exceeded the benefits at all times and without exceptions. One of these, Sir Henry Parnell, concluded in 1830: "This general reasoning, which the principles of trade suggest in refutation of the imaginary advantages of Colonies, is completely borne out by the experience of facts. The history of the Colonies for many years is that of a series of loss, and of the destruction of capital: and if to the many millions of private capital, which have been thus wasted, were added some hundred millions that have been raised by British taxes, and spent on account of the Colonies, the total loss to the British public of wealth, which the Colonies have occasioned, would appear to be quite enormous." *On Financial Reform* (London, 1830), pp. 239–40. Starting from the same doctrinal position, the *Westminster Review*, the organ of the Philosophical Radicals, calculated in 1836 that national revenues for the year attributable to the Australian colonies were only £264,559, while public expenditures were £395,464. "The Colonial Expenditure," XXIV (1836), 1–31. A recent collection of essays on various aspects of economic development during this period is G. J. Abbott and N. B. Nairn, *Economic Growth of Australia, 1788–1821* (Melbourne, 1969).

increased steadily during the first half of the nineteenth century as employment opportunities were demonstrated and the costs of transport and the effects of convict presence turned out not to be insurmountable deterrents.[6] The Australian reputation fluctuated, naturally, with the state of the highly volatile economy, reaching highpoints in the pastoral booms in the 1820's and 1830's; but generally by the 1840's, in the face of Irish famine and other economic dislocations throughout the British Isles, Australia at least held its own with other colonies in discussions of emigration before Parliamentary committees and in the press. Sir George Cornewall Lewis, who was particularly concerned with poverty in Great Britain and Ireland, specifically mentioned Australia in 1841 when he discussed the advantages a dominant country

6. At least through the 1820's Australia was usually given low marks as a home for the unemployed by such authorities as J. R. McCulloch, who wrote: "Whatever may be the advantages of New South Wales in respect of open country and climate, it is removed by distance beyond the *natural* sphere of European connexion; its future commerce must be Asiatic." "Emigration," *Edinburgh Review*, XLVII (1828), 206. See also J. R. McCulloch, "Value of Colonial Possessions," *ibid.*, XLII (1825), 271–303; and *idem*, "Emigration," *ibid.*, XLV (1826), 49–74. A *Westminster* reviewer in 1826 doubted that "emigration to New South Wales, on a large scale, can ever become expedient, or even practicable." "Emigration Report," *Westminster Review*, VI (1826), 371. See also James M'Queen, "The British Colonies," *Blackwood's Magazine*, XXIII (1828), 891–913, XXV (1829), 633–63; XXVII (1830), 223–53; XXIX (1831), 187–213; "New South Wales," *Quarterly Review*, XXXVII (1828), 1–32. In 1829 William Cobbett advised strongly against emigration to Australia. See *The Emigrant's Guide* (London, 1829), p. 40. A change in attitude was evident by the early 1830's. See, for example, the ambivalent discussion of "objections" and "advantages" to emigration in Lieut. Breton, *Excursions in New South Wales, Western Australia, and Van Diemen's Land* (London, 1833), pp. 462–65. However, as late as 1841 in the face of evidence of high wages in Australia, a *Westminster* reviewer still doubted whether the colonies could become a major receptacle for emigrants; "wages do not alone constitute happiness, and it will require a considerable transfusion of a sounder population before the colonies in question will be highly attractive to any class of persons. At the present moment *convictism* pervades every institution, influences every custom, modifies the very habits of the people, and affects the tone of society at large. This, no doubt, will be corrected in the course of time, but the process of correction will be necessarily slow—a disadvantage which is worthy the consideration of all who are engaged in choosing a country." H. S. C. [H. S. Chapman?], "Comparative Prospects of Our New Colonies," *Westminster Review*, XXXV (1841), 165. An exception to the early condemnation of Australia as an emigrant home was sometimes made for Van Diemen's Land, whose similarity to Britain in geography was noted and "where, it is to be hoped, a better race from the same parent stock is about to spring up, than that of the 'back woodsman' of North America." It was suggested even that the island's name be changed to "South Britain" or "Little England." "Van Diemen's Land," *Quarterly Review*, XXVII (1822), 99 and 101. See also *The Farmers: or Tales for the Times, Addressed to the Yeomanry of England* (London, 1823); and "Van Diemen's Land," *Westminster Review*, XXI (1834), 18–52.

gained from dependencies, including the following: "a field where the inhabitants of the former may find advantageous employment for themselves or profitable investments for their capital."[7] Australia, together with the other settlement colonies, was thought of or portrayed as an attractive emigration field during the 1840's by such prominent literary men as Thomas Arnold, Thomas Carlyle, Benjamin Disraeli, Edward Bulwer-Lytton, Arthur Clough, William Thackeray, Alfred Tennyson, and Charles Dickens. Carlyle in particular wrote persuasively of the need to provide for the hard-pressed British worker through schemes of organized emigration "a bridge built to carry him into new Western lands."[8]

Yet another advantage of Australia was that it seemed willing to follow a development pattern based on pastoral activity which most observers, whether adherents of Adam Smith or not, thought was wise, "natural," and coincidentally to Britain's special advantage. The wool industry was productive of a vital staple raw material for England's secondary industry and was non-competitive with any noteworthy domestic interests. Unlike the United States, Australia showed little vocal enthusiasm for starting large-scale manufacturing industries of its own (with the possible exception of distilleries), and it even seemed reluctant to move on from pastoral culture to the next appropriate development stage—settled agriculture—which also could be looked forward to as of special advantage to the imperial metropolis.[9]

7. Sir George Cornewall Lewis, *An Essay on the Government of Dependencies* (Oxford, 1891; first published 1841), p. 224. Nassau Senior said of this judgment: "There seems no reason for supposing that, if our American and Australian colonies were independent, they would offer less facilities to emigration than they do now." "Lewis on Dependencies," in *Historical and Philosophical Essays* (London, 1865), II, 238, first published in the *Edinburgh Review*, April 1846. Similar views to those of Lewis are contained in "Colonization and the Allotment System," *North British Review*, III (1845), 406–43; and John Barrow, "The Australian Colonies," *Quarterly Review*, LXVIII (1841), 88–145.

8. Thomas Carlyle, *Past and Present*, ed. A. M. D. Hughes (Oxford, 1932), p. 259, and *Chartism* (Boston, 1840), pp. 107–18. See also Sidney Rosenberg, *Black Sheep and Golden Fleece*, microfilm (Ph.D. diss., Columbia Univ., 1954), Chap. 5, pp. 81–105; and J. J. Eddy, p. 128.

9. The colonies did, of course, develop some manufacturing industries and settled agriculture in the early years. See G. P. Walsh, "The Geography of Manufacturing in Sydney, 1788–1851," *Business Archives and History*, III (1963), 20–52. However, the important consideration for this study is that the economic image in Britain remained primarily of convicts and wool.

British recognition of Australia as a valuable source of raw wool dates from the 1820's and especially from 1822–23, when three reports by John Thomas Bigge, a commissioner sent to examine the colony of New South Wales, were published as sessional papers both of the House of Commons and of the House of Lords. In the first and most general of these reports, on "the state of the Colony of New South Wales," Bigge examined the operation and effects of the convict transportation system. In the third, "on the state of agriculture and trade," he developed the thesis that Australia would be of long-run permanent economic value to Great Britain. He was optimistic about the possibilities of producing a variety of staple products, including timber, grain, tobacco, flax, and whale oil; but he was positively lyrical about the importance to Britain of the pioneer wool production initiated in New South Wales by the Macarthurs in the 1790's: "it renders her independent of foreign supplies, causes no interference with the natural and most beneficial course of her own agriculture, or with the produce of her own soil." In good Mercantilist tradition, Bigge recommended that favored treatment be extended to wool producers over other industries in the colony, and specifically that "encouragement" [assigned convict labor] be discontinued to "manufactures." [10] He concluded:

> Upon the expediency of promoting in the colony of New South Wales the growth of fine wool, and creating a valuable export from thence to Great Britain, no doubt can be entertained, as it appears to be the principal, if not the only source of productive industry within the colony, from which the settlers can derive the means of repaying the advances made to them from the mother country, or supplying their own demands for articles of foreign manufacture.[11]

In addition to recommending discouragement of manufactures, Bigge proposed a broad development policy for the colonies

10. *Report of the Commissioner of Inquiry Into the State of the Colony of New South Wales* (London, 1822; Australiana Facsimile Edition No. 68, Adelaide, 1966), pp. 158–63. For the circumstances of the Bigge reports see C. M. H. Clark, *A History of Australia,* I (Melbourne, 1962), 367–79. The export of wool rose from 74,284 pounds in 1809 to 323,995 pounds in 1825. A. G. L. Shaw and H. D. Nicolson, *Growth and Development in Australia* (Sydney, 1966), p. 20.

11. *Report of the Commissioner of Inquiry on the State of Agriculture and Trade in the Colony of New South Wales* (London, 1823; Australiana Facsimile Edition No. 70, Adelaide, 1966), p. 18; see also p. 53.

which came to be endorsed by many other British advisers in later years; he favored low tariffs, transport improvement, and restraint in construction of public works.[12]

An important reason why the Australian colonies retained a favored position in British eyes after the Bigge reports was that even the modest "encouragement" proposed by Bigge turned out not to be needed to make staple production, and especially wool, flourish in Australia. As Bigge himself had explained, the slow growth of agriculture was merely testimony to the strength of the pastoral industry. Observers reflected warmly on the prospect of steady development based on wool and on the possibility of trading expansion in the Pacific. John Barrow, Second Secretary of the Admiralty and enthusiastic geographer, who wrote occasionally about Australia, concluded in 1825:

> The prosperity of these colonies is the more gratifying to the mother-country, setting aside any direct advantages she may hope to derive from them, from the circumstances that, by their means, and probably at no very distant period of time, her laws and her religion, her language and manners, will spread themselves over a large portion of those numerous islands which rise out of the southern ocean, and are scattered around at no great distance from either of them.[13]

The historian Archibald Alison reported proudly in 1839 on the continued good prospects for mutually beneficial trade with Australia:

> I venture to predict, that before the year 1840 the colonists of New Holland, reinforced as they will be by our friends around us proceeding to New Zealand, will consume more of British produce and manufactures, though they may not number a hundred and twenty thousand souls, than the sixty millions of the Muscovite empire. Such is the wonderful difference between the commercial intercourse we can maintain with our own descendants—our own flesh and blood—the Anglo-Saxon race whom we have sent forth to civilize the world—and

12. *Ibid.*, pp. 17 and 101–2; *Report of the Commissioner of Inquiry Into the State of the Colony of New South Wales*, p. 163. The effect of the Bigge reports on colonial planning and administration is described by J. J. Eddy, p. 73 and *passim*.

13. J. Barrow, "The Australian Colonies," *Quarterly Review*, XXXII (1825), 312. See also John Barrow, "The Australian Colonies," *ibid.*, LXVIII (1841), 88–145.

the inhabitants of foreign states, subjected to the authority of hostile governments, or swayed by commercial jealousy.[14]

The Question of Transportation

Australia played visible parts in two active controversies of the first half of the nineteenth century which, in addition to the matter of trade, attracted the attention of prominent economists. The first controversy concerned the question which had prompted Bigge's mission, whether transportation was an effective, economic, and moral form of punishment. In the early years of the experiment in New South Wales, Sydney Smith, Jeremy Bentham, and William Paley, among others, declared that it was not.[15] A *Quarterly* reviewer in 1814 drew a typically dreary picture of the colony as a penal experiment and as an attempt at nation building. He declared that "no colony was ever formed of such bad and intractable materials . . . no colony ever had to struggle against so many difficulties and disadvantages."[16] Samuel Bailey, the moderate utilitarian radical, reaffirmed the verdict against transportation in 1823, just at the time of publication of the Bigge reports,[17] and throughout the 1820's Botany Bay was portrayed with regularity as a foul sink of moral iniquity from which neither reform nor discouragement to crime could be ex-

14. A. Alison, "Colonial Neglect and Foreign Propitiation," *Blackwood's Magazine,* XLVI (1839), 761. In a bitter denunciation of colonial appeals for tariff protection just at the time when Britain was herself liberalizing trade during the 1840's, G. C. Lewis conspicuously singled out the West Indies and Canada but not Australia. "Colonial Protection," *Edinburgh Review,* LXXXIV (1846), 236–66. The protectionist publicist John Barnard Byles was just as favorably disposed to Australia. *Sophisms of Free Trade and Popular Political Economy Examined* (1849; reprinted New York, 1912), pp. 97–98.

15. Rev. Sydney Smith, "Collins's Account of New South Wales," *Edinburgh Review,* II (1803), 30–42; Jeremy Bentham, *Panopticon: Postscript, Part II* (London, 1791); *idem, The Rationale of Punishment* (London, 1830); and "Principles of Penal Law," in John Bowring, ed., *The Works of Jeremy Bentham* (New York, 1962), I, 490–97; William Paley, *The Principles of Moral and Political Philosophy* (London, 1804), II, 288. See also F. L. W. Wood, "Jeremy Bentham versus New South Wales," *Royal Australian Historical Society Journal and Proceedings,* XIX (1933/34), 329–51; and Alan G. L. Shaw, *Convicts and Colonies* (London, 1966).

16. "Flinders's *Voyage to Terra Australis,*" *Quarterly Review,* XII (1814/15), 30. A pamphlet five years later had the same message: Henry Grey Bennet, *Letter to Viscount Sidmouth, Secretary of State for the Home Department, on the Transportation Laws, the State of the Hulks, and of the Colonies in New South Wales* (London, 1819).

17. S. Bailey, *Questions in Political Economy* (London, 1823), pp. 128–30.

pected. Thomas Hamilton, retired army officer and professional essayist, offered a description of the population and society of the Australian colonies in 1827; "they confessedly constitute," he wrote, "the most rascally and villainous population that ever congregated together on the surface of this habitable globe . . . a sort of moral Cloacina, into which the very scum and refuse of society is periodically discharged." [18] A *Westminster* reviewer in 1825 found it poignant that with their excellent climate and capacity to produce wool coupled with the "vice and barbarism" of convict settlements, the Australian colonies offered to prospective emigrants both the greatest economic advantages and the most serious social disadvantages.[19]

A thorough indictment of transportation came in 1832 from Richard Whately, Archbishop of Dublin. Like his predecessors, Whately rested his case mainly on the ground that transportation was not an efficient punishment either as a deterrent or as a means of criminal reformation, and he concluded that the "ill effects, in respect of the well-being of our Australian colonies, are also very serious." [20] An appendix to Whately's tract described New South Wales as "a colony founded and maintained on principles which, if acted on by an individual in private life, would expose him to the charge either of insanity or of shameless profligacy." The unidentified author of Whately's appendix asked whether one could "look forward, without a shudder, at the appalling spectacle which a few generations hence may be doomed to witness in Australia?" [21]

A leading strand in the transportation debate by the 1830's is

18. T. Hamilton, "Cunningham's New South Wales," *Blackwood's Magazine,* XXII (1827), 603.

19. "On Emigration," *Westminster Review,* III (1825), 448–87. James Mill, who was skeptical of all the alleged gains from colonies, wrote in his celebrated article on colonies for the Supplement to the *Encyclopaedia Britannica,* "New South Wales of all places on the face of the earth, except, perhaps, a British prison, is the place where there is the least chance for the reformation of an offender, the greatest chance of his being improved and perfected in every species of wickedness." Reprinted in *Essays* (London, n.d. [1831]), p. 14.

20. R. Whately, *Thoughts on Secondary Punishments, in a Letter to Earl Grey* (London, 1832), p. 8; also *Remarks on Transportation, and on a Recent Defence of the System; in a Second Letter to Earl Grey* (London, 1834).

21. *Ibid.,* pp. 201–3. For the effects of such views on some politicians of the day, see J. J. Eddy, pp. 39, 40, 49, 67. Through the issue of transportation a wide range of humanitarians had their attention drawn to Australia; e.g., *ibid.,* p. 51.

clear in this last statement. Debaters recognized that now the issues were wider than merely the best means to discourage crime and reform criminals. The prison had become an infant nation. One *Quarterly* reviewer stated the question succinctly in 1835 when he asked: "Who can doubt that this is a country which *must* make a great figure in the world, either for good or for evil, before three generations more shall have passed away?—or contemplate without alarm the existence of a powerful nation born and reared amidst such a moral atmosphere as at present shocks every new visitant of Sydney, and is but too apt to corrupt and harden the whole being of any one who protracts his residence there?" [22] Horace Twiss, formerly Undersecretary of War and the Colonies, wrote in a similar vein three years later and argued that if ever the case for transportation had been valid on grounds of Britain's domestic interests, it was so no longer, because of the social costs it imposed on this new country. "Society, in all its classes, is affected by the vast proportion which the convicts and their associates bear to the whole population. The lower ranks are corrupted, and the higher annoyed, by the juxta-position; so that everything either savours of the mischief, or suffers from it." [23] William Howitt, who later traveled in Australia (see below, Chapter 2) included a whole chapter in his study of European native policies in 1838 on the destructive effects of transportation throughout the Pacific region. He reported that "the convict system—the penal colony system—the throwing off the putrid matter of our corrupt social state on some simple and unsuspecting country, to inoculate it with the rankness of our worst moral diseases, without relieving ourselves at all sensibly by the unprincipled deed, has here shewn itself in all its hideousness. New South Wales and Van Diemen's Land have been sufficient to curse and demoralize all this portion of the world." [24] One observer in 1837 stressed again the apparent paradox which

22. "Bennett's New South Wales," *Quarterly Review*, LIII (1835), 9.

23. H. Twiss, "New South Wales," *Quarterly Review*, LXII (1838), 480. William Ashton described in graphic terms to a Sheffield audience "the vicious state of society" which was the inevitable result of transportation in Australia. *A Lecture on the Evils of Emigration and Transportation* (Sheffield, 1838).

24. William Howitt, *Colonization and Christianity* (London, 1838), p. 470.

others were to note in later years between the great economic potential of the Australian continent and what they considered to be the iniquitous social institutions which had been established there. "It [transportation] cannot be amended. It has completely failed as a punishment; it has been still more ineffectual as a means of reformation; it has produced the most degraded community in the universe, the most demoralized society on record in the history of nations; and at the same time the one possessing in proportion, to its population, the greatest amount of wealth." [25]

Blanket condemnations of transportation were seldom based either on informed consideration of alternative development opportunities open to the colonies or on a careful study of experience with the system itself. However, the repeated grim portrayals of transportation and of the colonies themselves helped to form British prejudices for a long time to come. Spirited defenses against misinterpretation by the colonial writers were nearly drowned out and were often denounced as unreliable special pleading.[26]

25. "Life in the Penal Colonies," *London and Westminster Review,* V and XXVII (1837), 92–93.

26. E.g., W. C. Wentworth's two large studies, *A Statistical, Historical, and Political Description of the Colony of New South Wales, and Its Dependent Settlements in Van Diemen's Land* (London, 1819), and *A Statistical Account of the British Settlements in Australasia* (London, 1824); Rev. John Dunmore Lang, *An Historical and Statistical Account of New South Wales* (London, 1834); and the activities in support of the emancipated settlers by Edward Eager described by Noel McLachlin, "Edward Eagar (1787–1866): A Colonial Spokesman in Sydney and London," *Historical Studies: Australia and New Zealand,* X (1961/63), 431–56. See also "A Colonist of New South Wales," *Transportation . . .* (London, 1832); and George Arthur, *Observations Upon Secondary Punishments* (Hobart-Town, 1833). A balanced survey of the effects of transportation in the *Edinburgh Review* in 1849 may have been written by one of the most prominent convicts of the day, the Irish leader W. Smith O'Brien. "Transportation as It Now Is," XC (1849), 1–39. Another moderate commentary was "Excursion to Port Arthur," *Fraser's Magazine,* XXVI (1842), 281–98. Examples of skepticism toward colonial writers are: John Barrow, "The Australian Colonies," *Quarterly Review,* XXXII (1825), 311–42, and Lieut. Breton, *Excursions in New South Wales, Western Australia, and Van Diemen's Land* (London, 1833), p. 40. Examples of media in Britain during the 1840's open to defenders of the colonies—merchants, former colonists, and current residents—are the *Colonial Magazine and Commercial-Maritime Journal,* edited by the historian of empire Robert Montgomery Martin, and *Simmonds's Colonial Magazine,* which capitalized on interest in both commercial and geographical affairs. In the latter, news of Leichardt and Sturt was mixed in with tables of wool and land prices. George Arden, Thomas M'Combie and William Westgarth were contributors. Notable articles in the *Colonial Magazine* were Mr. Justice Burton, "Observations on the Constitution of the Government of New South Wales," I (1840), 332–59; *idem,* "State of Society and of Crime in New South Wales," I (1840), 422–40, and II (1840), 34–54; and David

The debate over the virtues and vices of transportation continued right into the 1850's even as the institution approached its end.[27] The proportion of convicts in the population of New South Wales had fallen from around a half in the 1820's to a quarter in the 1840's. Nevertheless, when some colonists joined British reformers in calling for a rapid termination of transportation, this provided yet another reason for a group of critics to attack the colonies, in this case for selfishness of the residents and, in the words of Colonial Secretary Lord Grey, for "jealousy of the competition of convicts, and a fear that their coming might lead to a reduction of the extravagant wages they had been in the habit of obtaining." [28]

The Debate Over Colonization

The second economic controversy in which the Australian colonies played a part concerned the desirability of colonization in general and specifically of government encouragement to emigration. British economists tended to treat the question at a theoretical level and to play down detailed examinations of specific colonies as not central to the argument. On one side in the debate stood Malthus, Ricardo, and some of their disciples, who argued that an exodus of labor could only be a palliative to an old country's population problems and would at best afford temporary benefit while fundamental reforms were brought about in the domestic economy. The greatest danger in colonization was

---

Burn, "Van Diemen's Land: Moral, Physical, and Political," serialized in twelve parts from II (1840) to V (1841). In *Simmonds's* see J. Porter, "Australia: Past, Present and Future," III (1844), 358–63, 375–99; and IV (1845), 29–48 and 167–90; also Robert P. Welch, "Observations on Convict and Free Labour for New South Wales," XI (1847), 288–314. Few readers could fail to miss the extravagant tone of praise, approaching propaganda, in these journals. For example, a representative article concluded as follows: "On every mind, imbued with the ennobling spirit of independence, actuated by a pure love of their country, interested in the welfare of society, or engaged in the study of nature and of man, Australia possesses strong and peculiar claims." "Reflections on Australia," *Colonial Magazine,* VI (1841), 210–20.

27. See Margaret Ker, "The British Parliament and Transportation in the Eighteen-Fifties," *Historical Studies: Australia and New Zealand,* VI (1953/54), 29–44.

28. [Henry George] Earl Grey, *The Colonial Policy of Lord John Russell's Administration* (London, 1853), II, 47; see also II, 25, 26, 48, 55, 56, and 75–79.

that a considerable export of capital, needed to get colonies on their feet, would lead to a reduction in the domestic wages fund and cause a decline in wages and profits.[29] Thomas Chalmers, the Scottish theologian, stated this concern in 1832, announcing that "the near, the practical consideration is, that the relief afforded even now, by all the emigration, which even the most sanguine of its advocates can count upon, is but an insignificant fraction of what a population, left to its own unchecked spontaneity, would need; and every future year, this relief would become more insignificant." [30] William Thornton, economist and friend of J. S. Mill, reaffirmed this position in 1846; "for the present the resource offered by emigration is of no great value . . . the subtraction of so insignificant a proportion of the whole people cannot in the smallest degree ameliorate the condition of the millions left behind." [31]

At the operating level, the Colonial Secretary Lord Grey accepted the skeptical view of colonization and opposed all public assistance to emigration. He asserted that

> there is not (and never has been) any real redundancy of labour in this Country; consequently it would be most mistaken policy to seek relief from any temporary difficulties we may experience, by artificially promoting emigration at the public expense, instead of by removing any obstacles to the natural extension of the field of employment at home. It must be borne in mind that active and industrious labourers, by being sent to Australia, cease to become contributors to the wealth and revenue of the Mother-country.[32]

So long as production continued to increase in Britain at the same time as population, Grey argued, the country could expect to achieve economies of scale. For example: "It is clear, that the more the population and wealth of the British Islands increase, the lighter will become to their inhabitants the burden of our

29. Three accounts of the development of colonization theory are Klaus E. Knorr, *British Colonial Theories, 1570–1850* (Toronto, 1944), R. N. Ghosh, *Classical Macroeconomics and the Case for Colonies* (Calcutta, 1967), and Donald Winch, *Classical Political Economy and Colonies* (Cambridge, Mass., 1965).

30. T. Chalmers, *On Political Economy, in Connexion with the Moral State and Moral Prospects of Society* (New York, 1832), p. 274.

31. W. Thornton, *Over-Population and Its Remedy* (London, 1846), pp. 288 and 289.

32. Earl Grey, I, 333–34.

national debt, and of the taxes to which it compels us to submit." Grey even used a rough pre-Darwinian theory of social evolution to reject the principle of assisted emigration. The transfer of the least efficient workers in Britain to the more agreeable environment of the colonies, he said, would contravene the normal process of natural selection:

To establish the practice of giving relief to those who cannot find work at home, by sending them to Colonies where wages are higher than they are here, would therefore be to reverse the position of the good and bad labourers under the wholesome operation of the natural laws of society, and actually to give an advantage over the best labourers to the indifferent ones, on account of their inferiority, by considering their inability to compete with the others in the labour-market at home, a reason for giving them the means of carrying their labour to a higher market in the Colonies.[33]

On the other side of the colonization debate stood optimists who argued that temporary congestion was Great Britain's major obstacle to progress; this crowding, they believed, could be alleviated by rapid development of colonial territories. Robert Southey, the poet, provided in 1828 an especially eloquent statement of the need for immediate emigration, using biological metaphors popular at the time. He wrote:

But when a patient is suffering from plethora and in danger of apoplexy, where is the medical practitioner who would be withheld from bleeding him, because nature may again in a short time surcharge the vessels which have been thus relieved? A regular as well as a regulated system of emigration is required in the stage of society which we have attained: it becomes as necessary in the economy of a state as of an ant-hill, or a bee-hive.[34]

33. *Ibid.*, p. 332.

34. R. Southey, "Emigration Report," *Quarterly Review*, XXXVII (1828), 577. In 1794 Southey composed some of the earliest poems concerned with Australia, the *Botany-Bay Eclogues*. These had reference more to the contemporary state of criminal justice in Britain than to conditions on the new continent. They can be found in *The Minor Poems of Robert Southey* (London, 1823), I, 63–90. Apparently, Southey had hoped to receive an appointment in the colonies. He wrote to Sir Walter Scott in 1812: "For myself I know but one thing which would strongly tempt me to break up my quarters, and that would be if they would make me Governor of Botany Bay. I have a strong fancy for that situation—but unluckily Mrs. Southey has as strong an objection to it, and as her objection is sufficiently reasonable, the inhabitants of that choice colony are never likely to be benefitted by my good intentions and the honour of crossing the Blue Mountains must be reserved for some more fortunate person. Unless indeed I should find my

At a level designed to reach the lower classes, Harriet Martineau, the popularizer of political economy, explained by parable in one of her *Illustrations of Political Economy* how emigration to Australia benefited workers in the New and the Old Worlds.[35] Beginning in the 1830's a variety of emigrant's guides began also to provide bountiful information in an immediately practical form, especially about the new colony of South Australia.[36]

The economist G. Poulett Scrope, who was active in the founding of South Australia, complained in 1833 that "we have confined our growing energies too closely within the narrow limits of this little island, and have been slow to avail ourselves of the prodigious facilities for enlarging the superficial area of our industrial pursuits which are afforded by our colonies."[37] A critic of Chalmers insisted that the "produce of the soil" could "increase at the rate at which population *would* increase . . . in America, north and south, New South Wales, &c., where no artificial checks are in operation, where population has its full swing, and the only want experienced is that of *men,* to develope by their labour the infinite capacity of the soil, and to consume the abundance with which it is ready to reward their lightest ef-

---

way there in some deportation under the revolution which so many unhappy causes are now cooperating to hasten on." Kenneth Curry, ed., *New Letters of Robert Southey* (New York, 1965), II, 36.

35. H. Martineau, *Homes Abroad: A Tale* (London, 1832).

36. For example: *The Emigrant's Guide to New South Wales* (London, 1832); Charles Medyett Goodridge, *Statistical View of Van Diemen's Land* (n.p., 1832); Henry Walter Parker, *The Rise, Progress, and Present State of Van Diemen's Land* (London, 1833); Rev. Henry Carmichael, *Hints Relating to Emigrants and Emigration* (London, 1834); John Bowie, *Notes on Australia, for the Information of Intending Emigrants* (Edinburgh, 1837); Henry Capper, *South Australia: Containing Hints to Emigrants* (London, 1838); [David Lindsay Waugh], *Three Years' Practical Experience of a Settler in New South Wales* (Edinburgh, 1838); Samuel Butler, *The Handbook for Australian Emigrants* (Glasgow, 1839); Duncan Mackellar, *The Australian Emigrant's Guide* (London, 1839); Nathaniel Ogle, *The Colony of Western Australia: A Manual for Emigrants* (London, 1839); Theodore Scott, *Description of South Australia* (Glasgow, 1839); [John Stephens], *The Land of Promise . . . South Australia* (London, 1839); Peter Cunningham, *Hints for Australian Emigrants* (London, 1841); R. G. Jameson, *New Zealand, South Australia, and New South Wales* (London, 1842); Rev. David Mackenzie, *The Emigrant's Guide; or Ten Years' Practical Experience in Australia* (London, 1845); G. H. Haydon. *Five Years' Experience in Australia Felix . . . Interesting to Intending Emigrants* (London, 1846). Both the South Australian Company and the Colonization Commissioners for South Australia issued quantities of literature for prospective emigrants.

37. G. J. P. Scrope, *Principles of Political Economy* (London, 1833), pp. 377–78.

forts."[38] An argument for emigration to the Empire rather than elsewhere was that colonial trade with the metropolis would be increased thereby. One writer explained in 1845: "Paradoxical as it may appear, every emigrant to the colonies increases our power of supporting a more numerous population at home, by the demand which he causes as a colonist for British produce and manufactures."[39]

Naturally the optimists in the colonization controversy were as anxious to portray the colonial experience in a favorable light as the pessimists were to use darkness and shade. In fact, references to Australia from both sides were almost as extravagant and extreme as they were in the debate over transportation. For example, for the affirmative John Barrow celebrated the pathetic first settlement of Western Australia as a magnificant step in the continuing British policy of overcoming territorial limitations, a policy which he advocated as follows: "Let England, therefore, we say, plant her standard on every unoccupied spot, if insular so much the better, of the habitable globe. The expense is trifling when compared with the inestimable advantages which will one day result to her from these outstretched members of her little body."[40] Herman Merivale, later the permanent undersecretary of state for the colonies, in his Oxford lectures of 1839–41 declared that "the progress of New South Wales has been so astonishing, as far as regards the production and accumulation of wealth, as to afford the most remarkable phenomena of colonial history."[41] Of Victoria a *North British* reviewer wrote: "In the

38. Review of *On Political Economy* by Thomas Chalmers, Glasgow, 1832, *Quarterly Review,* XLVIII (1832), 39–69.

39. "Colonization and the Allotment System," *North British Review,* III (1845), 409.

40. J. Barrow, "New Colony on Swan River," *Quarterly Review,* XXXIX (1829), 340. A similar account is "Australind," *Monthly Chronicle,* 1841, pp. 385–405. An especially optimistic portrayal of Australia as an investment field was M. [Robert Montgomery Martin], "On the Employment of British Capital in the Australasian Colonies," *Colonial Magazine and Commercial-Maritime Journal,* III (1840), 423–27. Pablo Pebrer, who packed a remarkable number of errors into a six-page description of the colonies, told the British people that they "ought to feel the highest gratification in seing [sic] 300,000L. a year expended in such useful and magnificent objects." *Taxation, Revenue, Expenditure, Power, Statistics, and Debt of the Whole British Empire* (London, 1833), p. 423.

41. H. Merivale, *Lectures on Colonization and Colonies* (1861; reprinted, London, 1928), p. 120. For similar views concerning South Australia see James Spedding, "South Australia," *Edinburgh Review,* LXXV (1842), 140–62. Writers in

history of man, there has been nothing like the rapid prosperity of Port Phillip, and it should not be forgotten that in this prosperity the mother country is a sharer, for incidental to its progress is a demand for British manufactured goods, which would not have taken place had these settlers remained in Great Britain." [42] In the same spirit, the economist Richard Jones reported that emigration of Englishmen to Australia "will enable them to live like kings." [43]

The contrary view of the impact of colonization was expressed by the economist and journalist J. R. McCulloch, who wrote in 1834: "Those who emigrate in the expectation of finding an El Dorado in New South Wales, or in any part of Australia with which we are acquainted, will meet with nothing but disappointment." [44] A critic writing in the *North British Review* in 1846 prepared an interesting catalog of reasons why he believed Australia in the long run was unlikely to be an economic success. Above all he regretted the heavy dependence on wool and the relative insignificance of "minor staple articles" of production. The result to date of this monoculture, he said, had been ever-present uncertainty about levels of annual income and slow development of such stimuli to growth as that "one main element of social prosperity, the middle class between the producers and the exporters of those products, the class of dealers who, as store-keepers in every village, (often the first inhabitants, and even the founders of the forest-village,) or as travelling merchants going from settler to settler, buy up or barter for the smallest quantities of those products, and carry trade and civilization into the depths of the back woods." [45] Because of Australia's dependence on wool, this

Fraser's Magazine were especially optimistic about opportunities in Australasia. As one wrote in 1843, "when we look as far as the islands of the Pacific, we behold tracts of fertile land equal in extent to Russia, France, and Austria, put together, all lying waste, yet all owning our sway." "Colonisation—the only Cure for National Distress—Mr. Charles Buller's Speech," XXVII (1843), 739. See also "New South Wales," *Fraser's Magazine*, XXVIII (1843), 426–41; and "The Beagle's Discoveries in Australia," *ibid.*, XXXIV (1846), 105–17.

42. John Anster, "Colonization from Ireland," *North British Review*, VIII (1848), 237.

43. R. Jones, *Literary Remains* (London, 1859), p. 259.

44. J. R. McCulloch, "Sydney," in *A Dictionary, Practical, Theoretical, and Historical, of Commerce* (London, 1834), p. 1104. See also Denis P. O'Brien, *J. R. McCulloch: A Study in Classical Economics* (London, 1970).

45. "Australia," *North British Review*, IV (1846), 282.

author concluded: "As a seat for colonies, she is the poorest of countries, in natural sources of wealth."[46]

But more than export dependence on staple products worried this reviewer about the Australian economy: he considered wool to be almost the worst product imaginable upon which to construct a national life:

The tropical products, the mineral products of South America, the far more valuable industry and activity in fisheries, shipping, and trade of the Northern American States, are such a staple basis of a colonial prosperity. Wool is not. It is the worst product a new colony could have turned its capital and attention to, because the production of wool employs less of combined industry and art, diffuses less occupation among the people in proportion to the land it requires, and is thus of less civilizing and beneficial influence than almost any article raised for the use of man. The shepherd state, either in the individual, or in a class or a society, is a stationary state, out of reach of the civilizing influences of man working upon man. Each unit lives isolated, for itself and by itself, and not connected by industry with any other unit in the mass. Pastoral countries never advance until they get out of the pastoral state. It was a mistake in colonial policy to give encouragement to this social state in a new settlement.[47]

In the same way that many observers were able to prophesy great gains to Britain from Australia's concentration on wool production, this reviewer could discern little but loss. He listed various subsidiary ill effects of the industry—for example, the exploitation and near extermination of the aboriginal natives who might have constituted a valuable labor supply for other activities, such as the tropical productions of the West Indies. In addition, wool effectively excluded women from such "gainful" employment in non-monetized sectors of the economy as existed in the homestead agriculture of North America:

Cooking, washing, bed-making, and house-cleaning, are needful, but not gainful occupations; and modern colonies in which these are almost the only occupations in which one-half of the population are engaged, cannot advance so rapidly as the more ancient, in which all were, by the application of their time, labour, and skill, employed in giving a value to the raw material of the colony, and earning their own

46. *Ibid.*, p. 283.
47. *Ibid.*, p. 305.

subsistence by productive industry. These physical and social causes may account, in part, for the much slower progress of our Australian, than of our old American colonies in the same space of time. . . .[48]

Another ill effect of the wool industry was that it did not hold out opportunities for self-improvement to a substantial proportion of its labor force. Hence it did not provide for the long-run development of a broad spectrum of human capital; "wandering like the natives over the face of the country as their flocks may lead them, lodging by night in temporary bark wigwams, and unprovided with the comforts or decencies or education of civilized Christian life, and not even knowing the wants and habits of civilized Christian men, workers must inevitably become a mere white tribe of natives, as savage, ignorant, and uncivilized as the aborigines."[49] Like so many later critics, this reviewer applied standards of economic performance developed mainly for other parts of the Empire, particularly North America, to the conditions of Australia. The Australian colonies suffered in popularity in the eyes of these observers because, unlike the new lands of the Western Hemisphere, they did not promise continuing haven for the middle classes of the Old World.

Applications of Economic Doctrine

Some of the earliest comments upon the embryo Australian economy came from the Scottish essayist Sydney Smith. These are worth examining in some detail, not because of the insights they contain but because they were among the first attempts to apply new liberal doctrines of political economy to conditions in the Antipodes.

In 1803 Smith discerned clear economic danger in the British adventures on the new continent; even as an overseas prison, he feared, Botany Bay was too expensive and could become a seedbed for another American Revolution. "The moment after we have suffered such serious mischief from the escape of the old tiger, we are breeding up a young cub, whom we cannot render

48. *Ibid.*, p. 284.
49. *Ibid.*, pp. 305–6.

less ferocious, or more secure."[50] But Smith's views were not all pessimistic. Despite the youth of the colony, he urged social theorists to examine its experiences and thereby to gain understanding of Britain's own problems. "New circumstances will throw new light upon the effects of our religious, political, and economical institutions, if we cause them to be adopted as models in our rising empire; and if we do not, we shall estimate the effects of their presence, by observing those which are produced by their non-existence."[51] Already Smith could dream of the day when "the respectable part of the community" would be in better proportion to the "depraved inhabitants," and he urged the colonial government to formulate national policy from the beginning with an eye to sound economic principles. About the probability of such advice being accepted he was not optimistic: "The Governor, who appears on all occasions to be an extremely well-disposed man, is not quite so conversant in the best writings on political economy as we could wish; and indeed (though such knowledge would be extremely serviceable to the interests which this Romulus of the Southern Pole is superintending), it is rather unfair to exact from a superintendent of pickpockets, that he should be a philosopher."[52]

In this first economic appraisal of the colonies, Sydney Smith anticipated a crucial policy question which concerned many observers in later years: whether Australia should foster a subservient and cheap labor force or an enterprising and prosperous one. He himself favored the latter alternative and rejected the notion that wages should be kept low as a stimulus to capital investment. As one of the first philosophical prescriptions for Australian economic policy, his statement on this matter is worth citing at length:

50. S. Smith, "Collins's Account of New South Wales," *Edinburgh Review,* II (1803), 32. This and other contributions by Sydney Smith to the *Edinburgh Review* are reprinted in his *Collected Works.* A review of Collins's work similar in skeptical tone to that of Smith appeared in the *Analytical Review,* XXVIII (1798), 125–32. This reviewer found the account interesting, but doubted that the settlement effort was worthwhile. He concluded: "It is impossible . . . to peruse the volume, without perpetually recurring to the *cui bono?*"

51. *Ibid.*, p. 33.

52. *Ibid.*, p. 37.

The high price of labour is the very corner-stone on which the prosperity of a new colony depends. It enables the poor man to live with ease; and is the strongest incitement to population, by rendering children rather a source of riches than of poverty . . . the high prices of labour which the Governor was so desirous of abating, bid fair, not only to increase the agricultural prosperity, but to effect the moral reformation of the colony . . . the avaricious love of gain, which is so feelingly deplored, appears to us a principle which, in able hands, might be guided to the most salutary purposes. The object is to encourage the love of labour, which is best encouraged by the love of money.[53]

By 1819 Sydney Smith had before him a variety of fairly elaborate descriptive works upon which to base more extensive comments about Australia, in particular a book by the future Australian statesman W. C. Wentworth, *A Statistical, Historical, and Political Description of the Colony of New South Wales* (London, 1819), which gave a firsthand account of colonial growth, using the analytical framework of Adam Smith. Wentworth stressed the importance of transport development, free institutions, and the "natural" progress of economic growth. Sydney Smith found nothing here to make him modify his earlier views, and he remained worried about what he believed were Mercantilist follies perpetrated in the colonies, while he marveled at the progress which had been achieved "in spite of the afflicting blunders and marvelous cacaeconomy of their government." [54] He outlined three major criticisms of the colonies which later economists echoed for more than a century: excessive public works, geographical dispersion, and government control of prices. On the first point he said: "Regularity is of consequence in planning a metropolis; but fine buildings are absurd in the infant state of any country." On the second he said: "The difficulties of a new colony are such, that the exertions of all the arms and legs is wanted merely to cover their bodies and fill their bellies: The passage from one settlement to another, necessary for common intercourse, is a great waste of strength: Ten thousand men, within a

53. *Ibid.*, p. 39.
54. S. Smith, "Botany Bay," *Edinburgh Review*, XXXII (1819), 37. For a more extensive discussion of Wentworth's growth theory see my *Economic Enquiry in Australia*, pp. 300–303.

given compass, will do much more for the improvement of a country, than the same numbers spread over three times the space;—will make more miles of road, clear more acres of wood, and build more bridges." On the third point—the correct role for government in the marketplace—he offered a specific word of advice. "An examination on the principles of Adam Smith, and a license from Mr. Ricardo, seem to be almost a necessary preliminary for the appointment of Governors." [55] One of the few tasks which Smith prescribed for government in Australia was public education "to prevent the hereditary tendency to larcenous abstraction." [56]

Sydney Smith repeated his views on Australia in later years with few important changes, except for some increase in optimism and an expression of hope that the continent could become "a famous and potent nation" and a "new America." By 1828, perhaps as a result of the several editions of Wentworth's work and especially the expanded *Statistical Account* of 1824, he reported that his fears about creating a whole race of criminals had declined; "instead of treading in the steps of their progenitors, [they] almost invariably render themselves conspicuous by a course of life directly opposite; and are, in a more than ordinary degree, temperate and honest." [57]

Whereas Sydney Smith, without setting foot outside Britain, provided one of the first applications of Adam Smith's new economic doctrines to Australia, one of the first intensive applications of the older Mercantile principles was prepared by John Henderson, a military surgeon and visitor to the colonies from India. In a book entitled *Observations on the Colonies of New South Wales and Van Diemen's Land* (Calcutta, 1832) Henderson addressed himself to the question how best this colony could be organized and operated for the maximum gain and least cost to the mother country. He calculated that an amount in excess of 6 million

55. "Botany Bay," pp. 37 and 38. Governor Brisbane in the 1820's set out to apply principles of political economy to the colonies in a manner similar to that prescribed by Smith. See J. J. Eddy, pp. 130–33.

56. "Botany Bay," p. 33.

57. S. Smith, "New South Wales," *Edinburgh Review*, XLVII (1828), 94; see also "Oxley's *Tour in Botany Bay*," *ibid.*, XXXIV (1820), 422–30; and "Botany Bay," *ibid.*, XXXVIII (1823), 85–104.

pounds had been invested in Australia, which yielded an unsatisfactory rate of return in the form of raw materials of only around 1 percent.[58] He recommended a panoply of reforms to improve this yield. Above all, the rate of settlement and the range of goods produced should be increased so as to achieve economies of scale.[59] Female convicts should be encouraged to breed a growing labor force, and for every convict "the hopes of reward must be proportionally held out to him, as well as the fear of punishment." Strict economy should be observed in public construction, towns should be reduced in size, and a competent body of supervisory personnel should be attracted to operate larger and more efficient agricultural units.[60] He proposed that all the institutions of colonial society, from the banks to the law courts and the governor's office, be geared to encouraging the maximum production of export staples. In a word, "The object of all ought to be, therefore, to become productive."[61] He suggested that after their terms of office had been completed governors be judged strictly according to their economic performance:

> The facts required to be proved would be but few; namely, that in consequence of his, the Governor's exertions, the colony had advanced in happiness and prosperity. That the total wealth had accumulated in a greater ratio than the population. That the existing exports had increased by regular annual increments. That other sources of income had been commenced during his administration, and were about to succeed those exports, whose present supplies were becoming equivalent to the demand. Lastly, that the instruction of the rising generation had been properly attended to.[62]

Henderson laid heavy stress on the need for careful planning and strict social discipline. He warned especially against what he thought were certain wasteful tendencies in the colonization process which might be prevented through central direction; in particular, he feared the importation of larger quantities of capital

58. J. Henderson, *Observations . . .* , Australiana Facsimile Editions No. 103 (Adelaide, 1965), p. 24. The first part of the book is entitled "Observations on the Political Economy of New South Wales and Van Diemen's Land."
59. *Ibid.*, pp. 28 and 35.
60. *Ibid.*, pp. 16, 18, 22, 56, 63–65, 73, and 96.
61. *Ibid.*, p. 26.
62. *Ibid.*, p. 71; and also p. 87.

than could be employed effectively with existing labor supplies. Where the labor force was inadequate, the presence of excess capital caused inflation rather than economic growth; "the increase of specie into the new colony, or the investment of capital, whether by the Government, or by individuals, is prejudicial to its rising progress, and tends to restrain its productive power." [63] Anticipating the observations of many later travelers, Henderson suspected that Australian conditions were conducive to social and racial decline; "whatever be the causes, the fact is plain and undeniable, that the British character in both colonies is deteriorated; nor do I perceive any probable cause, why it should not continue still further to retrograde." [64]

In his book of observations, probably little-known in Britain but representative of an important and growing strand of British opinion, Henderson revealed clearly that in his view questions raised by colonial policy were similar to those encountered in the operation of a business enterprise. Criteria for policy formation should be aggregate exports, net cost, and profit to the owners, i.e., the mother country. Despite Henderson's clear statements that application of "the best known principles of political economy" in a colony would lead to "the greatest degree of human happiness through its increasing population" and his concern that in Australia "We are transplanting a sucker from an ancient tree to a different soil, and it will require our utmost attention to prevent it from degenerating," he paid little attention to such aspects of the colonial economies as patterns of income distribution or "balance" among industrial sectors. Unlike Sydney Smith, moreover, he was not at all hesitant about using the power of the state to achieve his objectives.

At first sight it may seem surprising that the principal British economists of the first half of the nineteenth century paid so little attention to the actual growth process in the colonies, for growth was a subject in which they had deep interest. An explanation for the want of interest may lie in the economists' confident belief that they had already discovered the main factors which

63. *Ibid.*, p. 36; and also p. 47.
64. *Ibid.*, p. 45; and also pp. 88 and 90.

determine the growth pattern of any economy: population pressure, resource scarcity, and capital accumulation.[65] The colonies clearly were parts of the world destined to be spared temporarily the nemesis of population pressure and to receive returns on labor and capital which would for a time be exceptionally high. Consequently, it was possible for economists to devote their attention to the Old World, where the growth-inhibiting forces had their greatest strength. An appreciation of the neglect by British economists of the rich development experience of their own Empire during the first half of the nineteenth century can be gained from Nassau Senior's remarks on the subject of colonization. In his celebrated *Outline of the Science of Political Economy*, published first in the *Encyclopaedia Metropolitana* in 1836, he made almost no comment on actual colonial experience. Instead he described in hypothetical terms what a "body of emigrants" "must" do when it "arrives on the coast of an unoccupied district." He explained how settlers in a new country, as in an old one, would gradually undertake more and more extensive and intensive agriculture while their growing stock of labor and capital pressed on the land and raised the costs of production:

> Every increase of wealth and population raises the price of raw produce. Increase of price occasions an increase of supply, raised at a comparatively greater expense. The price falls in consequence of the increased supply, but is prevented from falling to its former level by the increase which has taken place in the cost of producing that part of the whole supply which is brought to market at the greatest expense.
>
> The effect will be the same whether we select for the scene a continent or an island; a district containing soils of every degree of fertility, or of precisely uniform quality.[66]

This account remained unchanged in the many later editions of the work, and Senior ignored the obvious inconsistencies with the actual patterns of colonial development as they unfolded. Senior made little mention of the many pecularities of colonial economic history, not even the epochal technological changes which

65. See Erskine McKinley, "The Theory of Economic Growth in the English Classical School," in Bert F. Hoselitz, ed., *Theories of Economic Growth* (Glencoe, 1960), pp. 89–112.

66. N. Senior, *Outline of the Science of Political Economy* (1836; reprinted, London, 1938), pp. 107–8.

brought startling cost and price *reductions* in the colonies, such as the introduction of Merino sheep and the invention of Ridley's stripper in Australia. The clear implication of Senior's words was that analysis of colonial conditions was quite unnecessary to gain an understanding of the main forces in colonial development, and both he and most of his readers lived by his word.

To several prominent economists of the first half of the nineteenth century, notably Robert Torrens and Edward Gibbon Wakefield, Australia was of special interest because it afforded a convenient locale for experiments in the foundation of new communities.[67] But even in this respect, Australia's role was limited because its contribution was principally as a blank slate upon which the reformers could draw their schemes.[68] The economists'

67. Australia's place in this discussion has been described in R. C. Mills, *The Colonization of Australia (1829–1842)* (London, 1915); Douglas Pike, *Paradise of Dissent* (Melbourne, 1957); and Peter Burroughs, *Britain and Australia, 1831–1855* (Oxford, 1967). Like the other colonial theorists Torrens thought of training in political economy as a prerequisite for the Australian governors. J. J. Eddy, p. 251. As one of the foremost economist-statesmen of the day, Torrens' views are especially important. See Lionel Robbins, *Robert Torrens and the Evolution of Classical Economics* (London, 1958).

68. See, for example, Edward Gibbon Wakefield, *The New British Province of South Australia* (London, 1834); Robert Torrens, *Colonization of South Australia* (London, 1835). Torrens dealt with a specific proposal, and with the general theory of colonization, rather than with Australia itself. For evidence to support his contention that South Australia was well suited for agricultural settlement, he cited such authorities as Wentworth, Carmichael, Lang, Bennett, and Prinsep (pp. 81, 82, 89, 120, 212–17). See also William Hutt, *Emigration and Colonization: A Speech* (London, 1832); Robert Gouger, *Emigration for the Relief of Parishes Practically Considered* (London, 1833); Charles James Napier, *Colonization; Particularly in Southern Australia* (London, 1835); *The Great South Land* (Stirling, 1838). The unfamiliarity of systematic colonizers with actual conditions in the colonies was emphasized, above all, by critics in the *Westminster Review*. One said of Torrens' work that "there is not one new fact brought forward to show the peculiar eligibility of Australia. . . . The truth is, that there is no country in the world, of the same extent, of which the spontaneous products are so scanty and so worthless." "South Australian Colony," XXIII (1835), 213–39; and also "New South Australian Colony," *ibid.*, XXI (1834), 441–76. A scheme for social engineering in Australia, less well known than the Wakefieldian one, was presented to the Royal Geographical Society in 1838. Captain Vetch of the Royal Engineers outlined a "careful design and systematic arrangement" for the political administration of Australia which he said "would tend to promote the future welfare of the inhabitants." From European experience he concluded that the population might reach 153 million. He proposed ten administrative divisions, apparently drawn arbitrarily on a map with a ruler, with present-day Western Australia divided into "Victoria" and "Dampieria," part of the Northern Territories called "Tasmania," and much of Victoria and New South Wales "Guelphia." Apparently, economic considerations had almost no part in the distribution of territory. "Considerations on the Political Geography and Geographical Nomenclature of Australia," *Journal of the Royal Geographical Society,* VIII (1838), 157–69.

interest was far more in the structure of the experiments—what the colonies could become—than in the environment in which the settlement was to occur; and characteristically, neither Torrens nor Wakefield ever set foot in Australia. The main doctrinal innovation which passed from this discussion into the accepted corpus of economic theory was the alleged need for "systematic colonization" and the desirability of restricted land dispersal so as to achieve compact settlement.[69] Despite Wakefield's use of New South Wales as the backdrop for his fictitious *Letter from Sydney*, in which these ideas received their first popular expression, it is doubtful that Australian conditions provided the germ for Wakefield's schemes. The systematic colonizers, like most other Englishmen, were far more familiar with conditions in North America and the West Indies, where their ideas may have had some direct applicability and, in any event, were not new. It is questionable, moreover, whether the notion of land restriction had much validity in a continent like Australia which was dependent largely on pastoral and (later) mineral staple raw materials.[70]

The Economic Image Is Formed

Australia's small and ambivalent place on a British economist's horizon by the middle of the nineteenth century and the impact of the controversies described above can be appreciated by examining a few random comments from some important economic writers of the day. First, John Stuart Mill in his *Principles of Political Economy* (1848) was mildly complimentary. He noted good and bad examples of colonization practice and concluded with approval that "the effective desire of accumulation is strong" and all "who can possibly be born, can find employment without overstocking the market." Nassau Senior was more enthusiastic.

69. An influential convert to the compact settlement doctrine was Earl Grey. See *The Colonial Policy of Lord John Russell's Administration*, I, 303–45.

70. The treatment of the Antipodes by British economists around mid-century more as an abstraction than as a living reality has a parallel in the use during the same period of Australia and New Zealand as the backdrop for fictitious Utopian creations. See for example: Lady Mary Fox, ed., *Account of an Expedition to the Interior of New-Holland* (London, 1837); *The Southlanders: An Account of an Expedition to the Interior of New Holland* (London, 1849); and Samuel Butler, *Erewhon* (New York, 1961; first published in part in the 1860's).

He expressed amazement at the rapid growth of sheep and wheat, and he speculated: "It is not impossible that during the [existence] of some of us who [are now living] the population of Australia may be as large as that of England is now." The statistician George Porter, on the other hand, was relatively gloomy. In his comprehensive survey, *Progress of the Nation*, he declared that "it appears to be altogether improbable that the colony can ever assume anything approaching to the importance of our North American possessions, either in regard to productiveness or population." [71]

The London *Economist*, which has been described as the most influential "general practitioner" of contemporary liberal economic theory in Britain, presented a cautious but optimistic view.[72] The paper expressed concern at some evidence of retention of misguided practices in the colonies, such as those implicit in colonization "schemes"; but still when it surveyed the state of the colonies in 1850 it described the "rise and progress of our Australian colonies" as "one of the wonders of modern civilisation," especially as "they have been nourished into importance almost by the refuse of our society, deposited at a distance of half the globe." The *Economist* pointed out that "the colonies are of less importance to us as consuming our manufactures than as supplying us with raw produce, and affording a large field where our surplus population may both provide for themselves and minister to the wants of people at home." [73] The same paper was quick to add a year later that no exceptions could be made to sound economic principles in the case of the colonies, and in particular it insisted that subsidies should not be provided for transport development. The pronouncements of the *Economist*

71. J. S. Mill, *Principles of Political Economy*, variorum ed. (Toronto, 1965), pp. 65, 191–92, 194, 343–44, and 966. Nassau Senior, *Industrial Efficiency and Social Economy*, ed. S. Leon Levy (New York, 1928), I, 250, 253, and 357; George Porter, *Progress of the Nation* (London, 1847), pp. 131–32.

72. James Wilson, the *Economist's* founder, was editor from 1843 until 1859, when he was succeeded by Walter Bagehot. Nassau Senior was "responsible for the paper's news and views on foreign affairs under both Wilson and, for a time, Bagehot." Herbert Spencer was Wilson's assistant from 1846 to 1853. *The Economist, 1843–1943: A Centenary Volume* (London, 1943), pp. 3, 8, 12, and 18–20.

73. "The Australian Colonies," *Economist*, VIII (1850), 788; also "The Prospects and Progress of Australia," *ibid.*, I (1843), 50–51.

on this occasion are worth repeating, for in part they constitute the first of many sermons read to the colonies during the second half of the nineteenth century on this topic: "Public money voted by Parliament with a view to secure cheaper and quicker passages and cheaper and quicker freights than could otherwise be obtained, is a direct violation of those laws which forbid the State to interfere between competitors in different trades in their struggles to serve the public." [74]

Karl Marx, although poles apart from both Mill and the *Economist* on questions of social theory, was relatively close to them in views of Australia. He was aware of the colonies' role as efficient suppliers of raw materials, and thereby as inhibitors of economic revolution. He was also contemptuous of Australia's convict origins; it was, he said, "a State of unconcealed blackguards," a veritable "United States of deported murderers, burglars, ravishers, and pickpockets." [75]

Aubrey De Vere, as much poet as political economist, but soon to be appointed Professor of Political and Social Science in the New Catholic University of Dublin, expressed in pungent terms the root of the nagging concern many observers had about Australia. As he wrote in an article for the *Edinburgh Review*, "the rank deposit which we have left on those remote shores has blighted some of the fairest regions of the earth with its exhalations: the vices of the old and the new world have met there, in one fermenting mass. . . ." [76] With comments such as this and the vague awareness of what seemed to be fundamental colonial economic problems, it is not surprising that Englishmen approached the questions of gold and self-government for Australia at mid-century with some caution and hesitation.[77]

74. "The Australian Steam Postal Service," *Economist*, IX (1851), 1034.
75. Henry Mayer, *Marx, Engels and Australia* (Melbourne, 1964), pp. 100–104.
76. A. De Vere, "Colonization," *Edinburgh Review*, XCI (1850), 55.
77. See W. A. Townsley, "English Opinion on the Australian Colonies Government Act (1850)," *Historical Studies: Australia and New Zealand*, V (1851/53), 38–46; and R. Torrens, *Political Economy and Representative Government in Australia* (London, 1855), Part II. Australia's doubtful reputation had also spread abroad by mid-century. Simonde de Sismondi pictured the colonies, characterized by penal labor and large sheep stations, as responsible for undesirable dispersion and destruction of the aborigines. "The Colonies of the Ancients Compared with Those of the Moderns, as Regards Their Influence on the Happiness of Mankind,"

Important patterns of British perception of the Australian economy were well established by 1850 and are worth summarizing briefly at this point. First, Australia had been compared with and judged according to the dominant economic models of the time. Sydney Smith, using the new political economy of Adam Smith, looked from afar for departures from the policy norms of laissez-faire. John Henderson on the spot applied Mercantilist doctrine to assess the value of Australia to the mother country. Second, a variety of writers discussed aspects of the Australian colonies which were relevant to the controversies over penal reform and subsidized colonization; here they were used mainly to illustrate firm positions pro or con, and in the process they became the victims of much casual prejudice and unsupported calumny. Third, the Australian economy before 1850 began, albeit in a small way, to stimulate some flashes of new thinking on the subject of economic growth. Innovative thought came not from the great men in the field such as Senior or Merivale, whose ideas on the subject were already set, but from a *North British* reviewer in 1846 who speculated about the role of staple products in economic development and anticipated, at least in outline, the "staples theory" of Harold A. Innis in the 1920's and 1930's. This particular innovation came to naught, but it indicated that the existence of Australia could be an inspiration for creative thought in Britain as well as an excuse for cant.

After sixty years of existence, Australia was still understood by most Britons through secondhand, prejudiced, and partial images. These images were not only cloudy, they must have been barely recognizable to the residents themselves.

---

in *Political Economy, and the Philosophy of Government* (London, 1847), pp. 245–85. It was in recognition of British doubts about the wisdom of Australian self-government that Robert Lowe addressed the Society for the Reform of Colonial Government in 1850. See his *Speech on the Australian Colonies Bill* (London, 1850).

· 2 ·

Self-Government and Gold: "The Alsatia of the Antipodes"

Two events combined at the middle of the nineteenth century to draw the attention of British observers to Australia more urgently than before. The first was the grant of increased local autonomy through the Australian Colonies Government Act of 1850 and subsequent legislation. The prospect of colonists rather than the British Parliament determining many aspects of colonial affairs shifted the focus of interest from London overseas and raised serious questions about what Britain stood to gain or lose from this transfer of authority. British musings over the virtues of self-government and the value of the colonies were given a sudden impulse by a second event, the discovery of large quantities of gold in New South Wales and Victoria in 1851.[1]

Information about the new gold flowed from Australia to Britain quickly and in a variety of forms. Newspapers and other periodicals were full of comment on the riches pouring forth;[2] special government publications were issued;[3] and emigrants'

An earlier version of this chapter was published in the *Journal of Economic History,* XXX (1970), 405–26.

1. Accounts of the gold rush are contained in Geoffrey Blainey, *The Rush That Never Ended: A History of Australian Mining* (Melbourne, 1963); Charles L. Barrett, ed., *Gold in Australia* (London, 1951); and Jay Monaghan, *Australians and the Gold Rush* (Berkeley, 1966).

2. E.g., *The Times,* September 20, 1851, p. 8; April 7, 1852, p. 6; March 17, 1853, p. 5; January 12, 1856, p. 12; and December 30, 1856, p. 8. *The Times* and other papers reprinted extracts from Australian newspapers as well as original correspondence. Other early accounts are J. G. F., "A Trip to the Australian Diggings," *Colonial and Asiatic Review,* I (1852), 32–39; "The Gold Fields of Australia: Being the Substance of a Recent Lecture at Leamington; by Mr. Fairfax, of the 'Sydney Morning Herald,'" *ibid.,* 312–19; and W. Shaw, "Prospects of Australia," *Colonial Magazine and East India Review,* XXIII (1852), 237–49.

3. Beginning in May 1851, collections of official "Correspondence" and "Papers" relative to the gold discoveries were published in London. These contained considerable data about economic affairs as well as about other aspects of the

guides[4] with varying degrees of fidelity advised prospective settlers and gold seekers about what they would find in the new El Dorado and how to get there. Responding quickly to the sudden market for more extensive descriptive accounts, recent travelers and old colonists alike issued a stream of publications which ranged from sensationalist pamphlets to detailed historical and statistical compilations prepared with colonial government sponsorship.[5] The bulk of the literature now shifted dramatically

rushes. They included extracts from Australian newspapers and comments from such prominent local residents as William Westgarth (a complimentary contemporary review of Westgarth's work is *Eclectic Review*, October 1857, pp. 372–80), e.g., *Correspondence Relative to the Recent Discovery of Gold in Australia* (London), I (1852), pp. 3 f., II (1854), pp. 88 f., and 195–204.

4. Examples of emigrant guides are A. Mann, *The Gold Fields of Australia* (London, n.d. [c. 1852]); R. S. Anderson, *Guide to Emigrants to Australia* (Glasgow, 1852); publications of John Capper from 1852 to 1858 listed in J. A. Ferguson, *Bibliography of Australia*, V (Sydney, 1962), 537–38; George French Angas, *Australia: A Popular Account* (London, 1855); William Geddes, *On Emigration to New South Wales* (London, 1855); *Cassell's Emigrants' Handbook* (London, 1852); and publications of Frederic Algar listed in Ferguson, V, 54–57.

5. Examples of this large literature are M. Matheson, *Facts from the Australian Gold Diggings* (London, 1852); Rev. David Mackenzie, *The Gold Digger: A Visit to the Gold Fields of Australia in February, 1852* (London and Dublin, n.d.); Samuel Mossman, *The Gold Regions of Australia* (London, 1852, and later editions); Godfrey C. Mundy, *Our Antipodes* (London, 1852); John Henry Pepper, *The Australian Gold Fields* (London, 1852); John Skinner Prout, *A Voyage to Australia; and a Visit to the Gold Fields* (London, 1852); F. Lancelott, *Australia as It Is* (London, 1852; 2d ed. 1853); Henry Hussey, *The Australian Colonies* (London and Adelaide, n.d. [c. 1855]); Robert M. Martin, *Australia* (London, n.d. [c. 1855]); Robert Caldwell, *The Gold Era of Victoria* (London, 1855); Edward H. Hargraves, *Australia and Its Goldfields* (London, 1855); William Campbell, *The Crown Lands of Australia* (Glasgow, 1855); "Frank Foster," *The Rise and Progress of Australia, Tasmania, and New Zealand* (London, 1857, and later editions); John Askew, *A Voyage to Australia and New Zealand* (London, 1857); William Patrick Andrews, *Colonization in India and Australia Compared* (London, 1858); Frank Fowler, *Southern Lights and Shadows* (London, 1859); P. Just, *Australia* (Dundee, 1859); Richard Henry Horne, *Australian Facts and Prospects* (London, 1859); Rev. John Davies Mereweather, *Diary of a Working Clergyman in Australia and Tasmania Kept During the Years 1850–53* (London, 1859); William Kelly, *Life in Victoria* (London, 1859); Arthur Kinloch, *Letters from South Australia* (London, 1861); Henry Parkes, *Freehold Homes in a Gold Country* (Birmingham, 1861); Roderick J. Flanagan, *The History of New South Wales* (London, 1862); Benjamin Arthur Heywood, *A Vacation Tour at the Antipodes . . .* (London, 1863); Thomas McCombie, *The History of the Colony of Victoria* (London, 1858) and *Australian Sketches* (London, 1861; 2d ser., 1866); Sir Richard Graves MacDonnell, *Australia: A Lecture* (Dublin, 1863); Rev. Frederick J. Jobson, *Australia; with Notes by the Way* (London, 1862); and the numerous publications of William Westgarth. Publicity attached to the gold discoveries caused the non-gold colonies to advertise their attractions in the face of this new competition. See, for example, Hugh M. Hull, *The Experience of Forty Years in Tasmania* (London, 1859), published with government support in three thousand copies for distribution in Britain. The letters home of a French miner, Antoine Fauchery, published first in 1857, have recently been translated and republished as *Letters from a Miner in Australia* (Melbourne, 1965).

from material based on hearsay to the results of direct observation. The most influential single work was probably William Howitt's *Land, Labour and Gold; or, Two Years in Victoria*, which was published both in London and in Boston and went through two editions (1855 and 1858). Howitt was a well-known literary figure in whom educated readers could have confidence, and his writings were cited often by economists, journalists, and others.[6]

Gold attracted British attention to the Australian economy in a way that generations of colonization reformers and publicists had failed to do. A tripling of the population in the 1850's to a total of more than one million, and the production of gold worth more than one hundred million pounds were spectacular achievements indeed. In the short space of little more than a decade, views about the development process in the colonies were firmly established for the rest of the century.

The Significance of Gold: "Headlong Depreciation" or the "Great Society"?

The gold discoveries of the 1840's and 1850's in California and Australia were monetary events which, like the return to specie payments earlier in the century and the debate over bimetallism toward the end, caught the eye of economists and raised for them a wide variety of fundamental economic issues. Discussion of the probable effects of the new gold went in several directions. The greatest urgency was attached to the question of what the direct impact would be of the new supplies upon the world economy, and in particular upon price levels, interest rates, balances of payments, and the volume of employment.[7]

6. Charles Gavan Duffy turned to "Howitt's recent book" and then to Howitt himself for "information which I could rely upon" when contemplating emigration in the mid-1850's. *My Life in Two Hemispheres* (London, 1898), II, 107. A biography of Howitt by his great-niece is Amice Lee, *Laurels and Rosemary: The Life of William and Mary Howitt* (London, 1955).

7. The debate over effects of gold in the 1850's has been discussed by R. S. Sayers in "The Question of the Standard in the Eighteen-Fifties," *Economic History (A Supplement to the Economic Journal)*, II (1933), 575–601, and more recently by Frank Fetter, *Development of British Monetary Orthodoxy, 1797–1875* (Cambridge, Mass., 1965), pp. 240–49. Representative contributions to the dis-

The immediate reaction of most economists to the discoveries was to argue from the quantity theory of money that price levels would increase in the proportion which the new gold bore to the total gold in circulation. A subsidiary effect, they pointed out, would be that future patterns of income distribution would be altered as contracts over time remained payable in currency of depreciated value.[8] On balance, the quantity theorists concluded, the world would be no farther ahead after the inflation, and the resources used in mining gold were effectively wasted. Thomas De Quincey, economist remembered better as confessed opium eater, wrote in 1852, "Every ounce of Australian gold, were there no other addition, should locally be so much more than is wanted." There was considerable disagreement over the probable extent of inflation. De Quincey agreed with Professor Michel Chevalier of the Collège de France, who had raised the alarm first in France, that if the flow of gold were sustained, "a headlong depreciation must overtake us without warning." De Quincey concluded that

---

cussion, which paid only passing attention to Australia and were concerned mainly with currency effects in Britain, are D. T. Coulton, "Gold Discoveries," *Quarterly Review,* XCI (1852), 504–40; W. N. Hancock, "Should Our Gold Standard of Value Be Maintained If Gold Becomes Depreciated in Consequence of Its Discovery in Australia and California?," *Report of the British Association for the Advancement of Science,* XXII (1852), Transactions, 116–17; J. Crawfurd, "On the Effects of the Gold of Australia and California," *ibid.,* XVII (1857), Transactions, 160; Francis Jourdan, "The Effect of the Gold Supplies on the Foreign Exchanges Between the United Kingdom and Foreign Countries, and on the Price of Silver," *Journal of the Statistical Society of London,* XXIV (1861), 38–54; R. H. Patterson, *The Economy of Capital, or Gold and Trade* (London, 1865); G. B. Johnson, "The Influence of Gold Upon the Commercial and Social Condition of the World," *Blackwood's Magazine,* LXXVI (1854), 576–88 and 672–90; Percy Greg, "The Future Value of Gold," *Fraser's Magazine,* LIX (1859), 730–44.

8. *The Times* City correspondent reviewed the issues posed by gold in 1852 and noted an impending conflict between "annuitants" and "landlords." June 25, 1852, p. 5. After this article had raised a barrage of letters to the editor, the correspondent was compelled to state that in future he could treat the subject "only in a broad and axiomatic form, and that the responsibility should be declined of making good in detail all the abstract principles that are assumed or indicated. . . ." August 6, 1852, p. 2. The *Colonial and Asiatic Review* summarized the pamphlet literature which followed announcement of the discoveries, particularly works by Frederick Sheer, Edmund Head Browne, Andrew Johnson, and Leon Faucher, in: "Gold Discoveries and Their Probable Results," I (1852), 72–79; "The Gold Question," *ibid.,* 147–50; "M. Leon Faucher on the Precious Metals," II (1853), 129–45. The *Eclectic Review* discussed the descriptive literature in "Australia: Its Capabilities and Prospects," October 1852, pp. 389–407; and "Australian Progress," November 1852, pp. 565–78.

"the solitary hope is that the gold quarries may soon be exhausted."[9] Sir Roderick Murchison, the leading spirit of the Royal Geographical Society, who claimed that he had first prophesied the new gold in 1844, declared to the contrary that because of their superficial character there was high "improbability of any precipitate or violent disturbance being produced by the new discoveries."[10] John Ruskin, often a critic of political economy, illustrated the "waste of labour in obtaining the gold" by actually picturing a typical Australian farmer shifting his efforts from growing corn and cattle to working in the mines.[11] Bonamy Price, soon to be appointed Professor of Political Economy at Oxford, viewed the effects of the gold discoveries as so self-evident that the whole inflationary episode was worthy only of neo-Mercantilist curiosity.[12]

John E. Cairnes, still making his reputation as an economist, in the mid-1850's agreed with the pure quantity theorists about the main effects of new gold, but he thought that the incidence, the costs of inflation, and subsidiary effects throughout the world required more careful examination than they had received thus far.[13] Losses, he observed, were incurred by certain groups more than by others as a result of price increases which caused shifts

9. T. De Quincey, "California and the Gold-Digging Mania," in David Masson, ed., *The Collected Writings of Thomas De Quincey* (London, 1897), IX, 418–27. Chevalier made his famous prophecy in *De la monnaie* (Paris, 1850); *Remarks on the Production of the Precious Metals and on the Depreciation of Gold,* trans. D. Forbes Campbell (London, 1853); and later in a work translated by Richard Cobden as *On the Probable Fall in the Value of Gold* (New York, 1859). French economists were as concerned as were the English at the prospect of inflation. See also Pierre Emile Levasseur, *La Question de l'Or: les mines de Californie et d'Australie* (Paris, 1858). A typical brief summary of opinion on the subject is contained in "Money-Market and City Intelligence," *The Times,* September 19, 1856, p. 8.

10. R. Murchison, "Anniversary Address," *Journal of the Royal Geographical Society,* XXII (1852), lxxvi. See also "Anniversary Address," *ibid.,* XIV (1844), xlv–cxxviii, and "Anniversary Address," *ibid.,* XXIII (1853), cxxiv–cxxxi.

11. John Ruskin, "Essays on Political Economy. Being a Sequel to Papers Which Appeared in the 'Cornhill Magazine,'" *Fraser's Magazine,* LXVI (1862), 743.

12. B. Price, "The Great City Apostasy on Gold," *Macmillan's Magazine,* VIII (1863), 124–37.

13. The development of Cairnes' thought on the gold question can be observed in manuscript notes he took on the subject from 1856 to 1858, now contained in the National Library of Ireland (MS. 8984). Chevalier's work appears to have afforded the first inspiration. Cairnes obtained much of his information about events in Australia from the official *Papers on the Gold Discoveries,* William Howitt's *Land, Labour and Gold* (London, 1855) and various works of William Westgarth.

in distribution and "some illusion on the understanding." The big losers among nations were relatively primitive countries which suffered a depreciation of their currencies and were compelled to acquire more precious metals to balance their price levels. "Having parted with their commodities for the new money, they are unable afterwards to replace them. As their stock of coin increases, their means of well-being decline, and they become the permanent victims of the monetary disturbances."[14] Cairnes pointed out that "the new gold thus tended to enrich England and America and the gold countries at the expense of India and China and countries similarly situated."

From a worldwide point of view, Cairnes wrote, gold production could be seen to absorb productive resources and thereby reduce the output of consumable goods and services. A sequential analysis of events revealed exactly where and when the costs were incurred. The loss to the world, Cairnes explained, was visible first within a gold-producing country itself—"the country being once occupied and settled, the presence of rich gold-fields must operate unfavourably upon its agriculture . . . and this, I think, is sufficiently proved by the recent history of Australia,—a history which exhibits the strange, and I believe unprecedented, spectacle of a country, possessing an immense unoccupied territory, and a soil of more than average fertility, importing more than one-half its food."[15] Subsequently, other countries were compelled to pay the costs of gold through purchase of the metal with their commodities and revaluation of their currencies with respect to gold.

In a narrower sense, Cairnes believed, the economic effects of gold specifically upon the laboring class would be more favorable

14. J. E. Cairnes, "Essay Towards a Solution of the Gold Question," *Essays in Political Economy* (London, 1873), p. 99, reprinted from *Fraser's Magazine*, XV (1859), 267–78, and LXI (1860), 38–53; and "On Some of the Principal Effects of the New Gold, as an Instrument of Purchase, on the Production and Distribution of Real Wealth," *Report of the British Association for the Advancement of Science*, XXVII (1857), Transactions, 156–58. Other articles by Cairnes on the subject are "On the Laws, According to Which a Depreciation of the Precious Metals Consequent Upon an Increase of Supply Takes Place, Considered in Connexion with the Recent Gold Discoveries," *ibid.*, XXVIII (1858), 174–75; "Mr. Ruskin on the Gold Question," *Macmillan's Magazine*, IX (1863), 67–69; "Have the Discoveries of Gold in Australia and California Lowered the Value of Gold?" *Economist*, XXI (1863), 592–93; and "The Consequences of the Gold Discoveries," *ibid.*, pp. 704–6.

15. Cairnes, *Essays in Political Economy*, p. 33.

than those upon the entire population of a country. The mining operations increased the aggregate demand for labor and stimulated the settlement of new lands. Consequently, the increase in returns to labor would more than counterbalance the increase in the price of consumer goods. The political effects, he thought, were less predictable. All the evidence of the past pointed toward the possibility of a more authoritarian government emerging from the chaos of the discoveries, and Howitt's experiences with tyrannical gold commissioners seemed to support this prophecy. He summarized his conclusions thus:

> The discoveries of the precious metals in the 16th century resulted in the degradation and ruin of the inhabitants of the newly-found countries. It led to the introduction of negro slavery. The effect of the recent discoveries will be to raise the condition of the laborers all over the world. This is partly owing to the difficult physical conditions under which the new gold is found—but in a still greater degree to the facilities for emigration.
>
> It has been remarked on the other side that the tendency of the late gold discoveries is to lower the franchise, and then to increase the power of the democratic element in all constitutional states. In the 16th century, on the contrary, the greater portion of the new silver coming to general circulation through the treasury of Spain, its tendency was to strengthen the monarchical element. . . .[16]

In later years Cairnes termed the example of the Australian shift from agriculture to gold in response to altered conditions of comparative advantage "one of the most striking experimental verifications which a purely abstract doctrine has ever received."[17] The importance here of Cairnes' conclusions is that they helped to build in the minds of British observers an impression of gold-producing Australia as an instrument, albeit an un-

16. J. E. Cairnes, MS. 8984, National Library of Ireland. Cited with the generous permission of the Council of Trustees.

17. J. E. Cairnes, *Some Leading Principles of Political Economy Newly Expounded* (London, 1874), p. 377. Cairnes' analysis in this instance came to be viewed as a classic application of theory to practice. See "Politico-Economical Heterodoxy: Cliffe-Leslie," *Westminster Review*, LXIV (1883), 479–80; and William D. McDonnell, "Prediction as a Test in Political Economy," *Economic Review*, IV (1894), 477–89. Lord Courtney reminisced as follows for the Political Economy Club, "I do not know a more admirable illustration of economic thought and inquiry." *Political Economy Club, Minutes of Proceedings, 1899–1920* (London, 1921), p. 327.

witting one, for inflation, the wasteful use of resources, and the overall reduction of human welfare.

William Stanley Jevons, who was himself a participant in the gold rushes as an assayer at the Sydney Branch of the Royal Mint, had relatively little to say about gold. He accepted Cairnes' analysis and confined his attention to the geology of the goldfields and the extent of price fluctuations. His main contributions came in correcting some of the extravagant fears of inflation and in developing price indices to measure changes in the aggregate price level.[18]

On the controversial question of the wider "social effects" of gold Jevons was ambivalent. He argued that a modest rate of inflation of about 1 percent per year, such as that which had occurred recently, "putting out of sight individual cases of hardship, if such exist" had "a most powerfully beneficial effect":

> It loosens the country, as nothing else could, from its old bonds of debt and habit. It throws increased rewards before all who are making and acquiring wealth, somewhat at the expense of those who are enjoying acquired wealth. It excites the active and skilful classes of the community to new exertions, and is, to some extent, like a discharge of his debts to the bankrupt or insolvent long struggling against his burdens. . . . [To] overestimate the *indirect* effects of these discoveries, in creating new colonies, spreading the English people and language, and newly animating commerce, is not easy.

Yet after saying all this, Jevons concluded still that "in itself gold-digging has ever seemed to me almost a dead loss of labour as regards the world in general—a wrong against the human race, just such as is that of a Government against its people, in overissuing and depreciating its own currency." [19]

18. W. S. Jevons, "Remarks on the Australian Gold Fields," *Memoirs of the Literary and Philosophical Society of Manchester*, 3d ser., I (1862), 114–30; *A Serious Fall in the Value of Gold Ascertained, and Its Social Effects Set Forth* (London, 1863); "On the Variation of Prices and the Value of the Currency Since 1782," *Journal of the Statistical Society of London*, XXVIII (1865), 294–320; and "The Depreciation of Gold, 1847–69," *ibid.*, XXXII (1869), 449. The writings of Jevons in Sydney are discussed in J. A. La Nauze, *Political Economy in Australia* (Melbourne, 1949), pp. 26–44. Jevons pointed out in 1863 that the real inflation caused by gold might even be greater than index-number calculations revealed if the country were experiencing a depression. "Mr. Fawcett on the Depreciation of Gold," *Economist*, XXI (1863), 1041–42.

19. Jevons, *A Serious Fall . . .*, pp. 62 and 67.

In contradiction to Cairnes, Jevons, and others who viewed the Australian gold discoveries as mainly an unavoidable cause of price increases with some side effects on distribution patterns, a few economists suggested instead that Australia with its gold might be a divine instrument for social improvement and reform rather than redistribution and waste of production. They argued that Australian gold brought about beneficial developments which they had been unable to persuade government could be achieved with paper currency expansion. These included lower interest rates through an increase in the funds available for loan, gradual reductions in the real burdens of debtors through modest inflation, steadier employment from the stimulus to industry of real debt reduction, and higher wages generated by the accelerated departure for the colonies of surplus population. As early as 1853 William Newmarch, prominent economist and statistician, presented a variant of this view to a meeting of the British Association. Anticipating later Presidential rhetoric in the United States, he claimed that gold had led to the creation of a "great society":

> In the Australian colonies the effect of the new gold has been to add the stimulus of a very low rate of interest, and of an abundance of capital, to the other great and manifold causes of rapid development which they previously possessed.
>
> And, generally, we are justified in describing the effects of the new gold as almost wholly beneficial. It has led to the development of new branches of enterprise, to new discoveries, and to the establishment in remote regions of populations carrying with them energy, intelligence, and the rudiments of a great society. In our own country it has already elevated the condition of the working and poorer classes; it has quickened and extended trade; and exerted an influence which thus far is beneficial wherever it has been felt.[20]

20. W. Newmarch, "On New Supplies of Gold," *Report of the British Association for the Advancement of Science*, XXIII (1853), Transactions, 111. See also William Newmarch, "Facts and Statements Connected with the Question, Whether, in Consequence of the Discoveries Within the Last Six Years, the Exchangeable Value of Gold in This Country Has Fallen Below Its Former Level," *ibid.*, XXIV (1854), 143; "On the Emigration of the Last Ten Years from the United Kingdom, and from France and Germany," *ibid.*, XXV (1855), 183; "On Some of the Economical Questions Connected with the Effect of the New Gold in Diminishing the Difficulties of the Last Few Years," *ibid.*, XXVII (1857), 166 (title only); and "Results of the Trade of the United Kingdom During the Year 1860; with Statements and Observations Relative to the Course of Prices Since the Year 1844," *Journal of the Statistical Society of London*, XXIV (1861), 74–124. Newmarch devoted considerable space to these questions in his edition with

In 1864 a writer in the *Westminster Review* surveyed the aggregate export of gold from California and Australia after more than two decades and repeated Newmarch's optimistic conclusion. He suggested that gold had a fundamental regenerative effect on the world economy:

> To all the vital part of the population of the world—to every member of the productive classes—it is an unmixed good; it is a harvest of increased ease that they are the first to reap; and not only they, for even the unproductive classes, who live upon fixed incomes and salaries, or who draw their means of life from fees and settled payments, experience some relief in the diminished weight of taxation in a country where nearly one-half of the national revenue is collected for the purpose of paying the interest on a debt the capital of which would be so greatly reduced in value. Every capital that is invested in a non-productive manner would be lessened in its power of commanding the means and enjoyments of life; a fresh and lively spur would be applied to every form of active exertion. . . .[21]

The precise point at issue, of course, was how much the gold discoveries caused inflation and how much they increased employment and production. The extreme position that gold would stimulate only output and not prices was held by the orientalist John Crawfurd before the Society of Arts in 1863. He claimed that gold had "not only been useful to the colonists on the spot, but to the whole world, and, according to his view, gold had suffered no depreciation whatever, because it had been the stimulus which had produced goods equal in value to itself." [22] Most writers presented a case which was less absolute than this; but the more extreme writers acted as an effective spur to discussion. To give only one example of this effect, J. E. Cairnes began his study of the gold question after reading what he considered was "an ignorant and preposterous assertion" in an article on the subject in the *Examiner* in 1856.[23] He continued to be aroused by inter-

---

Thomas Tooke of *A History of Prices* (London, 1857). See esp. VI, 135–236 and 667–875. Some of the same optimism found in Newmarch was expressed by James Wyld, "Geographer to the Queen," in *Notes on the Distribution of Gold Throughout the World* (London, 1853).

21. "The Depreciation of Gold," *Westminster Review*, n.s., XXV (1864), 100.

22. J. Crawfurd, reported in Sir Charles Nicholson, *The Australian Colonies: Their Condition, Resources, and Prospects* (reprinted from the *Journal of the Society of Arts*, November 27, 1863), p. 8.

23. Cairnes, MS. 8984, National Library of Ireland.

pretations of the effects of gold such as that of William Newmarch.

Writers on the population problem in the 1850's stressed the impetus afforded by gold to the relief of population pressure in Britain. A contributor to *Fraser's Magazine* predicted in 1852: "By far the most important effects of the gold of Australia will be its influence in stimulating emigration, and improving the condition of the labouring classes." [24] William Westgarth, a prominent Australian merchant, said the same thing from the colonies with greater eloquence a year later:

> The comparative facilities held out by the circumstances of this colony to the rising generation of the mother country must prove a cause of permanent attraction to many thousands of our countrymen, whose annual emigration to the southern hemisphere will tend, by the constantly sustained identity of national character, and freshness of national feeling, to retain by the strongest of bonds the connexion of our great nation with the most prosperous and progressive of her colonial dependencies.[25]

The historian Archibald Alison, following Newmarch's argument, suggested that gold production would lead not to increased but to reduced emigration and to greater labor welfare by stimulating production and raising employment levels in Britain.[26] The journalist and assistant poor law commissioner John Lalor in his pioneering work on monetary theory *Money and Morals* (1852) accepted both of the arguments, first that new gold caused "a certain loss to mankind," and second that "the new demand will, of course, stimulate and increase production." [27] Marx and Engels drew gloomy implications from a similar conclusion. They believed that the Australian and Californian gold discoveries, by

24. "Gold and Emigration," *Fraser's Magazine*, XLVI (1852), 127–38.

25. W. Westgarth, "Minute on the Progress and Commerce of Victoria, Drawn Up for and Submitted to the Melbourne Chamber of Commerce by W. Westgarth," in *Further Papers Relative to the Recent Discovery of Gold in Australia* (London, 1853), 204.

26. A. Alison, "Gold—Emigration—Foreign Dependence—Taxation," *Blackwood's Magazine*, LXXII (1852), 203–17; "Free Trade and High Prices," *ibid.*, LXXIII (1853), 760–70; and "Gold and Emigration: In Their Effects, Social and Political," *ibid.*, LXXIV (1853), 117–28.

27. J. Lalor, *Money and Morals* (London, 1852), pp. 181–82.

providing markets, homes for emigrants, and opportunities for investment, had delayed the revolutionary crisis of capitalism.[28]

Henry Fawcett, just beginning his career as economist, used the wages-fund theory to supplement the effective-demand argument when he examined the effects of the new discoveries. He analyzed the impact on the aggregate wage bill of an increase in the currency. Gold, he said, constituted an accretion to capital. "The wage-fund is a component part of this capital. Wages are almost always paid in coin. This points to another way in which much of the new gold has been absorbed." [29]

The Irish economist T. E. Cliffe Leslie added still one more element to the argument that the total effects of Australian gold were not all wasteful. He agreed that a substantial proportion of the increase in the precious metals was used to facilitate the exchange of goods whose production it had stimulated, but in addition, he said, a part went to satisfy legitimate demands for liquidity in the East: "Even the hoards and ornaments in India, however, are not to be regarded merely as waste. They are not only as legitimate pleasures and uses of wealth as many of the modes of expenditure common in the West, but they are also the private banks and insurance offices of the Indian natives." [30] This currency "drain" to the East had long been observed in Britain, but it gained new interest during the gold years.[31]

28. Henry Mayer, *Marx, Engels and Australia* (Melbourne, 1964), pp. 104–10, 122, 124, 136–40.

29. H. Fawcett, "On the Social and Economical Influence of the New Gold," *Report of the British Association for the Advancement of Science,* XXIX (1859), 207, reprinted in *Macmillan's Magazine,* II (1860), 186–91. Leslie Stephen reported that this paper led to "the discovery of Fawcett." *Life of Henry Fawcett* (London, 1885), pp. 183–84. It is interesting that Marx agreed with this conclusion of Fawcett. K. Marx, *Capital,* Vol. III (1894; English trans., Moscow, 1959), p. 490. The *Economist* regarded Fawcett's paper to the British Association as one of those "very rare occasions" when "any absolutely new truth can be propounded to such a body. . . . Mr. Fawcett, at Newcastle, raised a question as to the effect of the gold discoveries in Australia and California, and thereby drew attention to several important but rather neglected facts." XXI (1863), 1011.

30. T. E. Cliffe Leslie, "The Distribution and Value of the Precious Metals in the Sixteenth and Nineteenth Centuries," *Macmillan's Magazine,* X (1864), 314. See also *Essays in Political Economy* (London, 1888), pp. 269–331. Cliffe Leslie's explanation was viewed with some skepticism by more orthodox economists. E.g., "Politico-Economical Heterodoxy: Cliffe-Leslie," *Westminster Review,* LXIV (1883), 479–80.

31. E.g., W. Nassau Lees, *The Drain of Silver to the East, and the Currency of India* (London, 1864).

Newmarch, Alison, Fawcett, and Cliffe Leslie all pictured gold discoveries as correcting or helping to counteract various defects in the British economy, and they had in common a weak basis in contemporary theory. They questioned the self-regulating character of the economic system pictured in the classical model, but like others in the same tradition, they were not able to present a convincing picture of how else the system could operate.[32] These authors rested their arguments in large part on the existence of what now we would call a liquidity preference demand for money and the possibility of long-term unemployment caused by inadequate effective demand. These concepts could not be defended convincingly until after publication of Keynes' *General Theory* in the 1930's. Australia's image as a gold producer was not substantially improved by the efforts of these pioneer macroeconomists.

The special economic problems created in Australia by the discovery of gold were not of central concern to British economists. One exceptional piece of analysis did come from Robert Torrens, who had a personal interest in the fate of South Australia and whose son, R. R. Torrens, was South Australian treasurer at the time. Torrens described the paradox of rapid gold production generating deflation because of inflexibility in the currency supply. He approved of emergency measures to issue a token currency in the form of stamped bullion, and he advocated a local mint as a long-term solution to the problem.[33] This, however, was not the type of subject which was able to fascinate British economists for long.

The Value of Australia

The discovery of gold precipitated serious questioning in Britain of the future role for the Australian colonies in the Empire.

32. See B. A. Corry, *Money, Saving, and Investment in English Economics, 1800–1850* (New York, 1962), esp. Chaps. 5–8.

33. R. Torrens, *Political Economy and Representative Government in Australia* (London, 1855). Torrens cited with approval in this pamphlet a similar analysis of the situation by William Purdy, London Manager of the South Australian Bank, entitled *South Australia and the Gold Discoveries* (London, 1853). An earlier defense of the South Australian Bullion Act by Lieut. Governor Sir H. E. F. Young was published in *Further Papers Relative to the Recent Discovery of Gold in Australia* (London, 1853), pp. 137–38.

The queries were given urgency by a number of coincidental developments. First of all, Australia by the 1850's had come to assume a value in the eyes of the British people which could only have been dreamed of by the most optimistic propagandist a few years before. The volume of trade with the colonies had grown steadily and—of equal significance—depressions, unemployment, and political rumblings in the Old World during the 1840's had placed a special premium on homes abroad for destitute and discontented labor and "redundant" capital. Economists such as J. R. McCulloch who had been lukewarm to the benefits of colonization in the 1830's could be lyrical on the subject in the 1850's. For example, McCulloch wrote in 1854:

> An extensive voluntary emigration has been going on for a lengthened period from Great Britain to which, as everybody knows, an extraordinary stimulus has been given by the discovery of the gold fields in California and Australia. And no one can doubt that this emigration has been signally advantageous not only to the emigrants themselves, but to all classes of the community. Wages have been raised, and the condition of the labourers materially improved. And at the same time that this has been done, the shipping interest has been enriched by the demand for vessels to carry away the emigrants; and a new and rapidly increasing demand has been created for all sorts of manufactured products. Hence the unprecedented increase of manufactures, commerce, and shipping; and the unexampled success that has latterly attended most sorts of industrial undertakings.[34]

The need for a safety valve against famine and unrest in Ireland and the Highlands of Scotland looms large in most discussions of the value of colonies during the 1850's and early 1860's.[35] More-

34. J. R. McCulloch, *A Treatise on the Circumstances Which Determine the Rate of Wages and the Condition of the Labouring Classes, Including an Inquiry Into the Influence of Combinations*, 2d ed. (London, 1854), p. 24. Cf. "Sydney," in J. R. McCulloch, *A Dictionary, Practical, Theoretical and Historical, of Commerce* (London, 1834), p. 1104. McCulloch argued that the increased employment afforded by colonization was an important reason why the gold discoveries caused only moderate inflation. See his two articles in the 8th ed. of *Encyclopaedia Britannica*, ed. T. S. Traill (Edinburgh, 1853–60) on "Precious Metals" and "Money," the latter reprinted in J. R. McCulloch, *Treatises and Essays* (Edinburgh, 1859), pp. 1–80.

35. William Rathbone Greg, industrialist and social critic, was one of the most eloquent exponents of the value of colonies to Britain in the 1850's. Unsigned articles by him on the subject are "Highland Destitution and Irish Emigration," *Quarterly Review*, XC (1851), 163–205; "Shall We Retain Our Colonies?" *Edinburgh Review*, XCIII (1851), 475–98; "The Modern Exodus in Its Effects on the British Islands," *North British Review*, XVIII (1852), 259–302; and "Our Co-

over, as Herman Merivale explained in 1862, the colonies assumed even greater significance for the "social well-being of the community" after the outbreak of the American Civil War, when they became the only secure destinations for British emigrants.[36]

There were several reasons why during the 1850's Australia, more than the other colonies, was viewed as specially valuable to Britain. First and above all else, the Australian colonies were conspicuously successful at producing valuable staple products at competitive prices and under terms of the new British policy of international free trade. Second, they were comparatively free of internal political and native problems, in contrast to the Cape Colony or British North America; in the latter the memories of two rebellions still lingered and talk was rife of annexation to the United States. In the British West Indies, a satisfactory adjust-

---

lonial Empire and Our Colonial Policy," *ibid.*, XIX (1853), 345–98. See also Rev. Henry Mackenzie, *A Sermon on Colonization from the Highlands and Islands of Scotland to Australia* (London, 1852). The annual meetings of the National Association for the Promotion of Social Science heard papers on the importance of colonies as outlets for emigration almost every year during the late 1850's and 1860's. Australia was usually viewed with wonder for its capacity to generate both jobs and trade. As a high point in 1863 the meeting of the Association contained a section headed "Emigration" with the following papers: R. R. Torrens, "On the Relations Between Great Britain and Her Possessions Abroad"; C. E. Bagot, "An Ample Fund for Emigration in the Colonial Crown Lands"; Henry Jordan, "Queensland—Principle and Operation of Its System of Emigration"; Thomas McLaughlan, "The Influence of Emigration on the Social Condition of the Highlands"; Jane E. Lewin, "Female Middle-Class Emigration"; Charles Drysdale, "Inadequacy of Emigration as a Means of Raising Wages in Old Countries. Being a Criticism of the Views of Mr. Hermann [sic] Merivale and Mr. Henry Fawcett"; *Transactions of the National Association for the Promotion of Social Science*, 1863, pp. 579–624. See also J. M. Mackay, "Emigration," *ibid.*, 1858, pp. 556–62; Nicholas Waterhouse, "The Results of Emigration," *ibid.*, 1858, pp. 562–75; C. H. Bracebridge, "Juvenile Emigration," *ibid.*, 1866, p. 793; Edward Jenkins, "Emigration and the Duty of Government Respecting it," *ibid.*, 1868, pp. 628–29; and a session on "Emigration," with papers by R. R. Torrens, Brooke Lambert, and others, *ibid.*, 1869, pp. 524–50.

36. Herman Merivale, "On the Utility of Colonies as Fields for Emigration (Read Before Section F of the British Association in 1862)," *Journal of the Statistical Society of London*, XXV (1862), 496. For similar enthusiastic statements see Henry Moule, "Emigration in the Nineteenth Century," *Home and Foreign Review*, III (1863), 472–96; "England and Her Colonies," *Fraser's Magazine*, LXVIII (1863), 454–70; Lieut.-Colonel Kennedy, "On the British Home and Colonial Empire in Its Mutual Relations," *Report of the British Association for the Advancement of Science*, XXXIV (1864), 169, in abstract; and Miss Rye, "On Female Emigration," *Journal of Social Science*, I (1865–66), 445–56. Miss Rye reported that in Australasia there was "a maximum of pay for a minimum of work," and in Queensland "if the men will only keep sober, and the women chaste, there are magnificent openings for hundreds of our countrymen yet" (pp. 446 and 454).

ment had not yet been achieved from slavery or the old Mercantile system, and India was in the throes of mutiny. Third, the Australian colonies seemed willing, at least for the moment, to continue accepting convict labor, the hardest portion of the redundant labor force for which to find new homes. Finally, the hope remained in at least a few British breasts that Australia would one day form the nucleus of a wider Empire in the Pacific.

The London *Economist,* accustomed to reacting quickly to topical matters, raised some of the significant issues posed by gold for Australia's role in the Empire as early as 1851, the year of the discoveries. First of all, the paper expressed serious concern about the possible loss to Britain from a shift in Australian production out of wool to gold. Whereas economists a century or so earlier might have welcomed the colonial production of precious metals with unalloyed joy, the *Economist,* in the classical tradition, was ambivalent. Gold was recognized as useful primarily to facilitate exchange; and as explained above, most respectable economists accepted a simple quantity theory of money which seemed to imply that if more gold were produced, the volume of trade would not increase but would simply take place at higher prices. True, gold could be exchanged abroad by the colonies for imported goods, causing foreigners to bear part of the real cost of inflation. But compared with wool, which stood at the basis of a major British industry, gold had to be ranked of secondary value. The *Economist* concluded that "as a matter of profit or loss . . . even gold may be bought too dear."[37] These fears grew in intensity when an observer such as William Howitt could report from the goldfields themselves: "The golden apple of temptation is here continually ejecting the children of Adam and Eve out of

37. "An Australian California," *Economist,* IX (1851), 979; "Sheep Farming in Australia," *ibid.,* p. 1097; "Wool, as Affected by the Australian Gold Digging, the Kafir War, and the State of the Continent," *ibid.,* pp. 1229–30; "The Australian Gold Diggings. The Supply of Wool," *ibid.,* X (1852), 557–58. A suggestion for subsidized emigration to assist the pastoralists is contained in "Australia: Its Gold Fields and Its Wool," *Colonial and Asiatic Review,* I (1852), 114–21. This article may be contrasted with another, one month earlier, where gold is prophesied to initiate an adequate flow of independent emigration. "Australian Emigration," *ibid.,* pp. 63–71. After gold, the work of emigration advocates such as Caroline Chisholm is viewed with special favor. "Mrs. Chisholm on Emigration. Being the Substance of an Address Recently Delivered by That Lady at Newcastle," *ibid.,* pp. 480–84; and "Colonial Wools," *ibid.,* II (1853), 221–26.

their paradises. The mania grows every day."[38] Discussions of the colonies came regularly to contain neo-Physiocratic assertions of the greater social value in agriculture than in mining. One typical writer reminded his readers: "It is a maxim of political economists that the basis of national prosperity rests upon the abundance of food to be obtained for the sustenance of the people."[39]

The Times feared that the labor attracted to the colonies by gold was not of a type which could easily be absorbed by a pastoral economy; "it is the quiet indolent people, unused to the activity of towns, or of hard labour, that are alone fitted for the shepherd life, and that would not be speedily induced to change it for the excitement of the gold fields."[40] After a year of careful observation in which an accelerated flow of emigrants of all sorts seemed likely to make possible the continued production of both staples, wool and gold, the *Economist* believed still that it "would clearly have been more convenient and more profitable if our imports of other commodities had been greater, and of gold less."[41]

The *Economist* and other observers as early as 1851 were concerned about the moral temptations of the industry. "The pursuit of mining, and especially of gold digging," the paper argued, "is essentially a lottery, in which the prizes are very alluring, but the blanks very numerous. . . . Hazard and speculation supplant steady industry; a spirit of gambling takes the place of patient endurance; and, in the search for gold, real wealth and solid character are alike sacrificed."[42] Evidence of the unstable character of the Australian colonists seemed to be everywhere. William Howitt reported from Victoria that "the Melbournians, from some cause or other, have shown themselves from the beginning of their brief history, a most mercurial race,—the maddest speculators in the world. At the slightest touch of prosperity, up they go

38. Howitt, *Land, Labor and Gold* (Boston, 1855), I, 37.
39. Samuel Mossman, *Our Australian Colonies: Their Discovery, History, Resources and Prospects* (London, 1862), p. 334.
40. *The Times*, 2 Dec. 1851, p. 3.
41. "The Production of Gold. The Effect on the Rate of Interest," *Economist*, X (1852), 1062; "Western Highlanders for Australia," *ibid.*, pp. 588–89; and "Highland Emigration Society," *ibid.*, p. 676. For similar statements see also John Lalor, *Money and Morals: A Book for the Times* (London, 1852), pp. 181–82.
42. "The Gold Diggings in Australia," IX (1851), 1062.

beyond the clouds, and if they met the man-in-the-moon in their flight, he would never convince them that they must descend again—till they actually fell." [43] Commentators said repeatedly that long-term wealth could never come to Australia from mining and that it was "her sheep-farms and her fertility to which she must look for a future of real abundance and prosperity." [44] The history of Spain, always chilling to an Englishman, was recalled, wherein national calamity had ultimately followed a shift from agriculture to the search for glittering hoards in the New World.[45]

The moral dangers of speculative mining were said to be compounded in Australia by the presence of convicts, the descendants of convicts, and an unhealthy proportion of non-Englishmen, especially Irishmen. Boom-town activities were described in lurid terms. For example, one account said as early as 1853: "The social condition of Victoria is the one odious blot on the fair picture of Australian life. Melbourne is a thieves' paradise, the Alsatia of the Antipodes." [46] Despite the optimism of such colonial planners as Lord Grey, who believed that the gold discoveries would afford fortuitous and honest employment for all kinds of labor supplied from the British prisons, the suspicion was firmly planted that convicts combined with gold could produce a monster.[47] Few features of colonial society struck British visitors as forcibly as what they took to be the prevalence of crime. Howitt remarked of

43. Howitt, *Land, Labor and Gold,* I, 294–95.

44. "The Old World and the New," *Fraser's Magazine,* L (1854), 305.

45. John Plummer, a "factory operative" and later a colonist himself, developed this analogy for a prize essay entitled *Our Colonies* (London, 1864), pp. 9–10. John E. Cairnes in 1856–58 undertook extensive reading on the Spanish experience to see if lessons for Britain could be learned from it. See MS. 8984, National Library of Ireland.

46. "The Social Condition of Melbourne," *Colonial and Asiatic Review,* II (1853), 193; and "Australian Gold Discoveries," *ibid.,* 453–75; Rev. H. Berkeley Jones, *Adventures in Australia, in 1852 and 1853* (London, 1853). "Alsatia" was a slang name for Whitefriars, a sanctuary for lawbreakers in seventeenth-century London. On this point also see William Howitt, *Land, Labor and Gold,* I, 77. Howitt warned the colonial government to watch carefully "the low, red-republican foreigners" on the diggings who were "a class of men far below the lowest English in a knowledge of the principles of moral reform and progress, who have no ideas but of physical force, and the demolition of any existing authority." *Ibid.,* pp. 440–41. On the question of convicts in the population, he said, "the old wound remains deep in the bosom of society, and will not cicatrize at present." *Ibid.,* II, 368.

47. [Henry George] Earl Grey, *The Colonial Policy of Lord John Russell's Administration* (London, 1853), II, 25–26, 47–56, 75–79, 109.

Victoria: "Of the number of thieves in this colony, the united contributions of Sydney, Van Diemen's land and the *purlieus* of dear old London, the *Argus*, one day this month, gave a singular evidence. It contained twelve columns of advertisements of stolen horses!" [48] Writers agreed that the combination of freedom and great wealth would be socially disastrous in these circumstances, where the "population is of a very mixed character, not very amenable nor much attached to any particular kind of law, and very much given to follow their own inclinations, and to regard their own will as their only law." [49] It was widely accepted in Britain by the 1860's that discovery of gold in Australia had sounded the death knell of the role of the colonies as convict receptacles.[50]

The New Zealand pioneer John Robert Godley argued after a visit to Australia that gold had made matters steadily worse by dislocating the economy and causing "a perpetual straining off of the best portion of society." [51] This type of attack was converted easily after the decline of gold into charges that irresponsibility, "commercial speculation," and "over-trading" had become part of the national character.[52] It also lent support to the argument that special efforts should be made quietly to improve the character of the Australian population before it was too late. One anonymous "Member of Parliament" declared that the economic development as well as the social and political health of the colonies depended upon the establishment of a true colonial aristocracy:

Probably, nothing has more tended to retard the advancement of our colonies in the development of their resources, and to check the stream of emigration among the more educated class of society, than the fact

48. Howitt, *Land, Labor and Gold,* I, 302; see also II, 8.
49. "New Position of Australia," *Economist,* XI (1853), 6. It should be noted that despite its strictures about convicts, the *Economist* was willing to sanction continued transportation to Van Diemen's Land to overcome the labor shortage. "Peopling the Southern Hemisphere," X (1852), 88–89; and "The Convict System in Van Diemen's Land," *ibid.*, p. 117.
50. E.g., "English Convicts: What Should Be Done with Them," *Westminster Review,* XXIII (1863), 1–32.
51. J. R. Godley, "Extracts from the Journal of a Visit to New South Wales in 1853," *Fraser's Magazine,* XLVIII (1853), 506–18 and 634–47. For attribution of this article see J. A. Ferguson, *Bibliography of Australia,* V (Sydney, 1963), 1079.
52. E.g., J. H. Tremenheere, "The Australian Colonies, and the Gold Supply," *Quarterly Review,* CVII (1860), 37–39.

that in leaving their native country, persons of position and of capital, or who had the means of living, if not luxuriously, at least in comfort in the mother country, have hesitated to quit all that, which, to so many, constitutes the charm of life. . . .

To them no wealth would repay the loss of social communion, and the interchange of thought arising from similarity of taste, and a like faculty of appreciating what is beautiful and desirable.[53]

William Howitt argued that land for the middle classes was the only reform likely to bring about improvement in the quality of the colonial population:

If there were land—land everywhere, and for everybody—the intellectual might come; the more the better, for intellectual men love country life, and are capable of cultivating cheap land of their own; and the more the better again, that they might breathe a soul through the brute mass, shed refinement and intelligence around them, and offer points of attraction to a superior class to come over and settle.[54]

A marked ambivalence toward Australia became characteristic of British writers as soon as it seemed likely that gold production would continue. On the one hand, they applauded with surprise the colonies' demonstrated ability to produce simultaneously both wool and gold, to absorb surplus population, and to import British manufactures. It was comforting to see the number of acres under cultivation double in the 1850's to a total of more than one million. William Hughes, a geographer, claimed that the "attractions held out by the 'diggings' constitute an inducement for the transference of our surplus labour to the other side of the globe, stronger than anything else could have supplied, and in the absence of which the truths of political economy might have been taught in vain, the dictates of philanthropy passed by unheeded, and lectures, essays, speeches, and pamphlets, treated alike with comparative disregard." It seemed even that automatic mechanisms operated to check ill effects of lost labor on the mother country. A contributor to the *Economist* pointed out: "A rise of

53. A Member of Parliament, *The British Colonies. Shall We Have a Colonial Baronage? or Shall the Colonial Empire of Great Britain be Resolved Into Republics?* (London, 1852), p. 8. Support for encouragement of "the aristocratic element" in Australia was given also in "Our Colonial Policy," *Colonial and Asiatic Review*, I (1852), 1–10 and 93–107.

54. Howitt, *Land, Labor and Gold*, II, 120. See also II, 316.

wages would immediately check emigration, and the process, therefore, contains within itself a self-adjusting principle calculated to prevent excess."[55]

On the other hand, writers began also to detect, in addition to gambling propensities, what they took to be unusual selfishness and extravagance amongst the colonists. First of all, they found that the level of personal consumption per capita was "quite enormous compared to the old stinted and frugal communities of Europe."[56] And of even greater seriousness, the infantile Australian colonies seemed bent on constructing public works with an almost manic fervor. With mounting ferocity the *Economist* read sermons to the colonies during 1854–55 on the principles of laissez-faire applied to government expenditure. For example:

> The Government expenditure on such works rarely or never promotes national welfare. It is especially the duty of Government to protect the people in creating and acquiring wealth, not to set about creating wealth itself. For a Government to borrow to make public works, expecting that the outlay will be so profitable as to pay the interest, and after a short period redeem the capital, is not warranted by experience. The plan has been very rarely successful. The wants of the public are, in most cases, the wants of private men. . . .[57]

55. William Hughes, *The Australian Colonies* (London, 1852), p. 281. "Effects of Emigration on Production and Consumption," *Economist,* XI (1853), 169. Other implicitly congratulatory statements are "Emigration and Population," *ibid.,* pp. 140–41; "The Mineral Riches and Labour of New South Wales," *ibid.,* pp. 335–36; "Exports to Australia," *ibid.,* pp. 922–23; "Latest from Australia," *ibid.,* pp. 1405–6; "The Australian Markets and Politics," *ibid.,* XII (1854), 614–15; "Australia," *ibid.,* XIII (1855), 756–57; "Protection to and Profits of Agriculture in Australia," *ibid.,* XVII (1859), 1120–21; "Agricultural Emigration. Who Should Emigrate?," *ibid.,* XXI (1863), 706–7; "Our Colonial Empire," *Westminster Review,* II (1852), 405; G. B. Johnson, "The Coming Fortunes of Our Colonies in the Pacific," *Blackwood's Magazine,* LXXVI (1854), 268–87; Richard Valpy, "The Progress and Direction of British Exports, and the Influence Thereon of Free Trade and Gold," *Journal of the Statistical Society of London,* XVIII (1855), 160–74; H. S. Chapman, "The Industrial Progress of Victoria as Connected with Its Gold Mining," *ibid.,* XXVI (1863,), 424–42; P. L. Simmonds, "On the Growth and Commercial Progress of the Two Pacific States of California and Australia," *Report of the British Association for the Advancement of Science,* XXV (1855), Transactions, 188–91; J. M. Mackay, "Emigration," *Transactions of the National Association for the Promotion of Social Science,* 1858, pp. 556–62; Nicholas Waterhouse, "The Results of Emigration," *ibid.,* pp. 562–75; "Sketches at the Antipodes," *Fraser's Magazine,* LIX (1859), 159–69.

56. "Australia—Gold and Markets," *Economist,* XII (1854), 531–32. A portrayal of Victoria as virtually a latter-day Sodom is "Social State of the Early Victorian Diggings," *Meliora,* 1863, pp. 63–82.

57. "Australia, Victoria," *Economist,* XIII (1855), 171.

Attempts by colonial administrators such as Lieutenant Governor La Trobe to explain the exceptional circumstances under which extensive public works were required in Australia did not mollify those critics who argued from high principle, including writers in the *Economist*.[58] Repeated claims by colonial experts such as William Howitt that the public works which had been constructed were not those most needed for development of the economy accentuated the skepticism still more.[59]

The gold boom in Australia had raised with dramatic suddenness a sharp conflict between the dictates of economic theory in Britain and the needs of colonial administration on the spot, a conflict which was to affect relations between the metropolis and the colonies for many years. Faced with a torrent of immigrants and a rush to the goldfields, the colonial governments had little choice but to offer vital services which had no prospect of being "remunerative," the approved test for public works, except in the broadest sense of contributing to national development in the long run. The *Economist* and other observers in the old country were prepared to attribute most subsequent disturbances in Australia, economic and political, to these departures from the true principles of fiscal parsimony.[60] Symbolically, when Herbert Spencer in the 1860's dealt with the subject of public works, he chose the notorious Australian gold rush case as his example. He pointed out that the needs of the diggers could have been answered either by the state or by private enterprise. Where the latter was employed, the result had been most satisfactory. Hence the following moral:

Until spontaneously fulfilled a public want should not be fulfilled at all. It must, on the average, result in our complex state, as in simpler ones, that the thing left undone is a thing by doing which citizens cannot gain so much as by doing other things—is therefore a thing which society does not want done so much as it wants other things done; and the corollary is, that to effect a neglected thing by artificially employing citizens to do it, is to leave undone some more important thing

58. See Despatch from La Trobe to Newcastle, May 4, 1854, in *Further Papers Related to the Discovery of Gold in Australia* (London, 1855).

59. Howitt, *Land, Labor and Gold,* I, 102, 116, 148–49, 166, 251, 319.

60. E.g., "The Condition of Victoria," *Economist,* XIII (1855), 222–24 and 307–8.

which they would have been doing—is to sacrifice the greater requisite to the smaller.[61]

Most serious of all for some British observers was the discovery of still another unfortunate proclivity among the Australian colonists—a willingness to adopt a widening range of restrictionist policies which seemed not only misguided in principle but likely to injure vital British interests. As early as 1855 the *Economist* appealed wistfully for homesteads on the American model and noted disapprovingly that large landowners in Australia were bent upon keeping immigrants from the soil: "we cannot comprehend the mismanagement that continually keeps land and labour severed, and keeps people in distress, or in a state of starvation, with all the elements of wealth around them." [62] The single theme which recurred most often in William Howitt's account of the gold rushes was the paradox of landless labor kept from settling on broad and fertile acres by the selfish cupidity of a shortsighted government.[63]

Yet the working classes too, observers noted, seemed captivated by monopolistic fallacies. The miscellaneous writer J. H. Tremenheere expressed in general terms the concern about the restrictive desires of Australian society. "It has its strikes and combinations. Agitation for objects both impracticable and unjust has found support from large masses of the people." [64] The high prices of goods and services during the gold boom were blamed on restrictive practices of settlers who were said to limit artificially the increase of supplies. William Howitt reported:

This rapacity seems to run through everything here. In the shops the prices they ask are actually amusing from their enormity, and if you seem to acquiesce in them pretty easily, they seem immediately to ac-

61. *Essays: Moral, Political and Aesthetic* (New York, 1868), pp. 86–87.

62. "Australia," *Economist*, XIII (1855), 1316; and "Australia—Land and Emigrants," *ibid.*, pp. 1064–65.

63. Howitt, *Land, Labor and Gold*, I, 17–18, 147, 325–26; II, 132, 138, 170, 247, 259, 311. He contrasted often the land policies of the United States with those of the colonies. For example, he wrote: "They are drawing daily from us the sinews of a gigantic empire, which, in Australia, we are repelling by all the force of idiotic folly." *Ibid.*, I, 254; see also I, 258, 261, 298–300; II, 134–35 and 181. Howitt attributed even the proverbial colonial taste for drink to an excessively restrictive land policy. "The drunkard will continue a drunkard till he can buy land." *Ibid.*, II, 119; see also II, 212 and 263.

64. Tremenheere, p. 39.

cuse themselves of having done themselves a serious injury by not asking more, and we have frequently found before leaving the shop, that they have quietly determined to lay on another fifty percent. on articles the price of which we asked.[65]

With respect to wage rates the charge was the same: the colonists manipulated the market for their own selfish advantage. As a general truth, Howitt remarked, "the one great principle of the colony is the Dutchman's maxim:—'Get honestly, if you can; but at all events get!' "[66] Although the *Economist* was of two minds about the virtues of convict transportation, the paper was furious at the "oppressive" and monopolistic behavior of Victoria in objecting to its continuation for Western Australia.[67] The very notion that the colonists should presume to dictate concerning disposition or use of lands which were Imperial property was anathema in Britain.

Sensitivity of colonists to the mounting criticism they faced from British commentators began to appear early in the 1850's. The Australian pioneer Samuel Mossman, in particular, reported that the "social and political" conditions of Australia were quite satisfactory and unlike those in the mining colonies of Spain. In fact, he said, Australia would "prove to the historian . . . that gold may be dug from the mine without degrading or enslaving the seekers."[68] Official sensitivity to criticism of departures from the policy precepts of classical political economy can be discerned in correspondence with the home government. For example, Governor Sir Charles Hotham provided for Colonial Secretary Sir William Molesworth a particularly interesting account of how standard principles of public finance had broken down in colonial circumstances. Faced with the emergency requirement of an increase in revenue, the colonial administration had at first imposed direct taxation at the mines in strict accordance with accepted principles. "Theoretically, nothing could be more just than that the man who profited by the gold should pay a proportion to the

65. Howitt, *Land, Labor and Gold*, I, 25.
66. *Ibid.*, I, 40; see also II, 304 and 332–33.
67. "Transportation and Australian Sedition," XXII (1864), 1339.
68. Samuel Mossman, *The Gold Regions of Australia* (London, 1852), pp. 10–11.

Crown for the right of extracting it, but practically nothing could be more unsound." Diggers who had not yet made significant "finds" were incensed at requests for fees, and they went into open rebellion. The simple answer to the problem was an export duty upon gold which, although disturbing market equilibrium like all indirect taxes, was levied only on successful miners and therefore was politically acceptable. "Leaving on one side . . . speculative questions which regard the political economist, the undoubted fact remains, that the export duty on gold has thoroughly answered its end; it has produced quiet, sustained the revenue, and is inoppressive in its character." [69]

Much of the enthusiasm for colonial self-government by the colonies which had been present in Britain before the discovery of gold had turned to skepticism by the end of the 1850's because of the change in the character of the colonial population and the number of policies adopted by the young colonial legislatures which contravened the wisdom of accepted economic theory. Approval or disapproval, of course, depended upon one's point of view; Karl Marx reported with delight in 1855 that revolutionary tendencies were mounting in the colonies.[70] A characteristic judgment of an Australian election by a *Cornhill* observer in 1862 was that "local influences, indifference, or drunkenness prevail." [71] The historian and essayist Goldwin Smith in his "Letters" on "Empire" to the *Daily News* in 1862–1863 could cite *The Times* as follows: "The fact is, that in Victoria and New South Wales, that has come to pass which was foreseen by founders of the American Constitution. Responsible government is rapidly reducing itself to an absurdity." He could also report that "I see nothing as yet among the Colonists of Australia that marks the opening life of a great nation." [72] As the gold rushes ended, the *Economist* could think only of colonial federation as a possible conservative counterweight to growing selfishness and radicalism in the colonies. A grouping of the dependencies, the paper hoped, might become a

69. C. Hotham, in *Further Papers Relative to the Discovery of Gold in Australia* (London, 1856), pp. 24 and 25.
70. Mayer, pp. 112–14.
71. "An Election Contest in Australia," *Cornhill Magazine*, V (1862), 34.
72. G. Smith, *The Empire* (London, 1863), pp. 66 and 179.

substitute for "the guidance and authority of historical traditions." [73]

The Golden Image

By the end of the "golden fifties," Australia was far better known to the people of Britain than at the beginning. The volume of literature based on direct perception, and often recorded on a traveler's trip home, had increased markedly. But all in all, Australia's reputation had not gained by the exposure. Observers recognized that the land had great pastoral and mineral wealth, but at the same time they accused the people of speculative mania, ingratitude, extravagance, radicalism, monopolistic proclivities, and participation in an inflationary process which robbed the poor to benefit the rich. The country was seen as providing at the same time remarkable examples of rapid economic development and the most extreme forms of democracy. Criticisms of the Australian economy during this period were based on class prejudice, the world view of the critics, and a priori reasoning from economic principles. Australia's defenders had begun to make themselves heard, yet they were not able with the time, resources, and theoretical equipment available to them to counteract many of the allegations of serious character defects.

The gold years brought Australia out of the mists of obscurity and identified controversial aspects of her economy for attention in the future. Perhaps of greatest importance, a framework for inspection and the outlines of a conventional image were created for literate persons in the mother country. Henceforth mere mention of many aspects of Australian society or economy would immediately conjure up visions in those who had never seen the land at first hand. Patterns of thought and outlook on Australia established during this period probably influenced not only the behavior of later colonial critics and defenders but also important facets of future relations with the metropolis and even the development pattern of the colonies themselves.

73. "The Australian Colonies and Their Federation," *Economist,* XVI (1858), 111–12.

• 3 •

Focus of Attention

Grounds for Fascination

Even after the decline in curiosity about gold, the concentration of British observers on the Australian economy was sustained throughout the second half of the nineteenth century. The first reason was simply recognition of long-term economic self-interest in this new land. Britain now imported much of the food products and raw materials she needed, some of the most important of which Australia had demonstrated she could produce with ease. Wheat exports began to Britain in 1866 and refrigerated meat in 1880. Increasingly as the years went on, the British became convinced of the value of the self-governing colonies for trade, investment, and emigration. Their views on each of these three advantages with respect to Australia are outlined below.

By the 1850's Australia was accepted as a commercial partner of steadily growing importance, with a volume of British trade per capita unexcelled by many other regions of the world. Not only did Australia provide wool, gold, and markets for British manufactured goods, she also produced an increasing variety of essential staple foods and raw materials such as cotton and wheat which events like the American Civil War proved could not always be obtained with any degree of reliability from independent trading nations.[1] Even Herman Merivale in his important article on "The Colonial Question in 1870," which was distinguished by a profound cynicism concerning the benefits of imperial soli-

1. Sir Roderick Murchison, the geographer, advocated in particular cultivation of cotton (see below, Chapter 4) as did also John Dunmore Lang in *Cooksland in North-Eastern Australia; the Future Cotton-Field of Great Britain* (London, 1847) and other publications.

darity, wrote ecstatically of Australia and her potential role as entrepôt of the Pacific: "She forms, in truth, the only division of our empire respecting which the question at issue is of any considerable importance. . . . It is difficult to exaggerate the scale of magnitude at which our relations in that quarter may arrive, or the part which Australia may have to play in connection with them."[2]

Another reason for British people to associate self-interest with Australia grew out of an extension of the views expressed in the 1840's that Australia could for a long time to come provide investment opportunities for the Old Country's capital. As Anthony Trollope, the novelist and visitor to Australia, explained, the colonies would open up "room for our capital, room for our intellects, room for our energies, and above all some means of redemption for a portion of our poor from that grinding poverty which we are unable to cure at home."[3] The rapid progress made in steam propulsion, in particular, suggested that Australia would be brought ever closer by the steamship and ever more open by the railway.

There were several variants of the case for colonies as a place for profitable investment. The first was that new countries offered essential opportunities for the maintenance of interest and profit rates in the face of sustained flows of savings. This argument was consistent with classical economic theory, even if not with the prophecies and policy recommendations of all classical economists.[4] The second variant was the old Wakefield argument that

2. H. Merivale, "The Colonial Question in 1870," *Fortnightly Review*, VII (1870), 160. Earl Grey, commenting on the Australian colonies in 1860, reported "incontestable evidence of their value to us, as well as of their own prosperity." "Anniversary Address," *Journal of the Royal Geographical Society*, XXX (1860), cxxix. A similar view is expressed by the social reformer Henry Richard Fox Bourne, in *The Story of Our Colonies* (London, 1869), pp. 198–367. Some aspects of the evolving economic relationships between Britain and Australia during the 1870's are examined in J. D. Bailey, *Growth and Depression: Contrasts in the Australian and British Economies, 1870–1880* (Canberra, 1956).

3. A. Trollope, *Australia and New Zealand* (London, 1873), I, 18.

4. The preoccupation of nineteenth-century British economists with a shortage of investment opportunities is described in A. K. Cairncross, "The Victorians and Investment," *Economic History* (*A Supplement to the Economic Journal*), III (1934–37), 277–88. George Baden-Powell waxed eloquent about the great investment opportunities in Australia. In addition to the mining of metals and agriculture, he singled out possibilities for development of the coal and chilled meat

the colonies provided employment for potential capital goods which otherwise would not come into existence in Great Britain at all. Rates of return in the Old World could not decline beyond a certain point, and thereby guarantee employment, this argument ran, because capitalists would not undertake what they considered unremunerative investments and would, reluctantly, hold funds idle. As Sir William Denison, the colonial governor, said in 1870 in explanation of colonial capital formation, "few or no Englishmen lock up the balance of their income, or their annual savings; they seek a profitable investment for these, and if they cannot find this in England, they ransack the whole world in search of it." [5]

The third variant of the investment argument was that colonies could act as a palliative for public and private economic mistakes in Britain. Whenever because of poor planning or misguided government policies domestic industry faltered, the colonies were available as a last hope for the unemployed labor and capital which resulted. John Plummer, who later emigrated to New South Wales and became a prominent journalist, explained in 1864 how this third variant did not necessarily depend on the second variant's assumption of declining profit rates:

> If nations would conform to the principles of political economy, as laid down by such writers of ability as John Stuart Mill, the evils of surplus labour and consequent pauperism would be comparatively unknown; but it is far easier to preach than to practice, and we must take the nation as it is, not as it should be, otherwise we shall only be striving after the unattainable. . . . whenever a stagnation of trade occurs, so long shall we be exposed to dangers, trials, and sufferings, like those with which the cotton manufacturing districts have lately been visited.

industries. *New Homes for the Old Country* (London, 1872), pp. 229 and 253. One of the most insistent worries was over the supply of coal. Typically, the London *Economist* greeted discovery of coal in Australia in 1854 with the remark that "as progress is made in obtaining it, there will be less occasion to press on our resources." XII (1854), 812. T. Mackay, the right-wing economic commentator, remarked to the Society of Arts in 1863, in response to a paper entitled "The Australian Colonies; Their Condition, Resources, and Prospects" by the Australian pioneer Sir Charles Nicholson, that it "must be a great consolation, after the paper lately read by Sir Wm. Armstrong at Newcastle, to find out that when the fuel of Old England was exhausted, we should have an abundant supply remaining in our own colonies." Reprinted from the *Journal of the Society of Arts*, November 27, 1863, p. 8.

5. W. Denison, *Two Lectures on Colonization* (Richmond, 1870), p. 12.

There is only one way of preventing this, and that is, the creation, or opening up, of fresh labour markets. Here such a thing is, at present, practically impossible; therefore we must look to our Colonies as the only means of supplying the deficiency experienced by us, and of rescuing our unemployed artizans from the state of pauperism with which they are continually threatened.[6]

In addition to being a field for surplus British capital, Plummer emphasized also that the empty Australian continent held land for the poor and unemployed workers of the Old Country for as far into the future as anyone could see. It will be shown later that Plummer was not exceptional in the excessively optimistic estimate he made of the opportunities there. He said:

The vast central region of Australia proves to be a country flowing—in the language of Scripture—with milk and honey. Instead of being an uninhabitable desert, recent explorers have found it to consist of smiling pastures, leafy groves, broad-running streams, extensive woodlands, and all that can tempt the enterprise, capital, and labour of men. . . . For years and years to come their resources can never be adequately developed, because of the comparative smallness of their population; and if every unemployed man, woman, and child, now living in the United Kingdom were sent thither it would be like pouring a drop of water into the ocean.[7]

Reasonable or at least respectable explanations were seldom provided for economic depressions in the nineteenth century, and unemployment continued to be offered as prima facie evidence of population "redundancy" and the operation of the Malthusian specter in the Old World. Homes and jobs overseas were suggested as the only long-run hope for excess people.[8] As the North American continent began to fill up and expansion reached the west coast, Australia seemed to many the best last resort for

6. J. Plummer, *Our Colonies* (London, 1864), p. 11; and see my *Economic Enquiry in Australia,* p. 470.

7. *Our Colonies*, pp. 18 and 23.

8. Baden-Powell took it for granted that "when England's population over abounds, it behooves her to provide an outlet for her surplus sons" (p. 440); and also *idem,* "An Empire Institute," *National Review,* VIII (1886/87), 433–42. Trollope remarked in 1875 that the colonies "should be regarded chiefly as a new and happier home for the labouring classes." *The Tireless Traveller* (Berkeley and Los Angeles, 1941), p. 93. Examples of the literature in which the colonies were pictured above all as an answer to British unemployment were plentiful in the *National Review*, e.g., J. F. Boyd, "The Depression of Trade," VII (1886), 40–53; Lord Brabazon, "State-Directed Colonization," IX (1887), 525–37; and Stephen Thompson, "The Lessons of Emigration," XIII (1889), 369–76.

surplus population.[9] Australia also had special advantages. Unlike the African, Asian, and West Indian possessions, it had minimal native problems; and unlike Canada, it seemed in no danger of being annexed by a voracious neighbor. A familiar theme in this argument, well-known earlier in the century, was that unemployment and redundancy affected all strata of society, and Australia could be a haven for all classes. Typically, a clergyman reminded prospective British emigrants to Australia in 1870: "To my mind it appears quite clear that in this great and famed land every profession and every business is *overcrowded.* The land cannot hold them, and continue to be healthy and vigorous, as of old. The remedy is emigration."[10]

In addition to feeling the spur of self-interest the British had an uneasy suspicion that in these colonies there might be seen a portent of Britain's own future. The same social forces were present in the New World as in the Old, it was thought, and in the young environment developments might move more quickly to their ultimate conclusion. A new country was the nearest equivalent to a laboratory for testing social theory. The *Economist* newspaper noted as early as 1862: "The experiments which the colonies have been making in the art of government since they became more or less independent of the Colonial Office are full of interest to the English people, and have the most important bearing on our mode of government at home."[11] Similarly, Charles Dilke in his report on the Empire, *Greater Britain,* urged that close attention be paid to the colony of Victoria; "the interest which attaches to the political condition of Victoria is extreme, since it probably represents an accurate view, 'in little,' of the state of society which will exist in England, after many steps towards social democracy have been taken, but

9. See esp. J. A. Froude, *Oceana,* new ed. (London, 1894), pp. 12 and 338; and "Colonies and Colonization," *Westminster Review,* CXXXI (1889), 13–25.

10. Thomas Henry Braim, *New Homes: The Rise, Progress, Present Position, and Future Prospects of Each of the Australian Colonies and New Zealand, Regarded as Homes for All Classes of Emigrants* (London, 1870), p. 13. A similar theme runs through *The Gentleman Emigrant,* by W. Stamer (London, 1874), wherein opportunities for large estates and sport in Australia are described, and also E. C. Booth, *Homes Away from Home* (London, 1869).

11. *Economist,* XX (1862), 233.

before the nation as a whole has become completely democratic." [12]

Whether an observer liked what he saw in the colonies did not necessarily affect the intensity of his fascination. Goldwin Smith, another influential commentator on imperial affairs, deplored almost all aspects of Australian life upon which he wrote, yet he concluded, "We see in Australia the image of what we have escaped in England, and may well profit by the spectacle." [13] The *Economist* speculated in 1864 that the current custom of prophesying the future of the colonies on the assumption that they were "all that is evil" might be a subtle maneuver by anticolonialists to accelerate the dismemberment of empire.[14] By the 1890's Edward Jenks, professor of Law at Melbourne University, could treat the notion of social prophecy from colonial experience almost as a cliché. He wrote: "Many tendencies, at present only latent in English politics, or kept in check by powerful counter-influences, have in Victoria run their unhindered course, and can therefore be studied under the valuable condition of abstraction." [15]

An important stimulus to the notion that Australian experience might be a guide for Great Britain was provided by the discovery that the advanced Australian democracy did not by any means correspond to the "liberal" economist's dream of maximum personal freedom and unencumbered trade; rather, it seemed to some that the opposite nightmares of restrictions, restraints, and government extravagance were the result.[16] Augustus Nash claimed that Australia afforded an opportunity to observe democracy developing "without let or hindrance" toward a corrupt state which "interferes with the natural energies of the people" and lives upon

12. C. Dilke, *Greater Britain* (London, 1868), II, 52. Sir George Bowen reported widespread acceptance of this notion by 1875 from a survey of contributors to the London *Times*. Stanley Lane-Poole, ed., *Thirty Years of Colonial Government: A Selection from the Despatches and Letters of the Right Hon. Sir George Ferguson Bowen, G.C.M.G.* (London, 1889), II, 49.

13. Goldwin Smith, *The Empire* (London, 1863), p. 68.

14. "The Antagonism Between England and Her Colonies," *Economist*, XXII (1864), 923–24.

15. Edward Jenks, *The Government of Victoria* (*Australia*) (London, 1891), p. vii.

16. E.g., David Wedderburn, "English Liberalism and Australasian Democracy," *Fortnightly Review*, XX (1876), 43–59.

"lavish expenditure."[17] Mounting controversy over specific social, political, and economic proposals in Britain increased interest in Australia to the point where the *Westminster Review* found it necessary by 1886 to caution against the custom of making facile comparisons. "The analogy between England and her Colonies is not complete, and the consciousness of this incompleteness should be always present with us whenever we institute a comparative study of the principles of representative government at home and abroad."[18]

A widespread conviction during the latter part of the nineteenth century that Britain had a fundamental obligation to watch over and nurture her overseas possessions gave reason for sustained attention to Australia. This doctrine of responsibility was expressed eloquently at mid-century by the Colonial Secretary Lord Grey:

> I conceive that, by the acquisition of its Colonial dominions, the Nation has incurred a responsibility of the highest kind, which it is not at liberty to throw off. The authority of the British Crown is at this moment the most powerful instrument, under Providence, of maintaining peace and order in many extensive regions of the earth, and thereby assists in diffusing amongst millions of the human race, the blessings of Christianity and civilization.[19]

This doctrine was intended principally for application to the nonwhite colonies of conquest, where it took the form later in the century of the notorious theory of "the white man's burden." But it was applied also to the white-settlement colonies, initially with regard to imperial supervision of native policies. Britain, the doctrine implied, could not leave the primitive Maoris, Kaffirs, Abo-

17. Augustus Nash, "Democracy in New South Wales," *Fortnightly Review*, XLI (1887), 312–15.

18. "Representative Government in Our Colonies," *Westminster Review*, LXIX (1886), 52. Henry Fawcett as a reforming Postmaster-General reported to Charles H. Pearson in 1883 of his "greatest interest" in Australian politics. John Tregenza, *Professor of Democracy* (Melbourne, 1968), p. 2.

19. [Henry George] Earl Grey, *The Colonial Policy of Lord John Russell's Administration* (London, 1853), p. 13. Equally eloquent statements came from the essayist W. R. Greg, "Shall We Retain Our Colonies?" *Edinburgh Review*, XCIII (1851), 475–98; *idem*, "The Modern Exodus in Its Effects on the British Islands," *North British Review*, XVIII (1852), 259–302; *idem*, "Our Colonial Empire, and Our Colonial Policy," *ibid.*, XIX (1853), 345–98; *idem*, "Our Colonies," *ibid.*, XXXVI (1862), 535–60; and "Colonial Policy," *Economist*, VIII (1850), 141–42.

rigines, or North American Indians to the tender mercies of their new colonist masters. As Charles John Bayley, Governor of the Bahamas, informed readers of the *Quarterly Review:* "Colonies are called into being, and are maintained, not only for the preservation of British interests and property, but for the limitation of British aggrandisement and the protection of the helpless, ignorant, and oppressed."[20] The theory of British responsibility toward natives in the settlement colonies was soon extended to other aspects of colonial life. The theorists accepted as a basic assumption that most British political and economic institutions were best for new countries and that these should be imposed upon the residents even if they were so misguided as not to appreciate their merit. But the principle of institutional transfer was not without paradox for British observers. A vital political institution which many of them believed deserved transplantation was self-government itself. Yet an increase in colonial autonomy, implied by self-government, seemed fraught with peril. The London *Economist* looked forward with foreboding to an increase in Canadian independence and reminded its readers in 1865 that "British rule and British institutions are better for a nation, more conducive to its welfare, its freedom, and its highest progress and development, than any yet invented."[21]

The doctrine of obligation to the settlement colonies even in the

20. C. J. Bayley, "Our Colonial System," *Quarterly Review,* CXIV (1863), 140. William Smith O'Brien, the Irish rebel leader, remarked in the treatise on politics which grew out of his transportation to Tasmania that native policy had to remain an exception to the arguments favoring colonial autonomy; "in regard to such a question as the introduction or maintenance of slavery, the mother country is manifestly entitled to prescribe conformity to the general policy of the empire. If one or all of the Australasian colonies were to take measures for establishing slavery even in a modified form, it would not only be right, but it would be the duty of the imperial Government to interpose its authority, and forbid such measures." *Principles of Government; or, Meditations in Exile* (Boston, 1856), p. 409. Similar expressions are contained in "The Duties of Civilised to Uncivilised Races," *Economist,* XVI (1858), 1036–38; Archibald Hamilton, "On the Economic Progress of New Zealand," *Journal of the Statistical Society,* XXXII (1869), 293–307; and Arthur Mills, "Colonial Policy in the Government of Coloured Races," *North British Review,* XLIV (1866), 388–410.

21. "Canada and England: The Connection and the Value," *Economist,* XXIII (1865), 464. See also, James Stephen, "On Colonization as a Branch of Social Economy," *Transactions of the National Association for the Promotion of Social Science,* 1858, pp. 96–109. On the progress toward self-government in Australia see A. C. V. Melbourne, *Early Constitutional Development in Australia,* ed. R. B. Joyce (St. Lucia, 1963).

application of control was given extra strength because it could be pointed out that in most cases fulfillment of British "responsibility" coincided with Britain's own self-interest. Colonies which were persuaded or compelled to operate on correct social and economic principles did not merely benefit themselves; they also relieved resource scarcity and population pressure at home; moreover, they would grow into strong trading partners. In the words of the statistician Stephen Bourne "a redundancy of population will become the means of producing abundant food, health, happiness, and wealth." [22]

The metaphor of Britain and Australia as parent and child was used often as a model for imperial economic relations during the nineteenth century. Britain, in the same way as a wise father, the argument ran, retained a familial obligation to watch closely the affairs of its adolescent child and to interfere where circumstances dictated, even when the child doubted the need any longer for a parental guiding hand. Anthony Trollope set forth this viewpoint eloquently in his account of the colonies:

> The need for guidance and control is that of the youth who is no longer a boy but is not as yet quite a man. He may be better educated than his father, of a higher intellect, of finer aspirations, giving promise of almost Darwinian improvement in his descent;—but he cannot be trusted to go quite alone till he has been taught by experience that paper, without gold to back it, will not long supply his necessities,—till he shall have learned that and other worldly lessons which will not come simply from high intellect and fine aspirations.[23]

E. Carton Booth, a writer on colonial topics, used the parental analogy to develop the notion of social forecast in the colonies. Discussing innovative Victorian legislation, he said: "On the principle embodied in the story of the old gentleman who, after teaching his grandson chess, was 'beaten by the boy,' England will, not improbably, follow the example of Victoria in these as well as in some other matters." [24]

22. S. Bourne, "On the Growth of Population with Relation to the Means of Subsistence," *Report of the British Association for the Advancement of Science*, XLVII (1877), 172.

23. Trollope, *Australia and New Zealand*, I, 156, and similar statements on pp. 10–11.

24. E. C. Booth, *Homes Away from Home* (London, 1869), p. 14.

Like so many other biological analogies used in nineteenth-century social theory, the comparison of imperial relations to family bonds was susceptible to a wide range of interpretations. The most obvious implication, and the one observed by Trollope, was that the imperial parent had a responsibility to keep a firm guiding hand on the colonial child and should even, where necessary, impose judicious discipline. "Childish" characteristics of colonies and their residents, including boastfulness, excessive optimism, and overall bad judgment, were noted frequently and disapprovingly by visitors such as the Austrian traveler Baron Hübner.[25] The policy dictates of this doctrine were the exact opposite of an immediate movement toward colonial autonomy deduced from economic principles by such noted liberals as Richard Cobden and Goldwin Smith. But the filial analogy was just as useful to spokesmen for the colonies and advocates of imperial unity who desired financial assistance from the metropolis. For example, Henry Kilgour explained: "The mother country ought to act towards the Colonies just as a kind, sensible father acts towards his children. When children are young, they require the paternal support, care, and protection. When grown up, they support and protect themselves." [26] In response to the suggestion that colonies assume a share of imperial defense costs, Thomas Braim, a clergyman who had served both in Britain and in Australia, said: "A young colony is like a young man, and at the best it is scarcely fair for the wealthier, older, and wiser nation, to impose upon feeble shoulders the whole burden of a responsibility so heavy and galling." [27] John Morison used the analogy in a negative way to charge that the British parent had stunted the growth of her colonial children through insufficient attention; "looking at the splendid resources of New South Wales, one thinks of the cradle of a great empire—of the child dwarfed and crippled through ignorance, neglect, and cruelty, who under wise

25. Baron Josef Alexander von Hübner, *Through the British Empire,* 2 vols., trans. from the French (London, 1886), I, 237, 252, and 305.

26. H. Kilgour, *The British Empire: Proposed Institution of a Joint Committee of the Legislatures and Governments of the Empire, Having Periodical Meetings in Great Britain* (London, 1869), p. 4.

27. Braim, p. 45. Sir William Denison used a similar argument (pp. 2–21).

guidance, might attain to the full vigour, strength, and stateliness of manhood."[28] Lord Rosebery when Undersecretary for the Home Office in 1883 told Edmund Barton, then speaker of the Legislative Assembly of New South Wales, that federation would be the signal that adolescent Australia had come of age. In the words of Rosebery's biographer, "Australia could thus speak to the mother-country with the voice of an eldest son who has attained his majority, and on whom the property is strictly entailed."[29] Charles Gavan Duffy, the Irish nationalist turned Australian immigrant, was suspicious of the parent-child analogy because it seemed to him to imply that the colonies should grow up to be near replicas of their imperial parent. He preferred a comparison with trees in a forest where variations among generations in response to environmental differences were quite normal; "the colonies are not mere branches of the Imperial tree, but saplings from the same root, flourishing in a soil and under conditions of their own, which render some modifications of structure inevitable."[30]

Flows of Information and Means of Interpretation

The development of British views toward Australia after the gold years is described in the following chapters. In this section an attempt is made to categorize very roughly some of the individuals and institutions who, in response to the interest just described, carried information about Australia to Britain and interpreted it there during the period roughly from the end of the gold fever in the mid-1860's to the late 1880's and the onset of deep depression.

The most prominent category of reporter was the stream of visitors from Britain who came to Australia for periods of several months or years and on their return home published descriptive

28. J. Morison, *Australia as It Is* (London, 1867), p. 272.

29. The Marquess of Crewe, *Lord Rosebery* (New York, 1931), p. 145. Lord Carnarvon, the former Colonial Secretary, expressed similar views after a tour through the colonies in "Australia in 1888," *Fortnightly Review*, XLV (1889), 432.

30. *Address of the Hon. C. G. Duffy, on Popular Errors Concerning Australia at Home and Abroad* (Melbourne, 1866), p. 13.

accounts of their travels. A wide range of attractions brought these wanderers to Australia: curiosity about the exotic flora, fauna, and social policies; hopes of making swift fortunes in wool or land; escape from the decadence of the Old World; [31] reunion with relations; enthusiasm for closer bonds of empire; and the search for good health.[32] Some of these visitors had intended to settle in the colonies, but returned home disappointed or disgruntled. A common pattern among those who later published their experiences was to stay for short periods with a succession of well-to-do pastoralists and businessmen as a means of "seeing the country." They made use of the long voyage home to write their observations, in which they kept in mind both the hospitality they had received and the probable interest in economic affairs of prospective emigrants.

The large number of books and articles of travelers' tales is evidence of the wide market for information about the colonies. It is possible here to provide only selected details about a few of the most prominent or representative visitors and works which had important roles in the development of opinion.

Many of the travelers' tales described little more than unusual

31. The vision of the Antipodes as a symbol of escape for British youth and as a blank slate upon which good could be written instead of evil can be seen in the experience of the Arnold family. Thomas Arnold, the elder, apparently contemplated emigrating to New Zealand in the 1830's. He wrote to Sir Thomas Pasley in 1840: "I have often thought of New Zealand, and if they would make you Governor and me Bishop, I would go out, I think to-morrow,—not to return after so many years, but to live and die there, if there was any prospect of rearing any hopeful form of society." The snake in the Antipodean Garden of Eden for Arnold was, as for so many other Englishmen, what he took to be the low quality of the residents. He continued: "I have actually got 200 acres in New Zealand, and I confess that my thoughts often turn thitherward; but that vile population of runaway convicts and others, who infest the country, deter me more than anything else, as the days of Roman Proconsuls are over, who knew so well how to clear a country of such nuisances." Arthur P. Stanley, *The Life and Correspondence of Thomas Arnold, D.D.* (New York, 1846), p. 357. Arnold expressed intense interest in both Australia and New Zealand in other letters, e.g., *ibid.*, pp. 367–68, 389–92. Arnold's oldest son, also Thomas, emigrated to New Zealand in 1847 with high hopes of escaping many of the features of the Old World. He was buoyed up in his hopes by his close friend, the poet Arthur Hugh Clough. James Bertram, ed., *The New Zealand Letters of Thomas Arnold the Younger* (Wellington, 1966). J. J. Eddy reports other proposals to implement the ideas of Robert Owen and Jeremy Bentham in Australia. *Britain and the Australian Colonies, 1818–1831*, pp. 41 and 53.

32. The common and often misguided practice of recommending a voyage to Australia as cure for everything from poor eyesight to pulmonary problems is discussed in Hübner, I, 162–63.

features of the countryside and colorful local practices such as mining, bushranging, and kangaroo hunting. They provided economic information only incidentally and to the extent that it might increase sales of their works to prospective emigrants. Several visitors, however, did arrive with a special interest in social and economic questions, and through personal reputations they were able both to obtain valuable data in the colonies and to reach large audiences with their ideas at home.

The first important traveler to Australia after the gold years was Charles Wentworth Dilke in 1866. Following a brilliant undergraduate career at Cambridge, where he was deeply influenced by Leslie Stephen and the economist Henry Fawcett, Dilke undertook an extensive fact-finding tour of the British Empire and the United States to observe and report on the worldwide expansion of the English "race." [33] Dilke's account of his travels, entitled *Greater Britain,* is marked by the brashness of youth, an arrogant condescension for much that he saw, snap judgments of people and institutions, and, on occasion, disregard for accuracy.[34] Nevertheless, the work was very perceptive on many points and was extremely readable. It went through four editions in England, was well reviewed and widely read elsewhere in the world, and brought Dilke the admiration of such distinguished economists as J. S. Mill, membership in the Political Economy Club, and assistance toward a seat in Parliament.[35] Only a portion of *Greater Britain* was devoted to Australia, and only a part of this to economic matters. On the economy Dilke's comments were neither especially profound nor trustworthy in detail, but his style was lively and comfortingly dogmatic, and he wrote with pride of what he considered were Anglo-Saxon triumphs at the Antipodes.[36] The literary success of Dilke's book helps to explain the

33. See Roy Jenkins, *Sir Charles Dilke: A Victorian Tragedy* (Fontana Books, 1968), Chaps. 1 and 2.

34. For example, when Dilke characterized Canadian statesmen as "blinded by their position" and like men "standing on the edge of a cliff . . . always wanting to jump off," he mentioned in particular "Sir James [sic] Macdonald." *Greater Britain* (1868; reprint, London, 1869), p. 69.

35. Jenkins, pp. 42–43.

36. The extent to which Dilke's work was considered authoritative can be appreciated from the references to it in C. B. Adderley's important book, *Review of the Colonial Policy of Lord J. Russell's Administration, by Earl Grey, 1853; and of Subsequent Colonial History* (London, 1869), e.g., p. 119.

stream of writers who traveled through the colonies in his footsteps.[37]

The next important visitor with a special interest in economic affairs was John Martineau, a product of the same environment which sent forth Dilke: Trinity Hall, Cambridge, and the intellectual circle dominated by Fawcett and Stephen.[38] Martineau differed from Dilke in the much stronger venom with which he described Australian social and economic institutions. His book, *Letters from Australia* (1869), is characterized by expressions of contempt for most things that he saw, especially the egalitarian and democratic aspects of Australian society. He was sympathetic to the pastoralists who were his hosts, and he feared the evolving economic system above all because it threatened the survival of this social class. Another visitor at about the same time, G. E. Carrington, reported that it had already become nearly impossible for a man of culture and education to earn a decent living in the colonies.[39]

George Baden-Powell visited Australia in the 1860's and published his impressions in 1872 in a handsome volume entitled *New Homes for the Old Country*.[40] His vantage point was similar to that of Dilke and Martineau, and his work reflects these earlier authors' sensitivity both to the hospitality of the pastoralists and

37. E.g., Sinclair Thomson Duncan, *Journal of a Voyage to Australia* (Edinburgh, 1869); Alice M. Frere, *The Antipodes and Round the World* (London, 1870); Charles H. Allen, *A Visit to Queensland and Her Goldfields* (London, 1870); George R. C. H. Pembroke and George Kingsley, *South Sea Bubbles* (London, 1872); and E. K. Laird, *The Rambles of a Globe Trotter* (London, 1875).

38. Biographical information about Martineau can be found in an obituary in *The Times*, December 20, 1910, p. 13. It is reported there that Martineau was "one of the few pupils who lived and read with Charles Kingsley at Eversley."

39. A University Man [G. E. Carrington], *Colonial Adventures and Experiences* (London, 1871). Another early example of this xenophobic genre is Robert Harrison, *Colonial Sketches: Five Years in South Australia* (London, 1862). A verse from Harrison's own composition "The Original Song of Australia" will indicate the tone of his work. He wrote:

> There is a land where money goes
> Not half so far as we suppose—
> Land of dear boots and dearer clothes!
> On many a plain the clost'ring vine
> Is spoilt—into colonial wine,
> Which makes us quaff some med-i-cine!
> Australia!

40. Also George Baden-Powell, "The Credit of Australasia," *Nineteenth Century*, L (1891), 3–12.

the prejudices of the middle-class British market for which the works were written. Baden-Powell was and remained one of the most vocal and doctrinaire advocates in Britain of imperial solidarity and absolute commercial laissez-faire, and he pursued these goals in writing about the colonies with remarkably few adjustments for the Australian scene. In describing Australia he presented arguments for an economy based predominantly on large estates operated by wage labor, and he reminded potential plantation owners of the opportunities for hunting and fishing. He employed a variant of the Wakefield case that immigrant labor should be kept from the land for its own good, at least for a number of years, but he appears to have withheld some of his more extreme criticism of colonial institutions from a desire not to discourage imperial unity or the immigration of workers.

Another British visitor who wrote on the Australian economy was the novelist Anthony Trollope. He deserves special attention if for no other reason than that he reacted vigorously to the tone and conclusions of his peripatetic predecessors. Trollope came to the colonies twice, apparently to visit his son, an unsuccessful sheep-station operator, and his writings were completed en route to provide income.[41] His rambling two-volume *Australia and New Zealand* (London, 1873) went through an initial edition of two thousand copies and was published also in fragments. It became one of the standard authorities on Australia for British readers for more than a decade.[42] It brought Trollope a return of thirteen hundred pounds for the fifteen months of "unflagging labour" it required, and he considered it "a better book than that which I had written eleven years before on the American States, but not so good as that on the West Indies in 1859." [43] He restated many

41. Anthony Trollope, *An Autobiography* (New York, 1950), pp. 341 and 348. See also Marcie Muir, *Anthony Trollope in Australia* (Adelaide, 1949); and James Pope Hennessy, *Anthony Trollope* (London, 1971), pp. 310–22.

42. Alfred Russel Wallace in his volume *Australasia* for *Stanford's Compendium of Geography and Travel*, 4th ed. (London, 1884) depended heavily upon Trollope and Howitt. E.g., pp. 137, 169, 242, and 250. A new edition of *Australia and New Zealand*, ed. with an introd. by P. D. Edwards and R. B. Joyce (Brisbane, 1967) has recently been published. Citations here are to the 1873 edition.

43. Trollope, *Autobiography*, pp. 348, 349, and 364. The *Westminster Review* compared Trollope's work with the most popular books by the colonists them-

of his views during a second visit in a series of letters to the Liverpool *Mercury* in 1875.[44] Trollope set out to correct and counterbalance what he thought were the false and uncharitable pictures of the Australian colonies drawn by his forerunners. Moreover, although even more than earlier observers a commercial writer, he gives the impression of not hesitating to run against the anti-democratic prejudices of many middle-class readers, especially in his admiration for free selectors and the working class. Yet Trollope was only partly successful in improving the accuracy and avoiding the biases which he sought to correct.[45] His sympathy with some radical aspects of social and economic policy in Australia was clearly greater than that of most earlier visitors, but he could not help feeling pity for the squatter and deep concern about the future effects of extreme democracy.

The late 1870's and early 1880's were not vintage years for reports from visitors to Australia, one exception being the youthful Socialist leader H. M. Hyndman, who cut his eyeteeth on social problems in Australia.[46] However, in 1885 James Anthony Froude, distinguished author, editor of *Fraser's Magazine,* and biographer of Thomas Carlyle, revived interest in the region with his tour and resulting volume *Oceana, or England and Her Colonies* (1886). Froude had long been an advocate of the Em-

---

selves and judged him to be both "readable" and "full of genial common sense." "The Australian Colonies," LIV (1878), 311–47.

44. Republished as *The Tireless Traveller* (Berkeley and Los Angeles, 1941).

45. By his own admission Trollope depended heavily upon secondary sources for historical background material, especially the work of the Australian historian George Rusden and a school textbook by F. Proeschel. *Australia and New Zealand,* I, 205 and 351.

46. See for example S. H. Jones-Parry, *My Journey Round the World,* 2 vols. (London, 1881); Fritz Geroldt, *Nine Colonies* (London, 1881); and Richard Tangye, *Reminiscences of Travel in Australia, America, and Egypt* (London, 1884); but also H. M. Hyndman, "The Australian Colonies and Confederation," *Fraser's Magazine,* XIV (1876), 641–52; and Chushichi Tsuzuki, *H. M. Hyndman and British Socialism* (London, 1961), p. 12–16, for an account of Hyndman's trip to Australia which began in 1869. Tsuzuki does not mention the *Fraser's* article and repeats some of the inaccuracies committed by Hyndman himself, e.g., "Hyndman met Charles Pearson, the author of *The Yellow Danger* [sic]" p. 14. Lord Rosebery was deeply moved to imperial fervor by a visit to Australia in 1883, but this did not lead to a published account. The Marquess of Crewe, *Lord Rosebery* (New York, 1931), pp. 144–48. The prominent Unitarian Moncure Conway also visited Australia in 1883 and met Rosebery while there, but he did not publish a full account of his journey until 1906 in *My Pilgrimage to the Wise Men of the East* (Boston, 1906), pp. 70–104.

pire, but heretofore in the abstract and from afar; as early as 1870 he had argued that the greatness of England depended on her possessions overseas.[47] Now, viewing the colonies from a vantage point twenty years farther into Britain's industrial growth than that of Dilke, Froude was able to see colonial development against a background of mounting social ills in Britain and a growing threat to Britain's commercial supremacy from aggressive rivals. He portrayed the colonies as far more than useful trading partners and heartwarming examples of racial adaptation to new conditions by Anglo-Saxon pioneers. They alone, he believed, provided secure markets and raw materials for British factories and amelioration for the human degradation of the Old Country. He wrote plaintively from Australia as follows: "If I had Aladdin's lamp, I would empty our towns of half the squalid creatures that draggle about the gutters, and pour them out here to grow fat and rosy again."[48]

There is both an urgency and a proprietary tone in Froude's writings which were not prominent in the accounts of his predecessors. On grounds of need rather than of sentiment he advised Britain to form an association among her dependencies. "With her colonies part of herself, she would be, as Harrington had foreshadowed, a commonwealth resting on the mightiest foundations which the world had ever seen."[49] Froude was not less critical of Australian government and society than were his forerunners, but he added a new poignancy to the attacks.

Just as Dilke in the 1860's and Trollope in the 1870's stimulated other travelers to follow their footsteps, so a succession of accounts in the 1880's may have drawn inspiration from Froude.[50]

47. Two essays by Froude in *Fraser's Magazine* in 1870, "England and Her Colonies" and "The Colonies Once More," are reprinted in his *Short Studies on Great Subjects* (London, 1907), III, 1–32 and 188–223.

48. Cited in Waldo Hilary Dunn, *James Anthony Froude: A Biography* (Oxford, 1963), p. 521. The Australian journalist A. Patchett Martin described the growth of Froude's interest in Australia in "James Anthony Froude: A Personal Reminiscence," *National Review*, XXIV (1894/95), 488–501. Froude told Martin that "Australia was of much greater importance than either Canada or the Cape; for the English in Australia have the whole country to themselves without any foreign competitors, or any serious native question to complicate the problem" (p. 490).

49. Froude, *Oceana* (1894), p. 10.

50. E.g., W. J. Woods, *A Visit to Victoria* (London, 1886); D. Vannorman Lucas, *Australia and Homeward* (Toronto, 1888); J. C. McCoan, "Seven Weeks in

One of the most reflective and most often cited works was by the Austrian scholar and diplomat Baron Josef Alexander von Hübner, entitled *Through the British Empire.* Hübner was said to be the illegitimate son of Prince Metternich, and after a career which included embassies to Paris and the Vatican, he devoted himself to world travel.[51] He made ample use of such secondary authorities as Trollope, but he also brought to the study of Australia a fresh viewpoint and wit.

The second major category of sources of information in Britain about Australia, after the travelers' tales, was the daily press and other periodicals. A few British papers for limited periods had regular correspondents of considerable distinction, such as the novelist David Christie Murray, the economist-journalist Arthur Ellis, and the Oxford historian Charles H. Pearson.[52] They also on occasion dispatched special correspondents, such as Flora Shaw (later Lady Lugard) for *The Times.* At the least, many periodicals reprinted articles from the colonial press, with or without comment. The *Economist* carried large quantities of economic data—increasing as the century went on—from which, in addition to businessmen and others, Karl Marx gathered much of his information about the continent.[53] A variety of literary and learned societies in their meetings, journals, and proceedings devoted attention to facts and commentary about Australia—in particular the British Association for the Advancement of Science, the Royal Statistical Society, the Royal Colonial Institute, the Political Economy Club, the Royal Geographical Society, and the National Association for the Promotion of Social Science; and just as the period covered in this chapter was ending, the British

Australia," *Westminster Review,* CXXIX (1888), 52–76; "Wanderer" [E. H. D'Avigdor], *Antipodean Notes* (London, 1888); and Carnarvon, "Australia in 1888," *Fortnightly Review,* XLV (1889), 420–43. One disgruntled visitor implied even that she had been duped into a wasted trip by Froude. She wrote: "Australia, as a whole, appears to me, I must confess, most uninteresting; a second or third rate England, with the substitution of a 'climate' for our own fogs and bitter winds." E. Katharine Bates, *Kaleidoscope; Shifting Scenes from East to West* (London, 1889), p. vi.

51. Obituary, *The Times,* August 1, 1892, p. 4.

52. Contributions by Pearson to such periodicals as the *Spectator* and the London *Speaker* are listed in John Tregenza, *Professor of Democracy* (Melbourne, 1968), pp. 259–63.

53. Henry Mayer, *Marx, Engels and Australia* (Melbourne, 1964), p. 142.

Economic Association (after 1901 the Royal Economic Society).[54]

The British government, directly and indirectly, provided information about the colonies. In Parliament and in the Sessional Papers, Australian affairs were discussed and data were published, particularly as they affected trade, migration, and investment. The development of responsible government in the colonies did gradually limit the policy areas upon which there needed to be official comment in Britain. But indirectly the British government continued to provide the means for interpretation of Australian economic affairs through the private efforts of returned colonial servants, especially such governors as Sir William Denison, Sir George Bowen, Sir Hercules Robinson, Sir Anthony Musgrave, Lord Carrington, and Lord Brassey.[55] These men usually were intensely loyal to the colonies in which they had served, but at the same time they were not unwilling to denounce policies and practices of which they disapproved.

A final category of commentator about the Australian economy was the colonists themselves, who as the years went on became increasingly self-confident and capable of defending themselves. The most outspoken group was the body of officials (many of whom had been colonial political leaders) posted to London as agents general or as official and unofficial representatives to hold discussions with government and raise funds. Among the most effective spokesmen at different times were William Westgarth, Archibald Michie, Edward Braddon, R. Murray Smith, B. R. Wise, George Reid, and Francis Labilliere.[56] Another group of colonists

54. The publications of these bodies which dealt with Australia are discussed more extensively in my *Economic Enquiry in Australia*, esp. Chap. 13.

55. Writings by all of these governors are mentioned below. Sir George Bowen's despatches and letters *Thirty Years of Colonial Government*, ed. Stanley Lane-Poole (London, 1889) document the important role of the governor as propagandist. The book was well reviewed in *Westminster Review*, CXXXIII (1890), 353–59.

56. Westgarth probably wins the prize for duration and volume of output. For almost half a century, beginning in the 1840's, he provided economic data and intelligent comment about the colonies for the daily press, the other periodicals, a variety of associations, and a wide range of public meetings. A typically complimentary review of articles on Australia he wrote for *Encyclopaedia Britannica* is in the *Economist*, XX (1862), 483. A discussion of the descriptive works about Australia available by the late 1870's is "The Australian Colonies," *Westminster Review*, LIV (1878), 311–47. This article was translated into French in *Revue Britannique*, January 1879, pp. 5–56. A discussion of colonial publicists earlier in

who helped to shape British opinion were men who had gone out to the colonies with a reputation already made, most notably the Irish nationalist Charles Gavan Duffy and the Oxford don Charles H. Pearson. Still another group which included men like the journalist-entrepreneurs David Syme and Edward Pulsford made a reputation in Australia through active participation in such worldwide controversies as those over commercial and land policy. The early Australian government statisticians Henry Hayter (Victoria), Timothy Coghlan (New South Wales), and R. M. Johnston (Tasmania) gained high reputations at an early date in Britain, and this increased their impact both at home and abroad.[57] Finally, a group of colonists which included the politician and cleric John Dunmore Lang and the historian-archivist James Bonwick became firmly identified as standard sources about Australia to which readers should look for information. Exhibitions which were held in Britain, Europe, and Australia itself, frequently provided the excuse for descriptive accounts of the colonies.[58]

The Meaning of the New Look

Conditions were remarkably well suited during the second half of the nineteenth century for a sharp focus in Great Britain, a relatively developed industrial nation, upon the economy of Australia, an undeveloped, semi-autonomous, staple-producing de-

---

the century is in J. J. Eddy, *Britain and the Australian Colonies, 1818–1831,* Chap. 4.

57. Examples of the bountiful testimony to the high quality of early Australian statistics are Dilke, p. 26; *idem,* "Presidential Address," *Journal of the Royal Statistical Society,* LXX (1907), 559; *Economist,* XXXVII (1879), 182; XXXVIII (1880), 211; LXIV (1886), 11 and 1474–75; LXV (1887), 1496–97; "The Growth of Colonial England: Australia and New Zealand," *Westminster Review,* LXVIII (1885), 412–43.

58. The Sydney and Melbourne Exhibitions of 1879 and 1880 seem in particular to have stimulated French commentators. E.g., Philibert Picrochole, *Lettres sur l'Australie* (Paris, 1880); Emile Montégut, *L'Angleterre et ses colonies australes* (Paris, 1880); L. Delavaud, *L'Australie* (Paris, 1882); E. Marin La Meslée, *L'Australie nouvelle* (Paris, 1883); F. Mournet, *L'Australie* (Paris, 1885); L. Simonin, "Le Monde océanique et les progrès de l'Australie," *Revue des Deux Mondes,* 15 March 1885, pp. 399–451; G. Verschuur, *At the Antipodes* (London, 1891). A representative descriptive work prepared for the Colonial and Indian Exhibition of 1885 in London was Edward Combes, *The Industries and Commerce of New South Wales* (London, 1886).

pendency. Discovery of gold afforded the initial stimulus for study, but interest grew steadily thereafter. In the quarter of a century from the decline of gold to the onset of depression in the 1890's the Australian economy was recognized in Britain as an important entity for careful monitoring and analysis. British writers perceived high actual and potential value to the mother country in the supplies and demands of the colonies. Moreover, they became fascinated by a wide range of economic and social phenomena which seemed of more than passing significance. To compliment the interest in Australia the media were present both at the point of origin and in the receiver to make possible a flow of information about institutions, policies, and events. This period provided both the reason and the means for the British image of the Australian economy to be well and clearly formed. What the British observers actually saw and how they interpreted it are discussed in the following chapters.

· 4 ·

Citadel of Heresy

Many British observers had their attention drawn to some specific Australian policy or institution before they came to reflect on the colonial economies as a whole. In the next chapter it will be shown that many commentators claimed they discerned common denominators throughout the economics in what they thought were rabid provincialism, pursuit of blatant self-interest, and toleration of economic heresy in many forms. In this chapter we shall examine how these commentators arrived at their impressions about the entire economic system through an initial concentration on individual elements of it. It should be emphasized at the outset that some of the colonies, notably Victoria and New South Wales, drew a disproportionate amount of attention. For the majority of observers, however, the impression prevailed that in Australia what held for one colony held for all.

Land and Immigration Policy

Most British observers who thought about the matter came to the conclusion that colonial disposition and management of public lands, which they saw as a valuable imperial treasure, deserved very sharp scrutiny.[1] Australia's success with wheat production, as well as with wool, through such technological improvements as Ridley's stripper, the stump-jump plow, and rust-resistant strains of grain sustained the interest at a high level. Two factors affected

1. Classic statements of the imperial significance of colonial lands were given by Lord Durham (*Report on the Affairs of British North America,* London, 1839, Part V) and by Lord Grey (*The Colonial Policy of Lord John Russell's Administration*, London, 1853, II, 375–76.) See also John M. Ward, *Earl Grey and the Australian Colonies, 1846–1857* (Melbourne, 1958), p. 2.

thinking on this subject: the first was the conviction that population pressure would remain an urgent threat to British welfare and that colonial lands could be a valuable safety valve; the second was widespread familiarity, at least at a superficial level, with land-settlement experiences throughout the world, especially in the western homestead areas of North America and the plantations of the Caribbean. The correct land policy for Australia seemed obvious: the colonies should maintain free entry to their territories for all British subjects, especially those who could not find employment at home, and they should make every effort to emulate the successful North American practice of encouraging small farmers—a model which held the admiration of the world. In circumstances where the North American pattern was clearly not practical, as in the northern latitudes of Queensland, the lessons of the West Indies should be remembered. Colored labor from other parts of the Empire, such as Polynesians or Indians, should be imported to assist the white settlers for the mutual benefit of all concerned. Special disciplinary practices would have to be followed for the natives' own good, the argument ran, to protect them from exploitation and to keep them from reverting to their natural state of idleness. Events which followed emancipation in the West Indies had shown that two techniques were especially effective in strengthening incentives to native labor. First, the workers must be kept from acquiring landholdings, and second they should be exposed to continued new immigration of their own kind, which would keep wages low and hold out the prospect of unemployment and starvation to laggards. British observers did not approach the Australian economy with a specific set of formal economic-development models to guide their judgment, as economists approach new countries today. But their shared experiences, values, and preconceptions were in some respects similar.

The observers did not have to wait long to discover that Australians were unwilling to follow strictly the precepts which were prescribed for them. As early as the 1840's, mounting opposition within the colonies both to transportation and to subsidized immigration of urban laborers sounded alarms in Britain. By 1863

Goldwin Smith could remark, without any personal knowledge of the colonies whatsoever, that Australian laborers had selfishly "cut away, I believe, the last pretence for saying that our nominal dominion over them is of any use to this country." [2]

Almost all the prominent visitors to the colonies from the 1850's to the 1880's were struck by what they thought were dog-in-the-manger attitudes of Australians toward land. William Howitt observed on his trip to the goldfields in 1852:

> Here you have immediately a proof of that ingenuity by which men contrive to defeat the intentions of Providence. Providence has given vast new lands, on which the overflowing population may settle; but selfish and purblind governments immediately lay hold on that which was meant to be a free gift of God, and dole it out in such modicums that the pressing necessities of arriving immigrants compel them to bid up at auction against each other, till the land of these new countries lying with millions of miles of unoccupied soil, becomes far dearer than the dearest of that which they have left.[3]

John Martineau wrote acidly of the notion that the colonists should be allowed to select new immigrants:

> It is unreasonable that colonies should claim to draw from the able-bodied and politically untainted population of the Mother-country just as they choose; that they should have the power to bribe them out, or discourage their coming, just as it happens to suit their ideas of what will benefit themselves; and that they should exclaim against taking at least their share of the criminally disposed, or even pauper, part, which their vast extent of country renders comparatively innocuous, and for the amelioration of whose condition it affords such advantages.[4]

Seventeen years later Baron Hübner described the Australian workingman categorically as "a sworn foe to immigration." [5]

2. Goldwin Smith, *The Empire* (London, 1863), p. 48. The formulation of land policy in the early years is described in P. Burroughs, *Britain and Australia, 1831–1855* (Oxford, 1967). Some of the complexities of settlement patterns and policies in the different colonies are described in (for Queensland) G. C. Bolton, *A Thousand Miles Away* (Brisbane, 1963); (for Victoria) Margaret Kiddle, *Men of Yesterday* (Melbourne, 1962); (for Western Australia) Frank K. Crowley, *Australia's Western Third* (London, 1960); (for wheat in South Australia) Donald M. Meinig, *On the Margins of the Good Earth* (Chicago, 1962).

3. W. Howitt, *Land, Labor and Gold* (Boston, 1855), I, 17.

4. J. Martineau, *Letters from Australia* (London, 1869), p. 151.

5. J. v. Hübner, *Through the British Empire* (London, 1886), I, 238–39. In a survey of the Empire in 1881 R. Acton reported, as if it were then common knowledge, that land legislation in New South Wales had been "always to the prejudice

Charles Dilke, fresh from an exhilarating tour of North America, deplored what he took to be misguided land policies at both the national and personal levels in Australia. Workers had been deluded into supporting immigration restraint, he believed, despite the fact that "there results an exceptional scarcity of labor, which cramps the development of the country, and causes a depression in trade which must soon diminish the wage-fund, and react upon the working men."[6] At the same time, he said, the practice of land squatting by large-scale entrepreneurs had tied up most of the potential settlement areas and prevented a vigorous frontier expansion such as he had witnessed in the United States. "The occupation of the whole of the Crown lands by squatters has prevented the making of railways to be paid for in land on the American system; but the chief of all the evils connected with squatting is the tendency to the accumulation in a few hands of all the land and all the pastoral wealth of the country, an extreme danger in the face of democratic institutions, such as those of Victoria and New South Wales."[7] Dilke believed that "small proprietors" were the great need of the colonies, and he viewed the policy of South Australia operating on "the Wakefield System" as the most promising move in the right direction.[8] Karl Marx, writing at about the same time as Dilke but avowedly "unconcerned" with "the condition of the colonies," viewed Australia's "shameless lavishing of uncultivated colonial land on aristocrats and capitalists" as an illuminating illustration of the artificial creation in new countries of the conditions for exploitation of labor.[9]

Many British visitors were torn between admiration for the large and hospitable landowners and squatters, who maintained habits of life with which they could feel comfortable, and sympathy for landless workers and would-be settlers. A number of

---

of the properly agricultural interests, which are comparatively backward and feeble in that colony." *Our Colonial Empire* (London, 1881), p. 93.

6. C. Dilke, *Greater Britain* (London, 1869), pp. 66–67.

7. *Ibid.*, pp. 40–41. Continuing the contrast, Dilke noted: "The want of railroads is incredible. There are but some 400 miles of railway in all Australia—far less than the amount possessed by the single infant state of Wisconsin" (p. 124).

8. *Ibid.*, pp. 102–3.

9. K. Marx, *Capital* (1867; English trans., Moscow, 1954), I, 773–74.

theoretical devices were contrived to resolve this dilemma. George Baden-Powell fell back on a stage theory of economic development, similar to that outlined in *The Wealth of Nations* and elaborated by German and American economists in the nineteenth century.[10] Forgetting the agriculturists who had preceded the pastoralists in the early days of settlement, he argued that pastoral "squatters" were crucial participants in the first stage of a natural growth process. Society should give these pioneers every encouragement, in the knowledge that ultimately they would pass away quietly and lead to smaller-scale successors:

> The first improvers of land, in all ages, have been owners of flocks and herds; and such a class are peculiarly fitted to be the first *occupiers* of land. Squatters are the Australian representatives of this useful class. With the rapid increase of their stock they reclaim unknown wastes, and, as it were, civilize them for the occupation of the agriculturists, who should ever be the first *owners* of land. After them arrive manufacturers and others, practising the more intricate arts of civilization.
>
> The Australian Governments should do all in their power to assist the squatters. The country would be wonderfully improved by them, could they but be certain of personally reaping the benefits of the money they lay out. This would be ensured by granting them long leases.
>
> They would then render the land in every way more valuable; storing water, fencing, clearing, or planting trees, and greatly improving the grass.[11]

What Dilke, Marx, and Baden-Powell all failed to grasp was that never for technological reasons would a large proportion of the Australian agricultural sector be able to support small-scale farming units.

The colonization doctrine of Edward Gibbon Wakefield, and specifically the contention that an adequate force of wage laborers should always be maintained in a new country, was a favorite means by which some observers reconciled the apparently conflicting objectives of large estates and small landholdings. Wakefield had argued for a land price "sufficient" to compel subsidized

10. Adam Smith, *Wealth of Nations,* Book II, Chap. 1; and Bert F. Hoselitz, "Theories of Stages of Economic Growth," in Bert F. Hoselitz et al., *Theories of Economic Growth* (Glencoe, 1960), pp. 193–238.

11. G. Baden-Powell, *New Homes for the Old Country* (London, 1872), pp. 457–58.

immigrants to wait through a period of landless employment while they accumulated sufficient capital to purchase property.[12] Anthony Trollope considered the failure of small-scale settlement by the 1870's sufficient proof of "the inexpediency of bestowing grants of lands on colonists." [13] Trollope emphasized repeatedly that in the long run, for workers who had accumulated sufficient capital, "free selection—or rather the purchase of land in small quantities by men who live upon it and cultivate it themselves" was "the system on which these colonies must chiefly depend for their permanent prosperity." [14] Baden-Powell endorsed Wakefield as a buttress to his stage-theory defense of large proprietors. He wrote: "It is a bad principle on which immigrants wish to become landowners at once. It is far better for them to spend several years in gaining experience in the country; at the same time accumulating coin of the realm, which will render their future possession of a home of their own really profitable." [15]

On the other side of this controversy stood William Howitt, who represented to some extent the views of new immigrants and gold diggers. He considered the Wakefield system to be iniquitous in every respect:

> The fatal Wakefieldian system of only selling colonial lands at a high price, and only where government pleases, has totally quashed that intermixture of tillage, that diffusion of cheerful villages up the country, which would have converted it from a desert to a place of happy and civilized life. The theory of preventing the too rapid spread of population in new lands, has here prevented it from spreading altogether.[16]

The colonies' own efforts at land reform were watched from Britain with deep interest and either high hopes or dark suspicion, depending upon the viewpoint of the observer. The usual charge

12. E. G. Wakefield, *A View of the Art of Colonization* (Oxford, 1914), pp. 331–345.

13. A. Trollope, *Australia and New Zealand* (London, 1873), II, 355.

14. A. Trollope, *The Tireless Traveller* (Berkeley and Los Angeles, 1941), p. 168; and *Australia and New Zealand,* I, 37, 104 and 109.

15. Baden-Powell, p. 465.

16. W. Howitt, *Land, Labour and Gold* (London, 1855), I, 147. After reading Howitt's account J. E. Cairnes remarked that the operation of the Wakefield system in Victoria seemed "analogous to that practiced by the Spanish Conquerors in America." MS. 8984, National Library of Ireland.

by writers sympathetic to the large landowners was that reform legislation was aimed, not at its declared goal of small-scale settlement, but rather at penalizing the middle and upper classes. John Martineau deplored bitterly the attacks of democrats upon "the old-fashioned Squatters . . . many of them sons of English gentlemen, with less wealth but with more education, knowledge of the world, and refinement, than those who are supplanting them."[17] Such skepticism seemed to be supported by the evident lack of success with declared objectives of many of the land reform schemes. Reports from prominent land reformers such as the Belgian Emile de Laveleye that the motivation behind land legislation in the colonies was in fact to reconstruct society on the basis of new ownership patterns did nothing to allay the fears.[18] During the violent political controversies of the late 1870's in Victoria, British reporters said that Australian land policy had reached its lowest point. Publication in Britain of some of the most vigorous denunciations of land policy by colonists themselves served to confirm these charges.[19]

The general reluctance of Australian governments to import non-white labor, and in particular vacillation on the subject in Queensland, was seen as one more indication of colonial intentions to persecute men of property. Both Baden-Powell and Trollope were vocal on this question; they had direct experience of the West Indies and could discern parallels with tropical Australia. Trollope viewed all colored races with unconcealed contempt, and he repeated the familiar post-emancipation argument that the transfer of colored laborers to places of employment and the imposition of necessary compulsion and discipline upon them benefited both employers and employed. He declared: "An ill-conducted enthusiasm may not only debar Queensland from the labour which she requires, but debar also these poor savages from

17. J. Martineau, p. 48.

18. Emile de Laveleye, "Alienation of Public Lands in Colonies," *Fortnightly Review*, XV (1874), 742–59.

19. E.g., Robert Niven, "Squatters and Peasant Proprietors in Victoria," *Fraser's Magazine*, XIX (1879), 511–18; and "The Deadlock in Victoria," *Economist*, XXXVII (1879), 116–17. George Ranken ("Capricornus"), one of the best known colonial critics of large estates—which he compared to decadent Roman latifundia —published two major works in Scotland: *Bush Essays* (Edinburgh, 1872) and *The Squatting System of Australia* (Edinburgh, 1875).

their best and nearest civilisation."[20] Attempts by some colonists and by British domestic humanitarians to explain the social grounds on which Asians and Polynesians should be excluded from Australia did not silence the critics. James Inglis, a journalist who visited the colonists in the 1870's, wrote:

From my own observation, which though short, has been searching and impartial, I do believe that a more improvident, lazy, self-indulgent, impertinent set of fellows never cursed a colony with their presence than those agitators and radicals, who falsely call themselves the leaders of the working men, organize themselves into leagues and unions, and are the originators of the present cry against cheap or abundant coloured labour.[21]

The tendency to generalize for all Australia and to discuss at the level of "principle" rather than of fact was especially strong in British comments on Australian land and immigration policy. The issues seemed clear in many British eyes and were especially familiar from having been raised in other colonies: whether to encourage small farmers or to make large grants to the middle and upper classes; whether to sell, to give away, or to tax land; whether to welcome newcomers from the Old World; and whether to use colored labor. In fact the limited experience of British observers with the details of land questions in other areas of the world may be the critical factor in explaining the generally low level of inquiry in the Australian case; it may have seemed that by the 1860's there was little more to learn about a problem which could be settled easily by appeal to theory. In any event outside of confidential government circles, few attempts were made to collect data and to understand developments in the special context of Australian conditions. In many discussions a

20. Trollope, *Australia and New Zealand*, I, 134. Later versions of this argument were Harold Finch-Hatton, "North Queensland Separation," *National Review*, VI (1885/86), 796–809; and J. C. McCoan, "Seven Weeks in Australia," *Westminster Review*, CXXIX (1888), 52–76.

21. James Inglis, *Our Australian Cousins* (London, 1880), p. 76. Critiques of the use of colored labor in Australia are F. W. Chesson, "The Polynesian Labour Question in Relation to the Fiji Islands and Queensland," *Proceedings of the Royal Colonial Institute*, III (1871/72), 34–56; and John Wisker, "The Coloured Man in Australia," *Fortnightly Review*, XXVI (1879), 82–97. A later defense of the practice was by the traveling statesman Lord Brassey (who became Governor of Victoria eight years later), "Recent Impressions in Australia," *Proceedings of the Royal Colonial Institute*, XIX (1887/88), 120–30.

distinction was not clearly drawn even between such dissimilar circumstances as those of Tasmania and New South Wales. The complexity of the land situation in Australia was probably appreciated only dimly in Britain; the problems of pests, erosion, storage, and marketing, the success of small-scale wheat culture in South Australia but not elsewhere, the encouragement of pastoralists in some parts while they were discouraged in others, and the steady and complicated debate over land reform all received limited attention.

Critics of the alleged misuse, or non-use, of Australian lands were given support by amateur and professional British geographers who repeatedly portrayed Australia as eminently suitable for plantation settlement in the north and homesteads throughout the south. Any interruption of steady growth, the geographers implied, must have a conspiratorial explanation. The geographers and their readers saw Australia as capable of becoming something like a combination India and Canada in the South Pacific.[22] By building up unreasonable expectations, the geographers set the stage for disappointment. Typically, in their discussions they paid little attention to such economic considerations as the markets

22. George Croly, a minor literary figure, commenting in 1848 on Sir Thomas Mitchell's recent discoveries, wrote that the opening of Australia was "the addition of a territory, almost boundless, to the possessions of mankind; a location for a new family of man, capable of supporting a population equal to that of Europe; or probably from its command of the ocean, and from the improved systems, not merely of commercial communication, but of agriculture itself, capable of supplying the wants of double the population of Europe. It is, in fact, the virtual future addition of three hundred millions of human beings, who otherwise would not have existed." "Colonisation," *Blackwood's Magazine,* LXIV (1848), 66. See also George Croly, "The Navigation of the Antipodes," *ibid.*, LXII (1847), 515–33; and Frederick Hardman, "Research and Adventure in Australia," *ibid.*, 602–14. A writer in *Fraser's Magazine* commented only slightly more cautiously on the explorer Sir Thomas Mitchell's discoveries. "There is room enough to bestow comfortably, in New South Wales alone, at least one-half of the entire population of the British islands." "Australian Colonies or Republics?" *Fraser's Magazine,* XXXVII (1848), 575. William Hughes, "Late Professor of Geography in the College for Civil Engineers," predicted in 1852 that Australia would exercise "an influence over the industrial destinies of Britain analogous to that which the colonisation of the western continent has exerted over the commercial relations of the different nations of Europe." *The Australian Colonies* (London, 1852), p. 307. See also Charles H. Allen, F.R.G.S., *A Visit to Queensland and Her Goldfields* (London, 1870). James Coutts Crawford, F.R.G.S., pointed out in connection with Northern Australia that "the moderate use of Chinese labour in thinly-peopled countries may be of immense use to every one concerned." *Recollections of Travel in New Zealand and Australia* (London, 1880). Henry Cornish envisaged Australia as a home for surplus "Eurasians" from India. *Under the Southern Cross* (Madras and London, 1879), Chap. 18.

for the goods which could be grown in the north, or principles of comparative advantage which would draw labor south. Rather, they exhibited mounting frustration as their settlement schemes and recommendations were not heeded. Sir Roderick Murchison, the dominant figure in the Royal Geographical Society around mid-century, was one of the most vociferous advocates of northern Australian settlement.[23] As early as 1844 Murchison had appealed for revival of the twenty-year-old scheme to develop Port Essington in the north.[24] In 1857 he said, with growing impatience, "it is scarcely possible to point to any region of the globe where British occupation is so imperatively called for, whether as a precaution, or with a view to future commercial interests." [25] The Indian Mutiny was an inspiration to Murchison: in 1858 he pointed out that the northern territories were an ideal location for the "rebellious sepoys," and in 1859 he pictured northern Australia as an important alternative source of raw cotton:

> Let it not be said that the heat of the climate, about 15°s. latitude, is a fatal impediment to the flourishing condition of any colony of which Englishmen are the leaders, but not the operatives. . . . To such a settlement Malays, Chinese, and Coolies would easily be attracted by English wages, and, under the influences of the sea breezes, cotton plantations might arise, and thus secure for us in our own Australia the very staple on which the chief manufacture of our country relies.[26]

Repeated failures of experimental settlements in the north did not discourage Murchison; he placed the blame on correctable human error. He said in 1864: "I am fully persuaded that, with the rich products of that region, the fine bays of the sea on the south shore of the great Indian Ocean must, sooner or later, be occupied by a great maritime nation like our own, which already possesses the

23. Murchison's role in the Society is described in Hugh Robert Mill, *The Record of the Royal Geographical Society, 1830–1930* (London, 1930), pp. 51–92.

24. R. Murchison, "Anniversary Address," *Journal of the Royal Geographical Society,* XIV (1844), xlv–cxxviii, esp. xcvii–ciii. For the northern settlement efforts of the 1820's see J. J. Eddy, *Britain and the Australian Colonies, 1818–1831* (Oxford, 1969), pp. 235–36.

25. R. Murchison, "Anniversary Address," *Journal of the Royal Geographical Society,* XXVII (1857), clxxix.

26. R. Murchison, "Anniversary Address," *Journal of the Royal Geographical Society,* XXXI (1861), clxxv. See also *ibid.,* XXVIII (1858), cxcvi; XXIX (1859), ccxi–ccxxi; and XXXII (1862), cxlvii–clvi.

other three sides of this vast continent."[27] If the greatest geographer of the age could hold such convictions, could mere laymen do more than keep their peace?

In the 1880's when interest in maintaining secure outlets for emigration from Britain reached a peak, disillusionment with Australian land policy became intense.[28] Critics charged that Australian governments had disposed of their public lands—the imperial patrimony—in the most profligate fashion "to the injury of the public, to the exclusion of agricultural later comers, and to trouble in the future."[29] The colonial governments, it was argued with even greater vehemence than before, were interested less in improving the pattern of ownership and achieving thicker settlement than in continuing their persecution of the landed middle class in favor of the urban proletariat.[30] Calls were voiced in the British press for tighter imperial control and for adoption of entirely new land policies in Western Australia, the last part of the continent in which direct action by the Colonial Office seemed practicable.[31] Some critics did not doubt the sincerity of Australian land reformers, but were concerned lest their genuine zeal ruin the economy which they sought to improve. Upon receiving a description of the proposed land reform schemes of New Zealand Prime Minister Sir George Grey, Baron Hübner reflected, "It remains to be seen whether the remedy is not worse than the disease."[32]

The only aspect of Australian land policy which usually received favorable comment from British observers during the nineteenth century was the method of property transfer known as

27. R. Murchison, "Anniversary Address," *Journal of the Royal Geographical Society,* XXXIV (1864), cl. See also *ibid.,* XXVI (1856), clxxxiv. The alleged misuse of the Northern Territories was a recurring theme in later literature: e.g., George Gascoyne, "Australia's Greatest Danger," *National Review,* LIX (1912), 502–13; and Edward Samuel, "The Northern Territory of Australia," *ibid.,* CVI (1936), 490–93.

28. An example of this interest is J. A. Froude, *Oceana* (London, 1885), pp. 10 and 338.

29. "The Future of Emigration: Colonial Lands," *Westminster Review,* CXXXI (1889), 169.

30. E.g., "South Australian Views Upon Class Taxation," *Economist,* XLVIII (1890), 552–53; "Queensland Finance and Class Taxation," *ibid.,* 1323–24; "New Zealand's Legislation Against Capital," *ibid.,* XLIX (1891), 1363–64.

31. "Western Australia," *Westminster Review,* CXXIX (1888), 163–73.

32. Hübner, I, 246.

the Torrens system. But even in this case the approval was often grudging or patronizing and did not lead to major reforms in Britain's own transfer practices. Sir Robert R. Torrens, the systems author, who returned from South Australia and served in the House of Commons, remained a pathetic figure as year after year he and a few disciples raised his proposals again for discussion.[33]

Growth of Cities

Critiques of the growth of colonial cities by British observers were in part merely the obverse of attacks on land policy. Government was so unsuccessful in settling the people on the land, the critics said, that would-be homesteaders had no alternative but to congregate in urban centers. In addition, however, Australian cities suggested to suspicious Britons that their rapid growth was not entirely involuntary. The city dwellers seemed too happy and prosperous and lacking in the signs of urban poverty to confirm the hypothesis that they were kept from the land against their will. An alternative or supplementary explanation of urban growth was that colonial cities grew spontaneously because the colonists, encouraged by their democratic leaders, had become addicted to luxury and the "fast" life. The ease and license of the city masses, the critics said, were made possible both by pillage of productive landowners and by borrowing from the Old World. Few commentators suggested that the rural-urban mixture in Australia might be a result of the technology of the pastoral industry, nor did they remember that a high degree of urbaniza-

33. Examples of comment in Britain on the Torrens system are "The Torrens System of Land-Transfer," which summarizes a paper by Torrens to the Law Amendment Society, *Economist,* XXI (1863), 425–26, and letter from Torrens correcting the article, *ibid.,* p. 456; "Mr. Lowe on the Land Laws," *ibid.,* XXXII (1874), 227–28; Robert R. Torrens, "On the Transfer of Land," *Transactions of the National Association for the Promotion of Social Science,* 1872, 159–77; *idem,* "The Land Laws," *Fortnightly Review,* XXX (1881), 98–107—probably the same as a paper presented to the British Association entitled "Results to Be Attained by Applying to the Transfer of Land in This Country the Methods Employed in the British Colonies," noted in *Report of the British Association for the Advancement of Science,* LI (1881), 760; J. Dennistoun Wood, "System of Land Transfer Adopted by the Colonies," *Proceedings of the Royal Colonial Institute,* XVII (1885/86), 343–59; "A New View of Registration of Title to Land," *Westminster Review,* LXX (1886), 76–99.

tion had been a feature of the landscape since the earliest days. They preferred more sinister explanations which were rooted in a sort of neo-Physiocracy and belief in the frailty of human nature.

Charles Dilke made a very unfavorable comparison of Australia with the United States in the matter of urbanization. "The rushing to great cities the moment there is money to be spent, characteristic of the settlers in all these colonies, is much to be regretted, and presents a sad contrast to the quiet stay-at-home habits of American farmers."[34] Trollope characteristically was not as dogmatic as Dilke, but he was no less concerned about city growth. He wrote:

> I do not know that any political economist has as yet cared to inquire what proportion of the population of a community should be metropolitan,—so that the affairs of the community might be ordered in the very best manner. Nor could such inquiry be made with any exact result, as the circumstances of countries and of towns vary very greatly; but the proportions of population as shown in the Australian cities above named cannot be taken as showing a healthy state of things.[35]

A variety of physiological analogies were used to bolster criticism of urban growth. For example, the concept of ideal proportion was said to hold as much between city and country populations as between parts of the body. A disgruntled immigrant clergyman explained this argument thus:

> as in the human frame, when the head is too large, or out of due proportion to the body, it is unnatural, and enervates the whole system, so when a metropolis monopolises too many of the inhabitants of a country, it is injurious to the healthy action of the whole. Paris is given as an illustration of this, and Melbourne may also be regarded in the same light; for its too rapid growth and size seem antagonistic to the necessary development of the country outside, for the lands outside are in an infant state of settlement, both as to roads and irrigation. Here we see an immaturity of growth, caused, doubtless, by the niggard

34. Dilke, p. 21. He added later in the study: "In face of the comparatively small amount of good agricultural country known to exist in Australia, the disproportionate size of the great cities shows out more clearly than ever" (p. 125).

35. Trollope, *Australia and New Zealand,* II, 173. By 1875 Trollope seems to have become harsher in his judgments. He wrote then: "Men prefer to live where they can be engaged in manipulating the production of others rather than in producing themselves. Consequently, though large districts of Victoria are capable of growing wheat, she is driven to import grain." *The Tireless Traveller,* pp. 112–13.

circulation of the wealth, people, and resources of the too populous capital.

Henry Cornish, a barrister, suggested after a visit to the colonies that the biological disproportion exhibited by Australian cities was merely a reflection of the inhabitants. Melbourne, he said, "like some of the gawky, weedy 'larrikins' in her streets, has grown too fast in her youth, and has thus run too much to arms and legs." [36]

By the 1880's, after the rapid and much-publicized expansion of Melbourne, James Anthony Froude could repeat the familiar charges of luxurious waste with even greater vehemence. Like Thomas Carlyle, whose biography he wrote, Froude viewed the Antipodes and other unsettled temperate areas as potential refuges from the urban vices of the Old World. Consequently, he reported sadly from New Zealand that the vices seemed to have been transported with the emigrants. "Here as elsewhere the labourers crowd into the town, for the high wages, the music halls, and the drink shops. The municipality finds them unlimited employment, by raising loans cheerfully in England in hopeful confidence of being able hereafter to pay them." [37] Indictment of Australasian urbanization had become so familiar a refrain by this date that many writers had probably ceased to regard the matter as an open question.[38]

Edward Jenks, an Englishman teaching at the University of Melbourne, offered in 1891 one of the few balanced explanations for Victorian urbanization. He thought that three "causes" were

36. Alex. Pyne, *Reminiscences of Colonial Life and Missionary Adventure in Both Hemispheres* (London, 1875), pp. 279–80. Henry Cornish, *Under the Southern Cross* (Madras and London, 1879), p. 63. Biological metaphors had wide attractiveness. For example, Lord Carnarvon observed after a visit in 1888: "to the injury of all parties, a disproportionate flow of population to the towns may be detected—a determination of blood to the head, which must, as in the old world, bring trouble and sorrow and pauperism, with all those distempers to the body politic which follow in their train." "Australia in 1888," *Fortnightly Review*, XLV (1889), 425.

37. Froude, *Oceana* (1885), p. 211.

38. E.g., Matthew Macfie, "Aids to Australasian Development," *Proceedings of the Royal Colonial Institute*, XXI (1889/90), 53–72. Roger Acton wrote: "An artificial show of manufacturing prosperity is thus produced or maintained in the city, while a large part of the industrial classes fail to learn those robust habits of life and labour in the open air, which should fit them for getting an independent livelihood out of the produce of the soil." *Our Colonial Empire* (London, 1881), p. 89.

crucial. First, Australian settlement had taken place at a time when city growth in the motherland had already progressed a long way; Australian colonists, in contrast to their North American predecessors, carried with them models of effective metropolitan organization.[39] The second cause was "the character of the immigration to Victoria," which contained a high proportion of city-loving gold diggers and relatively few homogeneous peasant groups such as in other lands had become stable settlement populations. The third cause was Australian geography, which, with its absence of natural barriers to travel, facilitated growth of large service centers and placed few obstacles in the path of disgruntled farmers who wished to move off the land.[40]

Commercial Policy

Tariffs were one aspect of Australian economic policy upon which almost all British commentators believed they could safely make judgments. The issues in this field had been threshed out thoroughly in the 1840's with victory for free trade and defeat for high rates of duty; adoption of protection by the colonies seemed downright sinful and inexplicable on any reasonable grounds. It was like a sane but perverted person selecting a system of inequity and inefficiency which in the long run verged on masochism. By the 1860's, serious advocacy of protection had become an insult to the pride as well as to the intelligence of free-traders who believed that they had destroyed the theoretical bases on which tariffs stood. The only possible reasons for protection in a modern and enlightened age, the free-traders concluded, were blindness, stubbornness, corruption, and the baneful influence of the United States. Karl Marx explained Australian protection as the natural selfishness of a new capitalist nation.[41]

Because of the widespread attention generated by gold and the work of colonial publicists, the early Australian tariff transgres-

39. Edward Jenks, *The Government of Victoria (Australia)* (London, 1891), p. 381. Note the similarity of this thesis to the spinoff argument of Professor Louis Hartz in *The Founding of New Societies* (New York, 1964), and esp. Chap. 8 by Richard N. Rosecrance on Australia.

40. Jenks, pp. 382–84.

41. Henry Mayer, *Marx, Engels and Australia* (Melbourne, 1964), pp. 128–29.

sions received prompt as well as unfavorable comment. The colonies aroused the ire of many of the major free-traders of the period. As early as 1863 the noted liberal Goldwin Smith speculated that the main reasons for the heresy were ignorance, selfishness, and habits of extravagance among the colonists:

In the first place, Protection is the natural resort of ignorant cupidity, and ignorant cupidity is the besetting sin of communities intensely commercial and wanting in education. In the second place, these communities are excessively impatient of direct taxation, and therefore if their taxes are high, heavy import duties are the inevitable result. Their taxes must be high while their public expenditure is extravagant; and the extravagance of their public expenditure arises in part, as has been shown before, from their being inoculated by us with the system of central Government, and the abuses which, under their social circumstances, central Government entails.[42]

Nine years later Thorold Rogers, Drummond Professor of Political Economy at Oxford, expressed similar sentiments in a publication of the Cobden Club. He reminded colonists that in the Antipodes as elsewhere, "The refutation of the protective theory belongs to the rudiments of economic science, and can never be doubtful, unless the real issue be evaded by appeals to a spurious patriotism, or to a self-interested prejudice." [43]

Travelers to Australia were only slightly more open-minded about commercial policy than were the sedentary British doctrinaires. Dilke thought that Australian protection, even though misguided, was at least sincere. He explained patronizingly: "Protection is no mere national delusion; it is a system deliberately adopted with open eyes as one conducive to the country's welfare, in spite of objections known to all. If it be, as we in England believe, a folly, it is at all events a sublime one, full of self-sacrifice, illustrative of a certain nobility in the national heart." [44] Anthony Trollope came to Australia with free-trade principles firmly before him as a standard, and he salted the account of his travels with condemnation of tariffs. The futility of protection was sym-

42. G. Smith, *The Empire,* pp. 90–91.
43. James E. Thorold Rogers, "The Colonial Question," in *Cobden Club Essays, Second Series* (London, 1872), pp. 447 and 449.
44. Dilke, pp. 58–59.

bolized for him in restrictions on imports of fruit jam, an example he used repeatedly. "No one eats more jam than a Victorian miner,—unless it be a Victorian stock-rider. But they eat pumpkin jam flavoured with strawberries,—and call that strawberry jam. The effect of protection all the world over is to force pumpkin jam, under the name of strawberry jam, down the throats of the people." [45] George Baden-Powell in the years after his first trip through the colonies became one of the most vocal spokesmen in Britain for free trade. He reported newsworthy events in "the race" between free-trade New South Wales and protectionist Victoria, and he noted in 1879 that in the eyes of the world "Victoria is in danger of occupying the unenviable position of the 'horrid example.' " [46]

The London *Economist,* as one of the most widely accepted guardians of free-trade principles, made serious efforts to understand as well as to condemn the colonial predilection for protection. In 1864 the paper concluded that a desire for premature economic diversification and a strong distaste for direct taxation were the causes of the disease, and "patience is the only remedy." [47] By 1873, however, the paper's patience had begun to wane, and it conceded that the wait for free trade might be a long one: "The level of colonial politics is not high, and ignorance of scientific finance is conjoined with arrogance in the advocacy of Protectionist [policies]." [48] The *Economist* believed now that the drive for protection in Victoria arose not from economic conviction as much as from irresponsible demagoguery made possible under unrestrained democracy. "For some time to come the mass

45. Trollope, *Australia and New Zealand,* II, 38.

46. George Baden-Powell, *Protection and Bad Times, with Special Reference to the Political Economy of English Colonization* (London, 1879), p. 365; and see *idem, State Aid and State Interference* (London, 1882), 112–37, and "The Doom of Cane-Sugar: A Colonial Problem," *Fortnightly Review,* LXI (1897), 284–91. Confirmation of Baden-Powell's fear that Victoria had, in fact, become a favorite "horrid example" among free-traders can be found in G. J. Shaw Lefevre, "Address on Economy and Trade," *Transactions of the National Association for the Promotion of Social Science,* 1876, pp. 103–23; Richard Tangye, *Reminiscences of Travel in Australia, America, and Egypt* (London, 1883), pp. 101–12; W. J. Woods, *A Visit to Victoria* (London, 1886), p. 52; and Alfred Caldecott, *English Colonization and Empire* (London, 1891), p. 181.

47. "The Causes of the Colonial Preference for Protection," *Economist,* XXII (1864), 1549–50.

48. "Intercolonial Reciprocity in Australia," *Economist,* XXXI (1873), 436.

of the colonists will be incapable of appreciating elaborate arguments on economical questions, and in the meantime it is to be feared they will vote as they have been accustomed to vote, in favour of a protection policy." [49]

Implementation of the highly protective National Policy in Canada after 1879 helped both to draw attention away from Australian practices and to open slightly the minds of writers in the *Economist* to the relatively complex arguments upon which the case for colonial tariffs stood. One contributor in 1879 admitted that there were at least two reasonable grounds for protection in Victoria: first, a pressing need for funds to construct public works such as railways, and second, a shortage of urban employment. Concerning the second ground, the contributor reported: "Protection, they affirm is a poor law worked in a way which prevents its objects from feeling pauperised. . . . There can be no doubt of the economic fallacy, and even the social fallacy, involved in all these arguments. . . . [But] they are paying for an idea." [50] The substantial British trade with Australia which grew even in spite of protection helped also to mollify the *Economist*.[51]

One of the reasons why Australian tariff policy was so well known in Great Britain was that numerous skirmishes in the battles between colonial free-traders and protectionists were fought in the British press. Prominent Australian free-traders such as B. R. Wise, Edward Pulsford, George Reid, Edward Langton and Max Hirsch published books and articles in Britain, in some instances under such prominent auspices as the Cobden Club.[52]

49. "Free-Trade in Victoria," *Economist,* XXXV (1877), 297. The paper was furious with the Victorian leader Gavan Duffy for suggesting that the free-trader John Bright and John Stuart Mill had approved protection in Australia. "An adherence to sound principles of financial policy, not a vain endeavour to support incorrect opinions by the influence of great names, will prove the best course for the statesmen of Victoria to pursue," "Protection in Victoria," *ibid.*, p. 1034.

50. "Protection in the Colonies," *Economist,* XXXVII (1879), 388.

51. E.g., "British Trade to British Colonies," *Economist,* XXXVII (1879), 820–21; and "Our Colonial Possessions: New South Wales, Victoria, and South Australia," *ibid.*, XXXVIII (1880), 1080–82, 1168–70, and 1365–87.

52. E.g., B. R. Wise, *Industrial Freedom: A Study in Politics* (London, 1892); Edward Pulsford, "The Beneficial Influence of a Free Trade Policy upon the Colony of New South Wales, Having a Special Regard to Her Industries," in *Prize Essays on Free Trade and Protection* (London, 1887); *idem,* "An Australian Lesson," *Nineteenth Century,* XXIV (1888), 393–409; Edward Langton, "Colonial Custom-Houses: A Reply from Victoria," *Fraser's Magazine,* XVIII (1878),

Protectionists could not find media for their views as easily as could free-traders, but periodicals such as the *Fortnightly Review* and *Fraser's Magazine* did provide space for prominent Australian spokesmen like David Syme and Archibald Michie, the latter converted from free trade to protection when he became Agent-General for Victoria.[53] Undoubtedly, the apparent predominance of colonial testimony against the colonies' own protectionist policies helped to strengthen the impression of waywardness in the minds of many British readers.[54]

Fragmentation of a Potential National Economy

An article of faith with most British economists during the nineteenth century was that economic efficiency was a function of the size of markets. Increasing returns to scale could be achieved in large production units which had opportunities for wide and growing sales. The economists deplored all commercial restrictions as impediments to the free development of the largest possible natural trading areas, and they argued that maintenance of such small political units as the individual Australian colonies perpetuated barriers and hindered the growth of free trade. In the case of Australia, two additional reasons were given why small political divisions were objectionable on economic grounds. First, costs of government to the colonies and of defense to the mother country were larger than they need be. Second, selfish, parochial, and restrictive public policies were more likely to be

482–89; and contribution by Max Hirsch to *Report of the Proceedings of the Free Trade Congress* (London, 1908), pp. 171–220.

53. David Syme, "Restrictions on Trade: From a Colonial Point of View," *Fortnightly Review*, XIII (1873), 447–64; Archibald Michie, "Colonial and Indian Custom-Houses, and Manchester," *Fraser's Magazine*, XVII (1878), 632–37; "Australia," *ibid.*, LXXVII (1868), 642–54; G. H. D. Gossip, "Protection *versus* Free Trade in Australia," *Fortnightly Review*, XLVII (1890), 841–63. Sir Anthony Musgrave, governor of two Australian colonies, questioned the universality of free-trade doctrine and suggested to his critics thereby that he had been hopelessly corrupted by his Antipodean experience. See my *Economic Enquiry in Australia*, Chap. 14.

54. The Indian civil servant and tariff reformer, Sir Roper Lethbridge in 1885 contradicted the familiar assertion that some of the Australian colonies more than others adopted free trade from conviction. He said that tariffs in New South Wales, which were lower than in Victoria, were the result simply of more successful sales of public land as an alternative revenue source. "Is an Imperial Fiscal Policy Possible?" *National Review*, V (1885), 32.

conceived and tolerated in small than in large units. Nations could look forward to economies of scale in wisdom and commercial morality as well as in capital equipment. With very few exceptions, British observers preached federation as an essential economic reform, and they greeted the colonists' hesitations on the subject either with amazement or with deep suspicion of corrupt motives.

Most British commentators did not regard careful examination of Australian conditions as a necessary background for judgments on the merits of federation. They simply could not imagine special political and social circumstances, geographical factors, or other data which might lead to a negative conclusion. As with land policy, successful North American experiences often were held up to view, notably that of Canada, which within a decade after Confederation had elected a liberal, free-trade government. No Englishman seems to have noted that the first Canadian prime minister, and the father of the protectionist "National Policy," Sir John A. Macdonald, in moving the proposal for Canadian Confederation looked forward to the creation of "another subordinate nation" in Australia.[55]

One of the earliest advocates in Britain of Australian federation was Colonial Secretary Lord Grey, who at mid-century saw colonial union as the clear dictate of economic theory. In the view of Professor Ward: "His federation policy was founded very little on reports that reached him of conditions in Australia, for he relied mainly on general principles of political economy and his exceptional knowledge of the empire as a whole."[56] A succession of later writers emulated Grey's method and repeated his conclusion. Charles Dilke laid particular stress on gains in improved defense and administration which would flow from federation. "Although union will tend to the earlier independence of the

55. *Parliamentary Debates on the Subject of the Confederation of the British North American Provinces* (Quebec, 1865; reprinted, Ottawa, 1951), p. 44. Early proposals for federation in Australia were described in the Confederation Debates by Alexander Morris. *Ibid.*, pp. 435–37. A. A. Dorion at one point denied vociferously that governmental arrangements in New Zealand were any precedent for federation. *Ibid.*, p. 689.

56. Ward, *Earl Grey . . .* , p. 3. See also C. D. Allin, *A History of the Tariff Relations of the Australian Colonies* (Minneapolis, 1918), Chap. 2; and *idem*, *The Early Federation Movement of Australia* (Kingston, Ont., 1907).

colonies, yet, if federated, they are more likely to be a valuable ally than they could be if remaining so many separate countries. . . . From the colonial point of view, federation would tend to secure to the Australians better general and local government than they possess at present."[57] In 1869 Charles Adderley, having recently as Undersecretary for the Colonies carried through the British North America Act (1867), used information provided by Dilke to call for "the aggregation of provincial power, to make available the full local resources both of wealth and vigour."[58] Anthony Trollope thought that the independence of single colonies was "absurd" and "mad." The virtues of union were so self-evident that federation was inevitable. "The colonies will join themselves together in some Australian federation, as has been done with our North American provinces, and will learn the political strength and commercial advantage of combined action."[59]

Several British periodicals at different times set out the benefits to be gained from colonial federation. Three articles in *Fraser's Magazine* in 1876–77 reviewed the question in considerable detail. First, the socialist writer H. M. Hyndman, just beginning his literary career, stressed the paradox he saw in the uncoordinated present condition of the colonies. Australia, he argued, might have a boundless future as a well-organized federal state. Hyndman observed proudly that Australians were "thorough Englishmen," without the incubus of the "sluggish French" or "sulky Dutch Boers," and with the added blessing that "the proportion of Irish to the whole population is by no means excessive."[60] Federation, he believed, would lead to unimagined gains. First of all it might restrain "that untrustworthy class of small professional

57. Dilke, pp. 96 and 97.

58. C. Adderley, *Review of the Colonial Policy of Lord J. Russell's Administration* (London, 1869), p. 104.

59. Trollope, *Australia and New Zealand*, I, 53. For similar statements see also *ibid.*, pp. 242 and 358, and *The Tireless Traveller*, pp. 172–73. Sir George Bowen expressed in his letters impatience characteristic of colonial administrators with the slow progress toward federation. Stanley Lane-Poole, ed., *Thirty Years of Colonial Government* (London, 1889), I, 210–11, and II, 21. A harebrained statement of the case for federation, but one illustrating clearly the influence of the North American model, was Charles Flinders Hursthouse, *Australasian Independence* (London, 1870).

60. H. M. Hyndman, "The Australian Colonies and Confederation," *Fraser's Magazine*, XIV (1876), 642.

'politicians' who are rapidly becoming the bane of Australia, as they have long since been of America." At the same time, federation would bring better railways, sensible land policy, population dispersion, and increased immigration. Hyndman concluded by expressing the Englishman's characteristic impatience with the colonists' apparent concern about political obstacles to union. He complained bitterly: "it is not the general combination for the development of the country of which people chiefly think, nor of the improvement of communications, but of the almost insuperable difficulty of overcoming the differences between the various colonies on the subject of Customs." [61]

In the second article, an anonymous contributor to *Fraser's* took a similar approach to that of Hyndman. He too admired the great economic potential and the pure racial stock which was happily lacking "the weak and nerveless French Canadians or the Kaffirs and Hottentots of the Cape and Natal." However, a special incubus in Australia was the large public debt: "the possession of so much land has had a baneful influence . . . in inducing this extravagant mortgaging of the future." [62] Federation would stimulate the increased production necessary to service this debt, would permit free trade, and would make possible better arrangements for defense.

In the third article within two years, still another contributor to *Fraser's* cited Adam Smith on the one hand and Canada's success with Confederation on the other to prove to Australians that their separatist policies stood in the way not only of their own self-interest but also of future imperial union.[63]

The London *Economist* elaborated over the years the argument that Australian federation would permit development of the best possible political structure for economic growth. It is worth while reproducing, for illustration, one representative statement in 1870:

61. *Ibid.*, pp. 644 and 649.
62. "British Trade: No. X. Australia and New Zealand," *Fraser's Magazine*, XV (1877), 704.
63. "S.," "Australian Federation and Imperial Union: By a Colonist," *Fraser's Magazine*, XVI (1877), 526–39.

Federation will be an advantage to the Australians themselves, because it will introduce into their politics just that amount of complication which is necessary to produce statesmen. The defect of colonial politics as a training school for Government is a certain simplicity, or—to take a phrase from a different region of thought—a certain lowness of type, as of an organism not yet fully developed. . . . The consequence is that, like Anglo-Indians, they become very clever but very narrow reasoners, think much too little of obstacles, and are apt to grow into vehement doctrinaires of the parochial kind. Federation does much to correct all this. . . . For instance, a central Government in Australia would soon require the control and the produce of the Customs, now the sheet-anchor of Australian taxation. Hence a new and a higher view of the pressure inflicted by tariffs, a readiness to endure direct taxation, and a new and much-wanted appreciation of the uses of economy.[64]

Despite the repeated reverses experienced by advocates of federation in Australia, the *Economist* remained optimistic and continued year after year to call for union as a fundamental reform from which other improvements would surely follow.[65]

The *Westminster Review* and the *National Review*, like *Fraser's*, published versions of the case for federation from the colonists themselves as well as from British protagonists. Advocacy by colonists must have seemed particularly poignant to interested Englishmen. By the 1880's the three arguments for federation—free trade, reduced costs of government, and more rational policy formation—were repeated almost like the Catechism.[66] A few more examples may be given. To emphasize the last argument, Robert J. Beadon from Tasmania cited De Tocqueville to prove that although Australian legislatures currently were marked by the "vulgar obscurity" of the United States House

64. "Australian Federation," *Economist*, XXVIII (1870), 1144.

65. E.g., "Australian Federation," *Economist*, XLIII (1885), 467–68; "Australasian Federation Conference," *ibid.*, XLVIII (1890), 168–69; "Australasian Indebtedness and the Prospects of Federation," *ibid.*, pp. 235–36; "Federation and Protection," *ibid.*, XLIX (1891), 232; and "Australasian Federation," *ibid.*, pp. 460–62.

66. E.g., "Australasian Federation," *Westminster Review*, LXIV (1883), 431–37; H. B. E. Frere, "Have We a Colonial Policy?" *National Review*, II (1883/84), 15; William Westgarth, "The Unity of the Empire: Federation, Intercolonial and Imperial," *ibid.*, IV (1884/85), 504–11; R. Acton, *Our Colonial Empire* (London, 1881), pp. 82, and 103–4.

of Representatives, under federation they could aspire to "the ability and distinction to be found in the Senate." [67] H. Mortimer-Franklyn, a former colonist living in London, explained in a little book on imperial federation that the economies of scale awaiting Australia were enormous and that the reasons for failing to federate promptly were selfishness, ignorance, and corruption: "A number of the leading men in Australia perceive the inestimable boon which would be conferred upon the Colonies, as a whole, were they welded into an indissoluble union. But this intelligent group, when compared with the whole people, forms a very select minority." [68] He blamed the breadth of resistance to federation on "the prejudices which are the inalienable concomitants of adolescent communities. . . . Suspicion and jealousy are the most conspicuous traits of young commonwealths. Before these are submerged by the mightier flood of national sentiment, the ills and disorders incident to such a transition must supervene." [69]

J. A. Froude shared the "earnest desire" of other Englishmen for Australian federation, but at the same time he exhibited unusual restraint in not scolding the colonists for their delay in achieving this goal. He also exhibited a rare humility in doubting that he had all the answers to questions of colonial federation at his immediate disposal.[70]

Friedrich Engels illustrated how accepted doctrine on the subject of federation could be used in at least two ways. He explained in 1891 that as a revolutionary he preferred the independent small units of Australia to the centralized, more efficient, and authoritarian federal system which was desired for them.[71]

Continuing pessimism about prospects for federation, even among some prominent Australian statesmen, kept strength in British criticism of economic fragmentation right into the 1890's.[72]

67. Robert J. Beadon, "Australasian Federation," *Westminster Review*, CXXXI (1889), 537–44.

68. H. Mortimer-Franklyn, *The Unit of Imperial Federation: A Solution of the Problem* (London, 1887), p. 130.

69. *Ibid.*, p. 156.

70. Froude, *Oceana* (1885), pp. 78–79, 91, and 138. Lord Rosebery, also enthusiastic for federation, was equally cautious in his pronouncements. The Marquess of Crewe, *Lord Rosebery* (New York, 1931), p. 145.

71. Mayer, pp. 139–40.

72. E.g., G. H. Reid, soon to be premier of New South Wales, told British

Public Works, Banking, and Native Administration

A variety of additional economic policies came under British fire in the years after the gold discoveries. Public works programs, whether for irrigation, fencing, or construction of marketing facilities, were viewed with deep skepticism and labeled the jobbery of an extreme democracy. Following the practice of the 1850's, British reporters consulted direct rates of return on public capital as the index of legitimacy, and they rejected suggestions that broader considerations such as community development might be appropriate criteria for judging public works.[73] Trollope stated the concern succinctly when he said: "That question of levying taxes and spending public money for other purposes than those of direct government, including the defence and protection of the nation, is very seducing and very dangerous."[74] The *Economist* pointed out in support of this principle that "the richest colony [New South Wales] is also that wherein the proportion of debt is lightest."[75] Pronouncements from prominent British writers of the need to seek out and exploit investment opportunities in the colonies were seldom reconciled with the charges of colonial extravagance in accepting such loans.[76] It will be shown in the next chapter that Australian public works policies came to be identified as one of the strongest proofs of general social decline.

Departures in Australian monetary and banking practice from

readers in 1891 that "the federal movement is not the result of any popular agitation or interest." "The Commonwealth of Australia," *Nineteenth Century,* XXX (1891), 150. Alfred Deakin, leader of the Liberal Party in Victoria, was only cautiously optimistic in the same year. "The Federation of Australia," *Scribner's Magazine,* X (1891), 549–61.

73. E.g., "The Progress of Victoria," *Economist,* XVI (1858), 1204–5; "Victorian Finance," *ibid.,* LX (1882), 736–37; Adderley, *Review* . . . , p. 124.

74. Trollope, *Australia and New Zealand,* I, 49. Trollope was willing to recognize the possibility of an "adequate profit of an indirect nature" in the case of railways. *Ibid.,* p. 256, and II, 372 and 441.

75. "The Assets and Liabilities of our Australasian Colonies," *Economist,* XL (1882), 1554, and see also *ibid.,* pp. 1488–89.

76. E.g., G. Baden-Powell, "Colonial Government Securities," *Proceedings of the Royal Colonial Institute,* XVIII (1886/87), 254–79. In a discussion of this paper the economist Hyde Clarke asserted, "It is totally impossible for any new country to provide out of its own resources the means to plunge, as it were, into civilisation." *Ibid.,* p. 285. See also "The Best Outlets for Capital," *Economist,* XXV (1867), 1037–38.

British precedents, such as direct loans to wool producers, often drew unfavorable comments.[77] Moreover, even murmured suggestions about the possibility of government notes drew horrified reactions. In a typical response to such a proposal, Governor Bowen wrote to Robert Lowe from Brisbane in 1866 that "the late Treasurer, at the instance of some irresponsible advisers, obstinately insisted on an issue of 'inconvertible legal tender notes,' like the *assignats* of the first French Revolution and the *greenbacks* of the recent Civil War in America." Bowen quickly pointed out that such schemes were "so strongly condemned by Adam Smith." [78]

Policies toward native labor in Australia generally drew critical reactions even though policies in other parts of the Empire such as the Cape Colony and the West Indies caused greater immediate concern.[79] Karl Marx, at one extreme, claimed in 1883 that Queensland was bent on nothing less than a slave trade with New Guinea.[80] The general assumption of most Englishmen on this question was that even the best of their colonial brethren could not be trusted with native labor.

The Darkened Image

No matter what aspect of Australian economic policy an average English reader might have examined during the thirty years after the gold rushes, he would have concluded from the literature that the colonies were strikingly lacking in wisdom and steeped in error. Observers were nearly unanimous in pointing out that from taxes to telegraphs the colonies endorsed false principles and accepted mistaken practices. With respect to some policies, such as those governing land disposal and immigration, the observers concluded that shortsighted selfishness and class bias were the explanation. In other fields, such as tariffs and public

77. E.g., "Australian Banking," *Economist,* XXVII (1869), 419. A defence of "advances against wool" was contained in A. B. Baxter, *Banking in Australasia from a London Official's Point of View* (London, 1883).

78. Stanley Lane-Poole, ed., *Thirty Years of Colonial Government* (London, 1889), I, 260–61.

79. E.g., Froude, *Oceana* (1885), p. 5.

80. Mayer, p. 136.

works, they detected ignorance of economic principles and political corruption. Concerning still other colonial practices, such as opposition to federation, they were merely dumbfounded. Critiques of the Australian economy were often mutually inconsistent, such as those against both large-scale and small-scale settlement and those against extensive foreign borrowing and discouragements to capital imports. But the critiques came one at a time, and the inconsistencies did not become an important defense.

The reasons for a mounting British intolerance toward the evolving Australian economic system are complex. One reason was akin to the disillusionment of a parent with an ungrateful child. Another was xenophobia. In relations with the rest of the world during the nineteenth century, Englishmen were notoriously unenthusiastic about all foreign institutions. They had difficulty in conceiving that in the long run any rational people could actually prefer social, political, or economic forms which were different from their own. Parliament, the Common Law, the Church of England, free trade, and commercial banking were, they believed, all the nearest approximations to perfection yet achieved in social organization. It was hard enough for Englishmen to accept the fact that Africans and Indians should question these institutions, but it was inexplicable and insulting that their own kin in their own colonies should do the same simply because they had moved their homes across the seas.[81] It was doubly inexplicable that transplanted British subjects should accept some institutions, such as the law and the church, but reject others in

81. The prominent journalist Archibald Forbes in 1883 noted the irony in the frequent claim that despite Australia's foundation as "a moral cloaca" she remained "British in thought, word, and deed." "The Present and Future of the Australasian Colonies," *Nineteenth Century,* XIV (1883), 720–32; This article was mentioned unfavorably by Lord Rosebery while in Australia. See the Marquess of Crewe, *Lord Rosebery* (New York, 1931), p. 147. Apparently observers in Britain were not alone among Europeans in their proclivity to misinterpret Australian mores and institutions. A Swiss visitor wrote regretfully in 1861: "what is deplorable is that, whatever descriptions we may give of this country and its inhabitants in our letters to our families in Europe, they will never be understood. They will always assume that we see things through rose-colored spectacles and that Australia is too far away to be anything but a land of savages and of Kangaroos." Cited in Werner P. Friederich, *Australia in Western Imaginative Prose Writings, 1600–1960* (Chapel Hill, 1967), p. 177.

the economy and in the political system. A typical early writer on the Empire reported confidently in 1863: "It is a proof of the robust vitality of our national character, that, notwithstanding these and many other differences between England and Australia, our great colony should bear so truly English a character." [82] Discovery as the years went on that this faith was unjustified naturally led to acute disappointment.

With few exceptions the early commentators on the colonies were orthodox practitioners of contemporary social theory. They were not innovators. They accepted conventional models for the operation of society, and they simply did not take seriously the challenge of creating revolutionary new institutions or even of making significant modifications. They explained events and judged operational structures in terms of patterns which were well known to them. They appraised colonial land policy, tariffs, banks, and political organizations less for the ability of these arrangements to fulfill stated objectives than for their conformity to known and accepted practices. To a considerable extent the facts about the colonies which were examined were selected for their relevance to models of the Old Country or of other new countries with which the observers were familiar. Tariffs might be imposed by the colonists to increase the volume of urban employment, but neither the statistics of this employment nor alternative means of achieving this goal open to the colonists were examined when evaluations of tariffs were made. A wide range of information which now seems important to a fair appraisal of national policies, and which might have changed conclusions a century ago, was rejected or ignored.

There were also deeply imbedded, in the models by which the Australian economy was judged, values and preconceptions which were accepted unconsciously by the British commentators. The doctrine of free trade, for example, received support from its advocates as much for its identification with the notion of personal morality and political liberty as for its economic effects. Similarly, small homesteads and large plantations were endorsed as much for their conservative political role as for their suitability as

82. J. H. Fyfe, *British Enterprise Beyond the Seas* (London, 1863), p. 158.

economic institutions, and urban growth was deplored in large part from class prejudice. The task of distinguishing social from economic objectives, difficult enough in the Old Country, made the appraisal of colonial policies that much more complex.

The picture of the Australian economy in the British eye which emerged after the decline of gold was darker and more clearly focused than before. The volume of descriptive material had substantially increased and was based both on direct perception and the "afterimages" of returning travelers. The need to depend on imagination and secondhand sources had declined. But at the same time a new element had come to affect the image; greater attention had led to the use of social theory for establishment of performance norms. Mining and agriculture had demonstrated the value of Australia. However, comparison of the country's social and economic policies with the standard guides to good behavior showed her wanting in many respects.

The widespread charges of economic heresy described above form a background for the next chapter in which attempts made in Britain to discover organic change in Australia are discussed.

• 5 •

The Aloe Flowers

Mounting suspicion that the colonies suffered from serious organic faults and were undergoing aggregate social retrogression lay behind much of the criticism of various Australian economic, political, and social policies and institutions reviewed in Chapter 4. This suspicion was voiced most vehemently during the depression of the 1890's, a period which is examined in the next chapter. The fears were present in the three prior decades as well. however, and their beginnings are examined here.

British observers believed that the importance for Great Britain of overall social decline in the colonies was far greater than an occasional policy error. Whereas poor judgment on its own might be corrected through education and counseling, organic deterioration seemed to call for more drastic reformatory action. In fact, when what observers thought first were individual mistakes were viewed as part of a total colonial retrogression, the whole appearance of the transgressions changed. They became symptoms of a deeper malady which pointed toward major surgical treatment for a cure.

The process of visualizing an image of the total social organism led to a changed perception of the organism's parts. In the first section of this chapter, the beginnings of British suspicions about Australian social decline are examined. In the second and third sections, important early statements of this argument and some replies from the colonies are described.

Causes of Social Decline

At least five different reasons were suggested for what was thought to be Australia's social decline. The first and most popular was that convict transportation had brought to the colonies a unique collection of the least competent, effective, and socially successful human beings ever gathered on the face of the earth. The faults of these colonial progenitors, it was argued, were magnified in their descendants through intermarriage and the stimulus of a favorable environment. Australia, founded on selection of the least fit in Great Britain, afforded a rare example of a reversal of the traditional evolutionary pattern. Instead of improvement in the species, natural selection brought deterioration.

Several early travelers ventured variants of this explanation for Australia's social condition. Charles Dilke observed that "the curse of the country is the indolence of its lotus-eating population," and he concluded that at least in Tasmania one principal cause of laziness was the remaining "traces of the convict blood." Looking to the future, he said: "It will be long before the last traces of convict disease disappear from Tasmania and New South Wales." [1] Baron Hübner two decades later thought that the effect of convict origins was still just as important even if by this date it was considerably more complex. "This stain, though half effaced by time, and invisible to the inexperienced eye of a stranger, still afflicts the colony. Men are known who have convict's blood in their veins, and the sons have to expiate the crimes of their fathers." [2]

Statements about Australia by influential commentators in Britain who had no direct personal knowledge of the colonies reflect clearly the travelers' views about the convict impact. For example, C. B. Adderley, drawing heavily on Dilke, expressed serious concern about "the traces of moral injury to the infancy of these offspring nations, from which South Australia alone wholly escaped." [3] To the complaint that transportation had permitted inferior specimens of humanity to survive, the economist J. E. Cairnes added the notion that early requirements of convict discipline had permanently associated Australian colonization with

1. C. Dilke, *Greater Britain* (London, 1868), II, 86 and 119. On the question of consumption levels in the colonies, Dilke commented: "The extravagance begotten of the tradition of convict times has not been without effect, and the settlers waste annually, it is computed, food which would support in Europe a population of twice their numbers." *Ibid.*, II, 126.

2. Josef V. Hübner, *Through the British Empire* (London, 1886), I, 281.

3. C. B. Adderley, *Review of the Colonial Policy of Lord J. Russell's Administration* (London, 1869), p. 92.

social policies of "centralization and absolutism" and "ideas of infamy and crime." [4] The implication observers usually drew from the argument that convicts were a main cause of Australia's condition was that time and immigration alone could bring a cure. Free settlers would have gradually to counteract the effects of these convict families whose genetic fault (original sin!) had been detected so unerringly by the British criminal courts.

The second explanation advanced for Australia's social decline was the effect of climate on humans in reducing their "motive for exertion." By the time interest focused intensely on Australia in the 1850's and 1860's, the climatic hypothesis had already been suggested for other parts of the Empire, such as the West Indies and India.[5] In fact, writers with experience in other colonies were among the first to extend the idea to Australia. A *Quarterly* reviewer as early as 1828 had been fascinated by evidence of physical adaptation in Australia which, he suggested, must be caused by the climate. He wrote optimistically that "not only the human race, but most of the quadrupeds produced from animals imported, improve their breed, and increase considerably in size. . . . the salubrity of the climate, and the absence of all disease, may be considered as the prime causes of these extraordinary effects." [6] More than forty years later George Baden-Powell enumerated a less complimentary set of racial characteristics which he believed had developed in Australians because of the temperate dry environment. "They have already taken to them-

4. J. E. Cairnes, "Colonization and Colonial Government," in *Political Essays* (London, 1873), pp. 24 and 30–31. Governor Bowen had suggested the same idea in a letter to Richard Cobden from Brisbane eleven years before. "The professional habits and instincts of the soldier and sailor Governors led them to establish centralised bureaucracies, which have now, by a few rapid and inevitable steps, become centralised democracies." Stanley Lane-Poole, ed., *Thirty Years of Colonial Government* (London, 1889), I, 197.

5. E.g., Thomas De Quincey, "The Logic of Political Economy," in David Masson, ed., *The Collected Writings of Thomas De Quincey* (London, 1897), IX, 213–16; Earl Grey, *The Colonial Policy of Lord John Russell's Administration* (London, 1853), I, 54–82, and II, 259–60; C. J. Bayley, "Jamaica, Its Disturbances and Its Prospects," *Quarterly Review*, CXX (1866), 221–59; "Coolie Labour and Coolie Immigration," *Cornhill Magazine*, XVI (1867), 74–83; "The Deficiency of Labour in the West Indies," *Economist*, XVII (1859), 784–86; R. D. Mangles, "The Progress of India," *Edinburgh Review*, CXIX (1864), 95–136; "Effects of Climate Upon Man," *Colonial Magazine and Commercial-Maritime Journal*, III (1840), 165–73 and 318–25.

6. "New South Wales," *Quarterly Review*, XXXVII (1828), 7.

selves a certain type: being usually of good height, but wanting in breadth and depth, they have gained for themselves the epithet of 'cornstalks,' which is saying a great deal for the value of their heads." Baden-Powell did not conceal his doubts about the long-term prospects for this new Australian type. "Natives speak slowly, and are uncommonly fond of taking life easily; though they show perhaps a more fiery nature than the typical Englishman." [7]

Even staunch advocates of the colonies felt compelled to accept a variant of the climatic thesis. For example, Thomas Braim, a colonial clergyman, set forth one familiar form of the case which said that the hot climate of Australia led to early bloom and maturity in humans as well as in plants. "So far as climate may be considered as influencing the organization of man, its effects in New South Wales appear to be analogous to those observed in countries elsewhere of a tropical or semi-tropical character. Rapid growth, with early development of the physical as well as the intellectual powers, characterises each sex, but more particularly the female. But this remarkable precocity appears to be compensated for by early and premature decay." [8] This version of the climatic doctrine implied that adult senility might explain many of the human foibles observable in Australia.[9]

Dilke with his usual candor was unequivocal about the weaknesses of southern Australians who, he said, "like all dwellers in

7. G. Baden-Powell, *New Homes for the Old Country* (London, 1872), p. 402.

8. Thomas Henry Braim, *New Homes: The Rise, Progress, Present Position, and Future Prospects of Each of the Australian Colonies and New Zealand, Regarded as Homes for All Classes of Emigrants* (London, 1870), p. 100. William Howitt reported from Victoria as early as 1855: "A very clever doctor here says that his wife, quite a young woman, has become ten years older in constitution in two years." *Land, Labor and Gold* (Boston, 1855), II, 45. He was able all the same to draw fairly optimistic conclusions from this gloomy piece of evidence. He wrote: "There appears already an obvious tendency in the Anglo-Australian to run up into height, and with a slightness of frame like the Anglo-American; and it is observed that the bloom of youth, as in the United States, more rapidly fades; but if the term of life should prove a little shorter, its general current will run under a pure and a cheering sky." *Ibid.*, II, 420.

9. A traveler in 1892 reported what he considered to be a plausible theory suggested by "doctors" that the breakdown of mature Australians occurred because "the bones of Australian-born children are much weaker than those of other people. The cause is supposed to be that almost all the drinking water is got from rain run into tanks, which is, of course, deficient in lime." Baden Fletcher Smyth Baden-Powell, *In Savage Isles and Settled Lands* (London, 1892), p. 59.

climates cool but winterless, are content to dream away their lives in drowsiness." He did add with more caution: "It is still an open question whether the change of type among the English in America and Australia is a climatic adaptation on the part of nature, or a temporary divergence produced by abnormal causes, and capable of being modified by care."

Lord Rosebery even explained regional differences within Australia on the basis of climate. He wrote from Melbourne in 1883: "The people here are much more energetic and pushing than the Sydney people, which is partly the effect of climate, partly the result of a strong American infusion at the time of the gold discovery." [10]

A third reason offered for what was said to be the degraded Australian racial type was systematic cultivation of the gambling propensity in these specimens. On the one hand, it was argued, the gold discoveries had strengthened this propensity in all residents. On the other hand, gold had also attracted gamblers and speculators from the world over, who had accentuated this feature of the national character still more. Experience with gold mining, the argument ran, left both entrepreneurs and workers unsatisfied with anything less than high-risk ventures and unwilling to undertake more prosaic activity such as wage labor or small-scale farming. Anthony Trollope remarked that "there is something in the very nature of gold when thus found which almost justified the poet who declared that it was best placed when hidden from mortal sight. It unsettles and demoralises the finder, and dissipates itself." [11] John Martineau stated the case clearly as it was related to the propertied class: "Few things disturb honest industry and breed discontent more than the contemplation of too easily and too rapidly acquiring fortunes. Those that were made

10. Dilke, II, 86–87 and 129. In the same fashion Dilke described New Zealanders as "burley, bearded, strapping fellows, physically the perfection of the English race, but wanting in refinement and grace of mind, and this apparently constitutionally, not through the accident of occupation or position." *Ibid.*, II, 12. He attributed part of the conspicuous success of the colony of Victoria to the fact that a larger proportion of its population was first-generation immigrants than was that of New South Wales (II, 24); the Marquess of Crewe, *Lord Rosebery* (New York, 1931), p. 141.

11. A. Trollope, *The Tireless Traveller* (Berkeley and Los Angeles, 1941), pp. 140–41.

in Victoria and elsewhere soon after the discovery of gold have left their demoralising and disheartening influence on all Australia."[12] Baden-Powell was more concerned about gold's impact on the worker, for "gold has much the same effect on the labouring man as 'busy times.' Many will be found holding a firm belief, filled with a sure presentiment, that there exists a large nugget waiting for them somewhere. And thus a man will live on, now at the goldfields, now wandering about the bush, until his whole nature becomes unsettled, and he can never more force himself to stick to any steady work."[13]

Sir William Denison, who had extensive experience as a governor in several of the Australian colonies, suggested to a British audience that colonial failings resulting from the gambling propensity could be understood best through their own introspection. Britons had brought to the New World in accentuated form "characteristics of the race" which even in the Old World had caused serious difficulties. Above all, a spirit of "independence (mind, I do not use the term, as is too often done, in a laudatory sense)" led to various forms of selfish behavior, the absence of a "feeling of community," and "indifference to society."[14] The process of accumulation of wealth in Great Britain had first "stimulated the gambling spirit, one of those unwholesome tendencies of the human mind which a sound moral and religious training only can combat." This disturbing tendency had been accentuated to alarming proportions in the colonies, "where gold and diamonds are held out as baits."[15]

The unique phenomenon in Australia of what was perceived to be a large, itinerant, emotionally unstable, unemployed, and nearly unemployable body of men who constituted a serious threat to social tranquillity, almost like Marx's industrial reserve army, was discussed as early as the 1850's. William Howitt wrote in 1855 that the solitary life of a shepherd created an extraordinary class of "nomadic vagabonds" made up of "dreamy, half-

12. J. Martineau, *Letters from Australia* (London, 1869), p. 92.
13. G. Baden-Powell, p. 429.
14. Sir William Denison, *Two Lectures on Colonization* (Richmond, 1870), pp. 4–9.
15. *Ibid.*, p. 11.

alive sort of men" with "the weight of the woods on their souls."[16] Even the wealthy squatter, Howitt said, "is a nomad*e* [sic] by his very name. He is not a proprietor; he is not a cultivator, but a king of the desert, and can reign there alone."[17] Trollope and later writers also referred to restless, gambling, and pathetically optimistic elements of the work force of Australia as a "nomad tribe."[18] An English clergyman who had operated a church in the goldfields reported how the daily activities of miners, shepherds, and other colonists generated an unhealthy skepticism and radicalism which contributed to social instability. "In colonial life the fundamentals of truth seem to have more assailants than in older lands; freedom of action seems to favour a libertinism in thought, and new theories are often adopted merely because they are original."[19]

The fourth strand in the explanation of Australia's supposed degradation came from an interpretation of the leadership characteristics of the resident citizenry and of new immigrants. Observers claimed that the colonies had failed to attract or to nurture competent political and economic leaders and consequently had been compelled to fall back upon men who in their countries of origin would unquestionably have been followers. This argument was merely a variant of that put forth by Edward Gibbon Wakefield in his *Letter from Sydney* in 1829 that the colonies lacked the full cross section of Old World society which was necessary for healthy economic and social growth. The critiques of Australian leadership seem to have rested above all on the prejudices of Englishmen who from training and experience felt certain that they knew what to expect in good leaders. They

16. W. Howitt, *Land, Labor and Gold* (Boston, 1855), I, 144–45 and 364–65. See also Russel Ward, *The Australian Legend* (Melbourne, 1965).

17. Howitt, II, 184. Be it said, Howitt was reasonably optimistic for the long future: "It will take a century to work this miscellaneous gathering of rude people out of the scum. As they get money, they will, however, as in America, in time give their children some education; but out of them will grow, as is plain to see, a go-a-head, self-confident, Yankee sort of people" (I, 367).

18. A. Trollope, *Australia and New Zealand* (London, 1873), I, 312; and James Inglis, *Our Australian Cousins* (London, 1880), p. 433. See also J. H. Davidson, "Anthony Trollope and the Colonies," *Victorian Studies*, XII (1968/69), 305–30.

19. Alex. Pyne, *Reminiscences of Colonial Life and Missionary Adventure in Both Hemispheres* (London, 1875), pp. 328–29.

believed leaders should come from the middle or upper classes, and they should have certain approved manners, education, habits, and even accent.[20] To most Englishmen high statesmanship or business acumen just did not seem compatible with rough behavior and a Cockney accent.

Despite the weak basis of this argument in prejudice instead of analysis, the concern of British observers with the quality of Australian leaders was intense. They justified their concern in some instances by solemn reference to the colonial experience of ancient Greece and Rome or to such authorities as Thomas Carlyle, who had emphasized the vital roles played by great leaders throughout history. Doubts about Australian leadership were often expressed indirectly in the form of scorn or ridicule for such Australian politicians of working-class background as Henry Parkes and Graham Berry. But there was also direct discussion of the question as a matter of principle.

Anthony Trollope touched upon the leadership problem repeatedly in his accounts of the colonies. He was particularly affronted by the "arrogance" and "conceit" (behavior characteristics which he dubbed in the aggregate "blowing") of leading public men, who clearly, he implied, should have recognized and accepted their inferior social position and the relative insignificance of the land in which they lived.[21] Trollope was not optimistic about improving the quality of leadership in Australia because conditions there were not conducive to the training and nurture of the necessary social classes:

> The colonies are peopled with men who have gone out to earn their bread and who are earning it,—and from these have to be chosen their members of parliament. There is as yet among them no class of men capable of devoting their time and their energies to the public cause

20. The Rt. Hon. Sir E. B. Lytton, Secretary of State for the Colonies, advised Sir G. F. Bowen in 1859 concerning the role of the colonial governor as follows: "Throughout all Australia there is a sympathy with the ideal of a gentleman. This gives a moral aristocracy. Sustain it by showing the store set on integrity, honour, and civilised manners. . . ." Stanley Lane-Poole, ed., *Thirty Years of Colonial Government* (London, 1889), I, 82, and also p. 15.

21. Trollope, *Tireless Traveller*, pp. 111–13. Trollope admitted that the characteristics he deplored were not uniquely Australian: "Victorians of the upper classes . . . both in their defects and their excellences . . . approach nearer to the American than to the British type." *Australia and New Zealand*, I, 474.

and to that only. There is no established wealth handed down from father to son, the possession or prospect of which enables the young legislator so "to learn the ingenuous arts that his manners shall be refined, nor ever allowed to become brutal." In the preparation of such a class of men much time is needed and many accessories.[22]

Sir William Denison thought that the regular additions to the colonial population were made up largely of social refuse which was, at best, capable of becoming only productive labor. "Emigration, as generally practised, is, in so far as its action upon the mother country is concerned, more like the sewer or scavenger's cart, which, while carrying away much that is offensive and injurious, does, in connexion with these, take with it a great deal of matter which is useful and beneficial." [23] It was hard to think of effective leadership coming from the sewer or the garbage wagon.

John Martineau cited Carlyle directly on the importance of effective leadership, and he argued that the unsatisfactory political condition of the colonies was the result of self-government which "tends to cut off the supply from home of educated men who used to go out in various official positions." [24] Beyond the political sphere, even partial autonomy led also to a reduction in the immigration of talented leaders for other parts of society. "The proportion of clergymen, barristers, and university men who go out now is very insignificant compared with what it once was, and anything which caused it to diminish still more would be a misfortune." [25]

Two articles in *Fraser's Magazine* in the 1870's dealt specifically with the leadership problem in Australia and served to highlight British concern. The first, in 1871, by "An Old Colonist," took a fatalistic evolutionary position that environment inevitably determined social institutions in the colonies as elsewhere and that the best Britain could do under the circumstances was take into account the inherent political weakness of the colonies when guiding their destinies. The following account was given of the determinants of Australian social development:

22. Trollope, *Australia and New Zealand,* II, 270.
23. Denison, *Two Lectures on Colonization,* p. 22.
24. J. Martineau, *Letters from Australia,* pp. 79 and 206.
25. *Ibid.,* p. 156.

Few now dispute that the physical conditions of a country mainly determine the industrial, and the industrial to a great extent the political: other influences contribute, but this is the main order. The process is governed by a fixed law, the law of natural selection, by which every organism, whether it be an animal or a plant, an individual or a community, tends to take its form and structure, its habits and character, from surrounding circumstances, and to fit itself to the conditions of its existence, whether these be favourable or unfavourable.[26]

The second *Fraser's* article, in 1874, also anonymous, was less fatalistic and more constructive than the first. The author recommended that special steps be taken to attract and reward effective leaders in the colonies. In particular, he advocated reconsidering W. C. Wentworth's proposal of a quarter century before that a titled colonial aristocracy be established as encouragement to a responsible leadership class. "He [Wentworth] spoke in vain, but subsequent events have shown that the good he endeavoured to acquire for his country had many sides, and that the rejection of his proposition carried with it the seeds of a social as well as political bane." [27]

The fifth and final reason put forward for Australia's social deterioration was closely related to the fourth explanation of a leadership vacuum. Australia, the critics said, was the supreme example of democracy run rampant; the country suffered grievously from the degrading effects of too wide a suffrage. Almost every British commentator after the grant of self-government at mid-century offered some reflections on the operation of Australian democracy, and few of these comments were complimentary. Most of the objections to democracy were against specific economic policies, such as immigration restriction and public works; these, the critics claimed, were formulated in ignorance and rooted in base human selfishness.[28] The evils of democracy were

26. An Old Colonist, "Australian Tendencies," *Fraser's Magazine,* III (1871), 604–5.

27. "Colonial Distinctions," *Fraser's Magazine,* X (1874), 321.

28. John Morrison, a clergyman who had spent "thirteen years resident in the interior of New South Wales" provided a typical critical account of "Democracy and Its Results" in a book of memoirs published in 1868. He pictured the colonies with their wide franchise as lawless, corrupt, and brutalized because of their unwillingness to enforce compact settlement. He said "the Australian radical spares nothing; he tears up everything by the roots." And as a final indictment he

not seen as unique to Australia; the Australians simply had carried the process further than any other country, with the possible exception of the United States, and they exhibited most fully the social deterioration which followed in democracy's train. Two moral lessons for Britain from Australia's experience seemed to be that democracy should be introduced on her own shores with extreme care, and that all practicable steps should be taken to reduce its effects in the colonies. Robert Lowe (later Lord Sherbrooke), a former colonist but now a British politician who spoke often on colonial affairs, warned the British people and Parliament of the evils which followed extension of the suffrage, and he informed them repeatedly of the "unworkable system" which had been created in Australia.[29]

C. B. Adderley saw some hope for the amelioration of Australian democracy in the natural growth of a propertied middle class.[30] Other observers were less optimistic. Trollope reported numerous economic travesties which he thought resulted from democracy, and he thought that only through the wisdom of British governors had the colonies in other instances been "preserved from crude legislation, which would be the certain and natural result of inexperience in statecraft."[31] On the practice of paying legislators, Trollope remarked: "I have but little faith myself in the moderation of a dog that has once tasted blood."[32] The natural results of democracy on the Australian model, he concluded, were that a colony became "over-governed, over-legislated for, over-provided with officials, and overburdened with national debt."[33]

Froude was an especially harsh critic of Australian democracy,

concluded: "The New South Wales Government does not believe in, if indeed it understands, political economy." *Australia as It Is; or Facts and Features, Sketches and Incidents of Australia and Australian Life, with Notices of New Zealand* (London, 1867), pp. 253 and 258.

29. See Right Hon. R. Lowe, *Speeches and Letters on Reform* (London, 1867), pp. 17, 37, 53, 72, 88, 92–93, 148, 153–54, 163–64.

30. Adderley, p. 110. He wrote, "freedom works out its own correction, however roughly, better than the wisest dictation."

31. Trollope, *Australia and New Zealand*, I, 154. See also, A Clergyman, *Australia in 1866* (London, 1868), reviewed in *Economist*, XXVI (1868), 736.

32. *Ibid.*, I, 508.

33. *Ibid.*, II, 340.

and he delighted in recounting the economic ill effects of the political system. Using a metaphor which symbolized effectively the impressions of many British observers, he wrote: "Democracies are the blossoming of the aloe, the sudden squandering of the vital force which has accumulated in the long years when it was contented to be healthy and did not aspire after a vain display." [34] Using still another analogy, he explained: "A ship of war administered on elective and representative principles would not be a dangerous combatant. There would perhaps be a corresponding improvement if a nation was administered as a ship of war." [35] Froude deplored the supposed demoralizing effects of payments to members of parliament, the arrogance of demagogues, extravagant use of public funds, and despite his professed admiration for the Australian people generally, what he thought were philistine elements in the citizenry which were democracy's product. "Middle-class democracy is not favourable to the growth of manners, and, with all my wish to find it otherwise, I had to contrast them [Australian young people], not to their advantage, with two or three English youths among us, who, though belonging to the same social class, might have been another order of beings." [36]

J. C. McCoan, an author and journalist who followed in Froude's footsteps only a few years later, was equally contemptuous of Australian democracy. A visit to the Victorian Parliament, he explained, "was instructive, as showing to what extreme democracy may lead." [37] Douglas M. Gane, another traveler, speculated that various social institutions spawned by democracy, such as strong trade unions, would worsen conditions in future: "whether they do not tend, in conjunction with compulsory edu-

34. Froude, *Oceana* (1885), p. 134. Froude referred to the century plant, *Agave americana,* sometimes called American aloe. This plant lives for about ten years and blooms only once—just before death!

35. *Ibid.,* p. 158.

36. *Ibid.,* p. 298. See also pp. 73, 76, 106, 107, 112, 131, 138, 227, 238, 285. Froude wrote, "of the heroic type of man, of whom poets will sing and after ages be anxious to read, there will not be so many, when the generation is gone which was born and bred in the old world" (p. 168).

37. J. C. McCoan, "Seven Weeks in Australia," *Westminster Review,* CXXIX (1888), 73.

cation, to increase the already far too independent spirit in their members will in time be seen." [38]

Concentration of Attention

The strands of thought examined in the preceding section were expressed in random statements by British observers of the Australian economy; the comments did not in any case constitute an organized treatment of Australian social development, and they were set forth to indicate the widespread origin of the thought. As early as the 1860's, however, direct and highly focused treatments of the subject began to appear, and these are outlined in this section.

Prominent British evolutionary writers provided both the body of theoretical doctrine and some of the direct stimulus for examination of Australian social development. Charles Darwin himself offered some penetrating reflections on the colonies after the voyage of the *Beagle* in 1836. His first impressions were "admiration at the whole scene" and self-congratulation at being "born an Englishman." [39] He was excited by the explorations in progress, and he communicated on the subject directly with the surveyor-general Sir Thomas Mitchell. But Darwin was "disappointed in the state of society." He deplored, among other things, the unsavory presence of convicts, the political wrangling, and the single-minded pecuniary motivation. He was alarmed that the "whole population, poor and rich, are bent on acquiring wealth," and more particularly that the prosperity seemed so dependent on wool and whale oil. He concluded: "I formerly imagined that Australia would rise to be as grand and powerful a country as North America, but now it appears to me that such future grandeur is rather problematical." [40] In small degree he anticipated his later theory of natural selection when he remarked concerning the doubtful survival of the aborigines. "The varieties of man seem to act on each other in the same way as different

38. Douglas M. Gane, *New South Wales and Victoria* (London, 1886), p. 43.
39. Charles Darwin, *The Voyage of the Beagle*, Everyman's Library (London, 1906), p. 415.
40. *Ibid.*, pp. 427 and 428.

species of animals—the stronger always extirpating the weaker." [41]

Herbert Spencer, one of the most prolific and influential social evolutionists, was deeply interested in the Australian aborigines.[42] In addition, he pointed to the colonies as good examples of "derivative" societies, and he deplored the numerous instances of illegitimate government activity in them.[43] Spencer rejected out of hand the thesis concerning the role of leaders in society which had been applied so often to the Australian case. The cause of social ills, he believed, lay within social systems themselves, rather than in the individuals of whom society was made up. "The ridiculous Carlylean theory of the Great Man and his achievements, absolutely ignores this genesis of social structures and functions which has been going on through the ages." [44]

Of greatest relevance to the colonies was Spencer's assertion that representative government, in contrast to a hierarchical system, was totally ill-equipped to take an active role in an economy. "Representative government, then, cannot be called a success, in so far as the choice of men is concerned. Those it puts into power are the fittest neither in respect of their interests, their culture, nor their wisdom. And as a consequence, partly of this and partly of its complex and cumbrous nature, representative government is any thing but efficient for administrative purposes." [45] For Australia, where government was more representative than any-

41. *Ibid.*, pp. 418–19.

42. E.g., see his *Principles of Sociology*, 3 vols. (London, 1876–96), *passim*. William Howitt discussed the aborigines in evolutionary terms as early as 1855 and had concluded: "that which will not go onward in the world's progress, must go down." *Land, Labor and Gold* (Boston, 1855), I, 274. Marx and Engels were both interested in the Aborigines and their evolutionary implications. See Mayer, p. 137. T. H. Huxley paid close attention to the Aborigines during the voyage of the *Rattlesnake* to Australia, but his assessment of colonial society was distracted by his courting of his future wife. Julian Huxley, ed., *T. H. Huxley's Diary of the Voyage of H.M.S. Rattlesnake* (London, 1935). Havelock Ellis spent several years as a schoolteacher in Australia during the 1870's, but his comments on the experience were mainly of an introspective character. Havelock Ellis, *My Life* (Boston, 1939), pp. 115–74.

43. Spencer contrasted favorably the emigration efforts of Caroline Chisholm with those of the Emigration Board as an illustration of the greater effectiveness of private than public enterprise. "Here are lessons for lovers of legislation. The State outdone by a working shoemaker! The State beaten by a woman!" Herbert Spencer, *Essays: Moral, Political and Aesthetic* (New York, 1868), p. 79, and see also p. 61.

44. Herbert Spencer, *Facts and Comments* (London, 1902), p. 23.

45. *Ibid.*, pp. 191–92.

where else in the Empire, the moral was clear. The state should adhere strictly to its legitimate role as policeman and judge. "To the question—What is representative government good for? our reply is—It is good, especially good, good above all others, for doing the things which a government should do. It is bad, especially bad, bad above all others, for doing the things which a government should not do." [46]

More direct comment on Australia's social evolution came from Walter Bagehot, who concluded that he could detect significant genetic changes taking place in all new countries. He explained in an article in the *Fortnightly Review* for 1867 which later became part of *Physics and Politics* (1872):

In America and in Australia a new modification of what we call Anglo-Saxonism is growing. A sort of type of character arose from the difficulties of colonial life, the difficulty of struggling with the wilderness; and this type has given its shape to the mass of characters because the mass of characters have unconsciously imitated it. Many of the American characteristics are plainly useful in such a life, and consequent on such a life. The eager restlessness, the highly strung nervous organization are useful in continual struggle, and also are promoted by it. These traits seem to be arising in Australia, too, and wherever else the English race is placed in like circumstances.[47]

Bagehot was cautious about naming either definite causes or clear effects of Australia's particular social evolution. He did suggest, however, that the operation of a voluntary selection process among emigrants from the Old World—a "process of attraction by similar faith"—might be part of an explanation for the unique racial type growing up in Australia:

all new settlements, being formed of "emigrants," are sure to be composed of rather restless people, mainly. The stay-at-home people are not to be found there, and these are the quiet, easy people. A new settlement voluntarily formed (for of old times, when people were expelled by terror, I am not speaking) is sure to have in it much more than the ordinary proportion of active men, and much less than the ordinary proportion of inactive; and this accounts for a large part,

46. *Ibid.*, pp. 206–7.

47. Walter Bagehot, "Physics and Politics No. I: The Pre-Economic Age," *Fortnightly Review*, II (1867), 535; and *Physics and Politics* (Boston, 1956), p. 27.

though not perhaps all, of the difference between the English in England, and the English in Australia.[48]

In 1884 Alfred Russel Wallace, a pioneer with Darwin in tracing the origin of species, was less cautious than Bagehot in assessing the effects of natural selection upon the colonies. In a popular account of Australian geography he attributed colonial economic progress since the discovery of gold directly to the bitter evolutionary struggle which this event had precipitated:

The influx of men of all classes from the mother country, and of almost all the races of the world, together with numbers of released or escaped convicts from the neighbouring colonies, led to a struggle for existence, in which the most hardy, the most energetic, the most patient, or the most far-seeing, could alone succeed. Thus, amid much trouble, much degradation, and much crime, the seething mass of humanity, drawn together by the love of gold, has worked itself into something like order; and the result is a population of almost unexampled energy, which is now steadily engaged in developing all the resources of a fertile and beautiful country.[49]

Bagehot's curiosity about the factors affecting social growth in Australia help to explain the sustained interest in the subject of the London *Economist,* the paper he edited from 1860 until his death in 1877.[50] As early as 1862 an *Economist* reviewer urged his readers to acquire "a thorough knowledge" of the "political and social history" of the colonies so as to view them as total entities and to assist them to fulfill their destinies as chosen offspring of the parent stock; "every English colony should be a centre for the radiation of English thought, English culture, and English principles in their highest aspects."[51] The reviewer warned that already circumstances were present in Australia which, if not modified, might lead to a truncated and inferior society, in particular—

the want of that variety of classes which we have at home, and the want, more especially, of that aristocratic, leisure-enjoying, highly

48. Bagehot, *Physics and Politics*, pp. 72–73.
49. Alfred Russel Wallace, ed., *Australasia*, Stanford's Compendium of Geography and Travel (London, 1884), pp. 174–75.
50. Attention paid by the *Economist* to specific economic policies of the colonies has been discussed above in Chapter 4.
51. *Economist,* XX (1862), 233.

educated class. May we hope that in time these latter may grow up to give completeness and stability to the fabric of society. Without them we never can hope to see that calm power of self-restraint, that love of law and order, that preference of moral to material interests, which at present make our mother country the wonder and admiration of the world.[52]

Another writer in the *Economist* pointed out in 1862 that a manifestation of colonial social failings would be acceptance of governmental institutions inferior in structure to those of the Old Country. Naturally, the colonial Parliament deserved the closest scrutiny, and he found it failed the test of comparison:

The legislatures which we have established directly or indirectly in our Australian colonies are by no means admirable or desirable. They are far too democratic, and the frequent changes of their executive administration and the unsatisfactory results of that administration have done much to weaken the confidence in democratic institutions, even of persons otherwise well inclined to them. They are not satisfactory bodies for an Imperial Government or for any one to be concerned with.[53]

In subsequent years the paper took careful note of works on Australia which seemed to confirm these early impressions, for example, the *Letters* of John Martineau.[54] The *Economist* was particularly reluctant to tolerate the Australian colonies making independent decisions in the international arena where bad judgment could be especially costly to Britain.[55]

During the 1870's and 1880's, safety of the substantial British investment in the Australian colonies was the *Economist's* main concern, rather than theoretical questions of social evolution. Nevertheless, the theme which runs throughout the articles of these decades is only a variant of that in earlier years: the familiar contrast in the colonies of nature's bounty and man's folly continues to be stressed. Moreover, a new air of foreboding and impending doom appears in the *Economist* reports. For example,

52. *Ibid.*
53. "The Australian Sovereign," *Economist*, XX (1862), 1068. Similar views are expressed in "The Lesson for England in the Australian Elections," *ibid.*, XXIV (1866), 442–43.
54. *Ibid.*, XXVI (1868), 736; and XXVII (1869), 533.
55. E.g., "The Anomalous Position of the Colonies," *Economist*, XXVIII (1870), 1453–54.

even when describing conditions of apparent economic health and high returns on capital the paper concludes, "when we find banking profits running up so rapidly as they have recently done in Australia, it argues a state of over-activity in the system which is not compatible with perfect health." [56] Investment in Australia was pictured still as an advantageous outlet for Britain's surplus capital, but increasing doubt was expressed about whether this opportunity might not be too much of a good thing: "it is very questionable indeed whether this extremely rapid borrowing has been quite prudent." [57] And again, "it would be better if New Zealand, Queensland, and perhaps South Australia, kept quiet for a time." [58]

A supposed colonial mania for "unproductive" public works was still seen by the *Economist* after thirty years as the major threat to continued Australian prosperity, especially as it seemed to have become an integral part of the political and social system. The paper complained in 1885 that "the widest interpretation is now given to the term 'reproductive' until wooden school-houses, police stations, fancy iron railings, wood-paving, immigration, forts, and war-ships, are all included; yet it is only by a wide stretch of the imagination that such works can be regarded as reproductive, or classed with railways and waterworks." [59] All the public construction "gives an artificial stimulus to the labour market, and, in fact, to all industries, from which an ultimate reaction is only too certain." [60] In 1889 an *Economist* cor-

56. "The Present Growth of Australian Banking Profits," *Economist,* XLI (1883), 910.

57. "The Gold Withdrawals for Australia," *Economist,* XLII (1884), 94.

58. "The Extent of Our Colonial Investments: III," *Economist,* LXII (1884), 228. See also, "The Assets and Liabilities of our Australasian Colonies," *ibid.,* XL (1882), 1488–89, and 1554–55; "The Debt of Queensland," *ibid.,* XLI (1883), 518; "The Extent of Our Colonial Investments," *ibid.,* XLII (1884), 160–61 and 196–97; "The Australasian Money Market," *ibid.,* 1321–22.

59. "The Debt of Australasia," *Economist,* XLIII (1885), 562.

60. "The Impending New South Wales Loan," *Economist,* XLIII (1885), 868–69. See also "Australasia—Silver Production and Land Speculation. From our own Correspondent," *ibid.,* pp. 1167–68; "A New Development of Australian Banking," *ibid.,* pp. 1349–50; "The Australasian Money Market," *ibid.,* XLIV (1886), 555–56; "The Australian Money Market," *ibid.,* p. 800. Towards the end of 1886 the paper reported: "The fact that, in order to maintain their expenditure upon public works, the colonies have, to a certain extent, been compelled to live upon capital, adds force to the opinion to which we have more than of late felt bound to give expression, that they have been running into debt rather more rapidly than is prudent." "Ten Years of Australasian Progress," *ibid.,* pp. 1474–75.

respondent reported from Sydney that in New South Wales public borrowing had reached "the last straw that breaks the camel's back."[61] Accordingly, the paper and its readers were well prepared psychologically for the seeming catastrophes which were shortly to follow.

The *Economist* was not the only periodical which contained elaborate discussions of Australia's social evolution or deterioration. C. W. Purnell in the *Fortnightly Review*, while calling himself a defender of the colonies from unreasonable critics, presented all the same an extensive catalogue of symptoms of national decline, in particular examples of governmental corruption and legislative misjudgment. He leaned toward the hypothesis of mental decline among the citizens as the most plausible explanation for recent history: "in place of the spirit of enterprise and love of adventure, we find a strong development of bumptiousness and self-sufficiency. I do not know in all these colonies of a single man of first-rate talent who is of colonial birth and breeding."[62] The disturbing questions raised by Purnell were kept alive in the *Fortnightly* through accounts of political events in the colonies from such reporters as the emigrant academic Charles H. Pearson, George Baden-Powell, and Augustus Nash.[63]

The *Westminster Review* published some of the most pessimistic and dreary prognostications of Australia's future of any British journal. An important article in 1868 entitled "Democratic Government in Victoria" drew a picture of racial decline in great detail. The anonymous author doubted that the evolutionary process had yet had time to work itself out fully in the colonies. "The national existences, such as they are, have not been produced by any process of natural selection. The types of character are embryonic, rudimentary, and transitional."[64] All

61. "The Borrowing Mania in New South Wales," *Economist*, XLVII (1889), 1468.

62. Charles W. Purnell, "Politics in Australasia," *Fortnightly Review*, XXIII (1878), 507. Alfred Deakin's first assignment in his long literary association with the Melbourne *Age* was a review of this article. See J. A. La Nauze, *Alfred Deakin* (Melbourne, 1965), p. 33.

63. Charles H. Pearson, "Democracy in Victoria," *Fortnightly Review*, XXV (1879), 688–717; G. Baden-Powell, "Reform in Victoria," *ibid.*, pp. 950–62; Augustus Nash, "Democracy in New South Wales," *ibid.*, XLI (1887), 312–15.

64. "Democratic Government in Victoria," *Westminster Review*, XXXIII (1868), 481.

the same, he was no less disturbed by the course of events, of which current political unrest in Victoria was only an example. He found the circumstances of Victoria's origin, especially the convicts and gold, profoundly disturbing and sufficient to explain current developments. Gold had been socially destructive both at the time of discovery and "in futuro." He anticipated terminology employed five years later by Anthony Trollope to describe the effects of gold on the populace. He said: "The pursuit of gold-digging tends inevitably to make nomads of those who follow it, and they in their turn infect and influence the whole current of the thoughts and the ambitions of the great mass of the people." [65] This author attributed the political deterioration of the colonies in part to their inability to profit from the experience of the Old Country:

> . . . whatever may be the advantages which the colonists as individuals may have enjoyed, it is abundantly evident that they have derived no instruction from the political history of the mother country: her knowledge of the inexorable laws of commerce—slowly acquired by costly experience—they persist in making a sealed book to themselves; they ignore the teachings of political economy, and would invent a new law of wealth to serve their selfish interests; while their statesmen are conspicuously destitute of any just conceptions of the sphere within which governmental action ought to be confined, and therefore of the true nature of the only reliable safeguards against the dangers of democracy.[66]

This *Westminster* reviewer argued that Australia's most pressing political problems could be explained in evolutionary terms by the absence in this fertile land of beneficial conflict. Self-government had been obtained with too great ease: "wholesome struggle for democratic principles . . . is needed to make any popular government sound or secure." [67] There were two ways, he said, in which a viable government could come into existence in any country: gradually and "naturally out of the character of the people" or suddenly on the model of a "scientific theory." The Australian colonies had taken neither of these courses and

65. *Ibid.*, p. 482.
66. *Ibid.*, p. 483.
67. *Ibid.*, p. 490.

in their haphazard flounderings were bound to face endless problems. Victorian government "was neither created, nor proceeding; but a jumble of old English ideas clumsily put together with what were supposed to be democratic principles. The garment with which the colony was indued was neither symmetrical in itself nor fitted to the shape of the wearer." [68] The depths to which politics had sunk in Victoria could be judged from the fact that "Mr. John Stuart Mill is openly denounced as a reactionist and a tool of aristocracy; and the mention of his name at any great public meeting of 'the people' in Melbourne is the sure signal for a chorus of jeers and groans." [69] At a personal level "for the most part the legislators are simple mediocrities, vacuous, empty, and null. They are active chiefly in corruption, in the practice of which they have acquired much skill and dexterity." [70]

Many of the evils which flowed from Victoria's political system, the reviewer suggested, were economic in effect. In private business corrupt democracy sapped the initiative of entrepreneurs:

> The chief dangers to which democracies have in all times been subject are those which arise from the suppression of individualism. . . . This passion for equality has tinged the whole course of government in Victoria. And the action of government under its influence has tended to make the people itself restless, unstable, intolerant, greedy of novelties, and impatient and suspicious of its own laws and ordinances. Self-government, which we might have expected would produce self-reliance, has only wrought self-indulgence.[71]

At the public level, extreme democracies inevitably rejected wise guidance and economic principle in formulating policy; without discipline or restraint, they embraced such heresies as tariff protection, immigration restriction, and extravagant public works:

> "What do we want with political economy?" is a favourite democratic cry. "Let us make our own science of wealth, our own theory of progress. The musty rules of Free Trade may be all very well for an effete old country like England, but for Australia is needed a separate

68. *Ibid.*, pp. 491–92.
69. *Ibid.*, p. 503.
70. *Ibid.*, p. 496.
71. *Ibid.*, p. 502.

law of being. That which is true of the northern hemisphere must not be accepted without question in the southern. We are in the possession of the government, and it shall be our business to try and discover a political economy better fitted for the working-man than the system which is in use among the English aristocrats." [72]

The reviewer denied that the economic success of Victoria could be attributed in any way to its democratic form of government. "If we were to say that the colony has progressed *in spite* of its government we should be much nearer the truth." [73]

The criticisms of specific Australian policies and practices contained in the 1868 *Westminster* article were similar in form to those described in Chapter 4 above. The article merits special attention here because it was one of the first attempts to treat Australia's alleged economic failings organically and to diagnose them as symptoms of total national decadence.[74] The article was an application to Australia of a principle which was rapidly gaining acceptance among mid-nineteenth century liberals throughout the Empire, that in addition to free trade and limited government, a satisfactory economy must have responsible and restrained political and social institutions.[75]

In later years the *Westminster Review* retraced the gloomy picture of the Australian economy painted in its earlier article. In 1870 readers were informed that, propaganda to the contrary notwithstanding, Australia contained as much poverty per capita as the Old World. There the poor were known as "swaggers"—"persons in the condition of dependence, whose wants are provided for by Government funds, aided by charitable efforts, and whose *status* is that of pauperism." [76] In 1878 a review of descriptive books on Australia afforded a convenient opportunity to reiterate at some length the opinions presented ten years before.

72. *Ibid.*, p. 504.
73. *Ibid.*, p. 506.
74. A relatively cautious earlier defense of Australia by Charles H. Pearson was rejected out of hand. "Mr. Pearson, though a tolerably candid and intelligent observer, betrays by many signs that his experience is but small and his opportunities limited." *Ibid.*, p. 498.
75. On this point see Lionel Robbins, *The Theory of Economic Policy in English Classical Political Economy* (London, 1965), esp. pp. 194–205; and Warren J. Samuels, *The Classical Theory of Economic Policy* (Cleveland, 1966).
76. "Colonial and American Pauperism," *Westminster Review*, XXXVIII (1870), 100.

The contrast between the natural fecundity of the country and its foolish citizenry was noted again, and the reviewer, like his predecessors in the *Westminster,* leaned toward racial deterioration as the most plausible explanation:

In America the physical degeneracy of persons of pure American extraction is acknowledged. The race would languish and become either extinct or effete, but for the fresh infusion of European blood. While the Australian cricketers are still among us, it seems rash to say that the "native" Australian is physically inferior to the Englishman. But he is certainly of lighter build—more agile, perhaps, and as enduring, but not so strong. Mentally they are, as contrasted with Englishmen, precocious and quick rather than sound. Manners, of course, are due rather to temporary environments than to inherent qualities. The rich men—the aristocrats—are often men of humblest origin; and there is *no* aristocracy of birth, or even of education, to give tone to society and establish a standard of manners.[77]

In 1887 the *Westminster* directed a particularly sharp attack in clear evolutionary terms against "Young Australia." The colonies' worst days lay immediately ahead, this reviewer said, because racial deterioration had proceeded so quickly. Geographical isolation, reduced immigration in proportion to the total population, and a wide range of misguided public policies, all contributed to catastrophe:

The great distance of the Australian continent from the centres of European civilization, the impossibility, except in the case of the most opulent classes, of much international intercourse, the cessation of any considerable stream of emigration for a number of years, and most of all, the growth to manhood of the colonial-born—now much the larger half of the population—under the narrow and restricted form of compulsory education provided by the State for the people, admirable as it is in many respects, are the chief factors in this very perceptible change.[78]

Proofs of Australia's racial decline were said to be bad manners, drunkenness, "the absence of any other ideal than wealth," and "the absurd infatuation for out-door sports and pastimes which prevails, engrossing the minds of the population to an extent

77. "The Australian Colonies," *Westminster Review,* LIV (1878), 346–47.
78. "Young Australia," *Westminster Review,* CXXVIII (1887), 549.

almost beyond the Teuton comprehension." Finally, "One of the keenest wants felt in Australia is an atmosphere of sympathy in intellectual aims." [79] The only clear solution offered on this occasion for Australia's problems was accelerated immigration of Englishmen to raise the overall quality and tone of the population.[80]

As uncertainties and fears of approaching collapse in Australia increased during the late 1880's, British periodicals were especially hospitable to what seemed to be penetrating accounts of recent developments. Cyprian Bridge (later Admiral, K.C.B.), recently returned from service on the Australian station as deputy commissioner for the Western Pacific, wrote anonymously in the *Edinburgh Review* of the waste and political corruption he himself had witnessed. Such matters, he indicated, had not received sufficient attention in Froude's *Oceana.*[81] Archibald Alison, son of the eminent historian of the same name and apparently resident in the colonies, wrote in *Blackwood's* that Australia's democracy was leading it straight to ruin. Manhood suffrage had been followed by immigration restriction, extravagant foreign borrowing and public works, strong trade unions, and the eight-hour day. These in turn had led to endemic laziness and acceptance of sloth as part of the national character.[82] In the same vein, Ernest W. Beckett in the *Nineteenth Century* reminded Englishmen once again that Australia's degradation might be prophecy for themselves.[83]

General William Feilding, who had spent some time in the colonies, made the literature on colonization come full circle after half a century by presenting a body of doctrine in the *National Review* almost identical with that set forth by Edward Gibbon Wakefield in his *Letter from Sydney* fifty-eight years before. Without mentioning Wakefield, Fielding argued that social decline in the colonies had proved beyond a doubt that haphazard

79. *Ibid.*, p. 553.
80. *Ibid.*, p. 555.
81. "Froude's *Oceana*," *Edinburgh Review*, CLXIII (1886), 405–36.
82. "Labour and Capital in Australia," *Blackwood's Magazine*, CXLI (1887), 677–82.
83. E. W. Beckett, "Australian Sidelights on English Politics," *Nineteenth Century*, XXV (1889), 110–32.

settlement of new countries must end in disaster. He suggested that there still was time to introduce in Australia a scheme of planned and controlled development based on restricted use of land which would "enable the social group to become self-supporting from the moment of its arrival on its new home 'location.'" The clearest indication of Feilding's contempt for existing colonial societies can be found in his prescription for the ideal. He listed the following as the first six requirements for establishment of a successful new community:

1. There must be capital, and in a model state of society this should be held in moderate proportions by several individuals.
2. There must be gentlemen, energetic, persevering, and of fair birth and education, to direct the intelligent use of capital towards the remunerative development of the soil or of trade, to set an example to those of less refinement and of lower tastes, and to lead public opinion into sound channels of thought and action.
3. There must be women of education and refinement to keep up the tone, which is apt, in the absence of good female influence, to degenerate into a coarse animalism. Their presence would conduce to cleanliness, tidiness, and comfort at home, to a due regard to decency and sanitation out of doors, and to the encouragement and maintenance of a proper attention to religious and educational matters.
4. There must be small farmers, with their families (the more numerous the better), accustomed not only to direct field work, but to take an active part in all the labours connected with farming occupations.
5. There must be a proper proportion of men of all trades, such as one baker, one shoe-maker, one saddler, one carpenter, two sawyers, &c. to each of the "social groups," or villages. The grocery and chemist's store should, in the first instance, be considered as part of the preliminary provision, and should be in existence prior to the arrival of the settlers.
6. There should be, in suitable proportions, men of the labouring class, agricultural labourers, gardeners, navvies, and good woodmen, if in a well-timbered country.[84]

It is clear that Feilding perceived few of the conditions necessary for successful settlement in the Australian colonies. His work

84. William Feilding, "Imperial Migration and Settlement," *National Review*, VIII (1886/87), 778, and 781. Obituaries of Feilding, a son of the Earl of Denbigh, are in *The Times*, 26 and 27 March 1895.

reveals that, if he was at all representative, Englishmen by the 1880's had lost little of their affection for colonization schemes aimed to reproduce British society in the New World and their suspicion of arrangements designed to take account of the special conditions of a developing country.

Counterattacks from the Colonies

Much of the descriptive writing by colonists about their own economies during the nineteenth century was inspired in a general way by the type of vigorous attack described in this chapter and the last. In part the inspiration took the form of a literary market and audience in Britain stirred up by controversy and willing to hear both sides of the lively argument. There was also growing appreciation that, as the Victorian statesman George Higinbotham wrote to Gavan Duffy in 1866, "English opinion has at present an extraordinary, and, I think, a pernicious influence on our affairs." [85] Many of the defensive writings were simply straightforward accounts designed to correct obvious errors and misinterpretations and with only occasional references to the various critiques of the colonies.[86] A few works do deserve special attention here, however, because they were designed as direct

85. Charles Gavan Duffy, *My Life in Two Hemispheres* (London, 1898), II, 271. Australians were made aware of British disapproval both by works published in Britain and by such outspoken commentaries as that of Earl Grey for the editor of the Melbourne *Victorian Review* in 1880. Grey confidently attributed Victoria's difficulties to "unwise legislation, and to mismanagement and want of economy in the administration." *Victorian Review*, I (1880), 857–75.

86. E.g., Anthony Forster in his large history of South Australia deplored the anticolonial comments of Goldwin Smith. *South Australia: Its Progress and Prosperity* (London, 1866). Similarly, all of the following works were to some extent defensive in tone: Christopher Rolleston, *New South Wales* (London, 1873); Samuel Mossman, *Our Australian Colonies* (London, 1866); George Sutherland, *Australia, or England in the South* (London, 1886); Waldemar Bannow, *The Colony of Victoria Socially and Materially* (Melbourne, 1896). A *Cornhill* reviewer in 1868 appealed for greater sympathy for Australia on the ground that "a new country, it must be remembered, requires legislation specially adapted to its needs." "Colonial Parliaments," *Cornhill*, XVIII (1868), 484–95; and see also "An Australian's Impressions of England," *ibid.*, XIII (1866), 110–20. Some of the defensive descriptions seemed ironic soon after publication. For example, an elaborate account of the Australian banking system issued just before the financial crisis of 1893 began with the question, "Where, in the banking world, can we find a record so stainless?" Robert Lucas Nash, *The Banking Institutions of Australasia* (London, [c. 1890]), p. 7. Other general accounts are discussed in Chapter 3 above.

refutations of the major derogatory accounts, and hence may have had some effect on British images.

First of all, an occasional word of sympathy or support came to Australians from residents of other parts of the Empire who, presumably, understood more fully than did people in the Old Country the problems of new countries and saw their own experience reflected in that of Australia. For example, the Canadian protectionist J. Beaufort Hurlbert said of Australia in 1865: "We have no example in history of better-governed states. Some of them were at first encumbered with the feudal system, and other establishments of a past age and a widely different civilization; these they have quietly rid themselves of, without endangering the peace or well-being of society." [87]

Some of the most effective statements by the Australian colonists came from visitors in London to sell securities, recruit immigrants, or conduct negotiations with the British government. Often the colonial spokesmen were responding directly to the charges of critics. Henry Parkes, as Government Commissioner for New South Wales in London, attempted repeatedly during the 1860's to counteract the notoriety produced by the gold period. He concentrated on reciting the positive achievements of the colonies (number of acres settled, buildings constructed, population added, goods produced, etc.), and he emphasized the fundamental similarity of colonial society to that of Britain, in sharp contrast to what most of the critics reported. He told an audience at the Working Men's College in London in 1862, "It would be difficult indeed for the most fastidious of social critics to discover in the face of things in the colony at the present time any visible traces of its penal origin, or any marked features distinguishing its cities and towns from the cities and towns of England, except it be that they generally are cleaner and look much happier." [88]

87. J. Beaufort Hurlbert, *Britain and Her Colonies* (London, 1865), pp. 216–17.

88. Henry Parkes, *The Mother of the Australias* (London, 1862), p. 8. In letters back home to New South Wales during this period Parkes pictured the defenders of the colonies as largely successful and the colonial reputation as improving: "If political mistakes have been made, they know that worse mistakes have been made nearer home, and in the midst of it all they see that the colony is making real progress . . . the alarm about Australian democracy is beginning to lose its

Charles Gavan Duffy responded directly to critics of young Australia in an eloquent address to the Society of Arts in 1866. He complained that "there are few countries in the world of which the people of England have received impressions so erroneous and untrustworthy as of the Australian Colonies."[89] Duffy was amazed at the lack of sympathy of most Englishmen for Australia's problems and their lack of pride in the continent's remarkable achievements. The colonies, he admitted, were "without the counterpoise supplied at home by the personal influence of the sovereign, and of hereditary rank and wealth, but in connection with a franchise which, from the circumstances of the country, was necessarily nearly as wide as the adult male population." Yet "under these conditions colonial statesmen have undeniably preserved public order, maintained public credit, and fostered national prosperity." Despite these accomplishments:

> Instead of regarding this great social expedition of our people to new regions with some of the interest and sympathy never denied to military expeditions—instead of recognising their remarkable labours in the cities which they have founded, the wealth which they have added to the storehouse of human comfort and prosperity, and the states which they have created and governed (conquests to be proud of)—they are habitually represented as little better than the semi-barbarous and chaotic republics of South America. When one comes to inquire what is the root of this prejudice it will be found, I think, generally to spring from a belief that the Australians, having a great trust committed to them in the complete power of self-government, have abused it, and run riot in licentious excesses.[90]

The causes of British skepticism of Australian society, Duffy concluded, were ignorance of the true facts of the new com-

---

potency to English ears." *Australian Views of England: Eleven Letters Written in the Years 1861 and 1862* (London, 1869), p. 56. Sir Charles Nicholson presented arguments similar to those of Parkes to the Society of Arts in 1863. See *The Australian Colonies; Their Condition, Resources, and Prospects* (reprinted from the *Journal of the Society of Arts,* November 27, 1863). An example of publicity by a former governor is Sir Charles Du Cane, *Tasmania—Past and Present: A Lecture Given at the Town Hall, Colchester* (Colchester, 1877).

89. *Address of the Hon. C. G. Duffy, on Popular Errors Concerning Australia at Home and Abroad* (Melbourne, 1866), p. 4. Duffy reflected also the opinions of other friends of the colonies such as Hugh C. E. Childers that "Australia is very imperfectly understood at home." Charles Gavan Duffy, *My Life in Two Hemispheres* (London, 1898), II, 256–57, 263, 270–71, 280–81.

90. Duffy, *Address,* pp. 4–5.

munities, and alarm at apparent "political instability" indicated by frequent changes of ministry. To meet the charge of incompetent leadership Duffy reported that there were in high places throughout the Australian colonies representatives of Britain's most distinguished blood lines, for example,

> The families of Wordsworth, Coleridge, Arnold (of Rugby), Brougham, O'Connell, Jenner, Faraday, Babbage, Whewell, Stephen; or, to come still closer to present tastes and sympathies, Dickens, Gladstone, Kingsley, William Carleton, Macready, Helps; or, to take the immense community which is sometimes called the religious world, sons of Edward Irving and Baptist Noel, and a brother of Frederick Lucas, hold public appointments in Melbourne.[91]

Duffy then went to considerable pains to explain the impact of geography upon colonial politics, a series of effects which he believed the insular Englishmen could not easily appreciate. First of all, he said, distance made even more impractical the colonial federation advocated by most Englishmen than it did a European political union. "Berlin or Vienna is much nearer to London than the capitals of the colonies lying farthest apart are to each other." [92] Within a single colony distances made the process of political integration and attainment of consensus exceptionally difficult and helped to explain the changes in ministries, which, upon investigation, turned out after all to be no more frequent on average than in Britain itself. Finally, Duffy explained, geography required men of ability to take as active a part in economic life as in the political affairs of the new nation. The part-time political lives of Australia's leaders should be applauded not condemned. "The discovery and development of the wonderful resources of the country; rendering easier the extraction of gold; improving the quality of stock; planting new industries, and enriching the land with plants and animals which nature has denied to it, are works as urgent as perfecting the laws and institutions." [93]

The main result of widening the franchise in Australia, Duffy said, had been improvement in political morality and social

91. *Ibid.*, p. 4.
92. *Ibid.*, p. 7.
93. *Ibid.*, p. 12.

stability. In response to Robert Lowe's suggestion that the Colonial Office reinstate government from Downing Street for the colonies' own good, he replied: "it has never been my fortune to meet with a colonist who had the smallest desire to replace his free government by the sort of thing which constituted a stable executive." In conclusion, Duffy appealed for greater sensitivity and discretion from British critics of Australia. Apart from leading to mistaken colonial policies, unfounded attacks by observers in the metropolis could severely affect the pattern of development and even the survival of a new country:

> In England the bones and sinews which sustain and move the body politic, and constitute the vital machinery of the State, are covered by flowing robes of ceremony, and custom forbids too close an inspection of the august and mystic organism beneath. In Australia you have only the naked ribs and vertebrae, possessed with a vigorous principle of life indeed, but with scarce a rag of traditional veneration to shelter them from inquisitive eyes. Reverence and custom, such powerful agents in the government of States, can scarcely be said to come at all in aid of authority which has to depend in a large degree upon its intrinsic strength for acceptance and support. It is not, surely, the part of an English constitutionalist, whether in parliament or the press, to increase the natural difficulties of government under such circumstances. But he does so by unjust criticism, whether he makes people discontented with its system of government or angry at the mother country for the misrepresentation of it.[94]

It is doubtful that many were listening to Duffy's advice.

The first elaborate defense specifically of "Australian Institutions" came from Charles H. Pearson, an Oxford history don of liberal sympathies who had migrated to the colonies and who came to play an important role in Australian politics and letters. In a collection of articles by various authors, entitled *Essays on Reform* (1867), Pearson set out to correct the impression in Great Britain "that society has been inverted in the Antipodes,

94. *Ibid.*, pp. 12 and 14. Concerning Lowe, Duffy wrote in his diary at that time: "we felt that he [Lowe] had not been kind to his old country; articles which we attributed to him disparaged everything Australian. He said his hopes of a future for Australia were greatly mitigated. When men educated in Europe ceased to go there, and that the governing men had to be taken from colonial classes, it would fall very low. You tell me what great things you are doing now, he said, smiling, but wait till the larrikin comes on the stage." *My Life in Two Hemispheres* (London, 1898), II, 264.

so that what is low here is high there" and that "the great prosperity of the Australian colonies is due to the accident of the gold fields and the circumstances of a new country, and is only retarded by their self-government under institutions that may be called Democratic." [95] To begin, he denied the charge that the convict element was still significant in Australian society. "In fact, convicts are no longer a visible evil in any part of Australia. They have died without founding families, or have been killed off, or are filling the State prisons in Victoria and New South Wales." [96] The ruling principle of Australians in most things, he said comfortingly, was "to reproduce England in their new home"; adjustments in institutions were made only as circumstances dictated. Pearson applauded the operation of democratic self-government in the colonies and compared it favorably to rule from Downing Street in the early years. He listed such manifestations of respectability in the colonies as extensive church construction, large expenditures for education, and a low crime rate. Government operations, he contended, had been fiscally responsible despite such minor "blemishes" as tariff protection; ironically, the main problems of colonial finance were created by "a dread of democracy in the English investing class." [97] Above all, Pearson claimed, the colonies had succeeded in establishing a strong and conservative agricultural lower-middle class. "Each colony has solved the problem of creating a yeomanry in its own fashion." At the same time, they had provided bountiful encouragement to the propertied upper middle class.[98] Pearson's message to Great Britain was, in essence, that Australia followed the mother country in most important matters, especially the nourishment of liberal institutions; charges of profligacy and radicalism could not be substantiated.[99] As a recent immigrant to

95. Charles H. Pearson, "On the Working of Australian Institutions," *Essays on Reform* (London, 1867), pp. 191–92. See also, John Tregenza, *Professor of Democracy* (Melbourne, 1968), pp. 42–43.

96. Pearson, *Essays*, p. 193.

97. *Ibid.*, pp. 200–202.

98. ". . . the present legislation of Australia, which sits so easily that it has never even been murmured at, is in no way opposed to the legitimate interests of the capitalist." *Ibid.*, p. 212, and see also p. 206.

99. In the light of Pearson's comments on Australia's future twenty-six years later, discussed below, Chap. 7, it is ironic that he ended this early essay by stat-

Australia from British intellectual circles, Pearson was able both to present a plausible defense of the colonies and to identify clearly the main causes of concern.[100]

Fraser's Magazine in particular among British periodicals opened its pages to colonial counterattacks. W. Jardine Smith, a prominent political journalist writing from Victoria, responded with eloquence and depth of feeling to the harsh commentaries of the 1870's. First of all, he rejected as contrary to fact the accusations of racial deterioration:

> We are disagreeably struck by the tone of assumed superiority which characterises every comment on our affairs in the columns of the press, or on the platform—a superiority which we are by no means inclined to admit. We know, although it is no merit of ours, that our population, compared man for man with a similar number taken promiscuously from among the lower and middle classes of English society, would carry off the palm for superior physique, intelligence, enterprise and education.[101]

Smith pointed out that much criticism of the colonial economies was not only misinformed, it was inconsistent. British commentators complained at the same time of the failure to develop a class of yeoman farmers in Australia and of the violation of the sacred principles of laissez-faire—principles under which small

ing "I cannot predict the future, and I am slow to believe prophecies from others." *Ibid.*, p. 216.

100. Pearson was applauded and joined in his denunciation of Australia's attackers by the Victorian politician Archibald Michie. In an address to a Melbourne audience Michie answered point by point charges in the *Westminster Review* article entitled "Democratic Government in Victoria." He concluded: "I regret that a periodical like the *Westminster Review*, which for so many years after its foundation, under the auspices of Jeremy Bentham, did such yeoman's service in the promulgation of a wise liberalism in politics, should have become the vehicle of wholesale detraction, on insufficient grounds, of an entire community." *A Lecture on the Westminster Reviewer's Version of Victorian History, Delivered at St. George's Hall, on Friday, 18th September, 1868* (Melbourne, 1868), p. 25. Michie continued his defense in later years. See, for example, his *Readings in Melbourne* (London, 1879), *passim*. A similar intention to that of Pearson, to defend colonial institutions from unfair attack, was evident in a work by "A Colonist of Twenty Years' Standing, and Late Member of a Colonial Legislature," C. R. Carter, entitled *Victoria, the British "El Dorado," or Melbourne in 1869* (London, 1870). This author wrote proudly: "We have had to make the country and provide certain special laws for its government. We have *fitted* it with social and political institutions, imported it is true, from our native country, like so many manufactured goods for general adoption, if not consumption. Yet we have done this during the life of the present generation" (p. 184).

101. W. Jardine Smith, "The Imperial Connection, from an Australian Colonist's Point of View," *Fraser's Magazine*, IV (1871), 385.

farmers could not always prosper. Colonists had learned, Smith declared, that in a new country small proprietors were seldom able to survive the predatory competition of their larger neighbors without protection and assistance from the state. It was the colonists' "very faith in the teachings of political economy which led them to adopt those expedients which are denounced by their critics as pernicious errors. They understood so well the action of the law of supply and demand, and the practically unlimited power of capital if left to its natural operation, that they sought by legislative enactments to check the forces which, if left unfettered, would have prevented the development of the very class which they were anxious to foster." [102] Smith outlined some of the complex challenges which faced colonial legislators in the formation of economic policy, and he conceded that some mistakes had been made. But he denied that over the years Britain had had a more distinguished legislative record than had the colonies, or that the mother country was equipped to offer very much useful guidance to its offspring. Again, on the land question—

> in all these things which we have done, we have violated the idol of the political economists—the sacred doctrine of "*laissez faire.*" Accordingly we are twitted by some of our home friends with our lamentable ignorance, and pitied by others for our perverse blindness. But while claiming for our endeavours to promote the happiness of the greatest number, only a moderate amount of success, and acknowledging the impossibility of entirely counteracting by legislation the operation of those economic laws the unchecked action of which as regards land we believe to result in the enrichment of the rich and the impoverishment of the poor, we would ask our English critics, "Where shall we turn for a model on which to fashion our land policy?" [103]

Certainly not to Britain was Smith's own reply to his last question.

Counterattacks by other Australian defenders took a variety of different forms. A colonist writing in *Fraser's* in 1873 assumed that a good offense is the best defense and demanded that Britain put its own political and social house in order so as to generate "fresh energy" and effective leadership for the colonies. Similarly

102. *Ibid.*, p. 391.
103. *Ibid.*, pp. 392–93.

Edward Morris, professor of modern languages at Melbourne University, asked Great Britain a year later please not to send any more of the dull and the sick about whom the Social Darwinists complained as breeding stock.[104] Dudley Adams, writing from New South Wales two years later, pictured Australia as absolutely vital to the continued social good health of Great Britain which was "the 'hive of the world,' whose bees must perforce 'swarm' periodically."[105] He implied that the evidence of Australia's continued economic growth was proof enough of the legitimacy of her economic policies. A number of other writers such as Robert Christison, Francis P. Labilliere, and Harold Finch-Hatton, reported the presence of warm imperial sentiment in Australia which unreasoning criticism would certainly destroy.[106] Some defenders attacked the credibility of specific critics. For example, the Victorian politician James Mirams delivered a scathing attack on George Baden-Powell for his presumption of authority on Australian affairs after only two visits. Queenslanders, understandably, were particularly sensitive to the "mistaken impression" given by the work of Baden-Powell and others that white labor degenerated in the tropics, and they replied with accounts of economic success.[107]

Three categories of colonial defenders who maintained a steady level of skirmishing with critics of the colonies during the 1870's and 1880's were the colonists themselves, visiting in Britain or at home, former colonists now living in Britain who retained a proprietary interest in their former homes, and agents-general whose official task was to protect colonial interests in London. Prominent members of the first and second groups were J. Lang-

104. E. Morris, "A Proposed Reform of the English Constitution," *Fraser's Magazine*, VIII (1873), 600–607; Edward E. Morris, "On Sending Out to Australia," *Longmans' Magazine*, 1883, pp. 173–83.

105. D. Adams, "Letter from New South Wales," *Fraser's Magazine*, XII (1875), 799.

106. Robert Christison, "United Australia and Imperial Federation," *Westminster Review*, CXXX (1888), 335–48; Francis P. Labilliere, "The Contraction of England and Its Advocates," *National Review*, III (1884), 467–80; and Harold Finch-Hatton, "Lord Bury and Imperial Federation," *ibid.*, V (1885), 207–19.

107. James Mirams, *The Progress of Victoria: A Reply to an Article by G. Baden-Powell, Esq., on "Protection in Young Communities," Published in the "Fortnightly Review"* (London, 1883). See also: J. C. White, *Queensland the Progressive!* (London, 1870); Charles Haynes Barlee, *Queensland Australia* (London, [c. 1870]); Augustus G. Perceval, *Northern Queensland* (London, 1881).

don Parsons, J. Henniker Heaton, Finch-Hatton, Labilliere, William Westgarth, and Sir George Bowen. In the third category were Saul Samuel, R. Murray Smith, and Julius Vogel, the latter a New Zealander who tended to speak for the colonies as a whole. These spokesmen used any forum open to them, but favorite outlets were meetings of the Royal Colonial Institute, letter columns of the newspapers, and sympathetic periodicals such as the *National Review*.[108] Many of the colonial defenders were British-born, and Alfred Deakin expressing a true native's viewpoint at the Colonial Conference in 1887 was still a relative novelty.[109]

The Survival of the Worst

Analysis in evolutionary terms of the Australian economy and society confirmed the impression of heresy created by examination of specific economic policies. Observers who looked for overall social progress or retrogression reached the same gloomy conclusions as did those who looked at the colonial economic systems for conformity to the various policy dictates of political economy. Whereas in the pure economic sense, the Australians seemed bent on interfering with or destroying the basis for a

108. The role of these colonial defenders as transmitters of information is examined in Chapter 3 above. Examples of additional defensive replies to attacks on the colonies are Harold Finch-Hatton, *Advance Australia!* (London, 1885); an address by Sir George Bowen at Eaglehawk in 1874 in which he deplored "mistaken comparisons" of Australian public debts with those of Great Britain, in Stanley Lane-Poole, ed., *Thirty Years of Colonial Government* (London, 1889), II, 22, and also p. 114; Henry Parkes, "Our Growing Australian Empire," *Nineteenth Century*, XV (1884), 138–49; *idem*, "Australia and the Imperial Connection," *ibid.*, 867–72; J. Henniker Heaton, "The Centenary of Australia," *National Review*, X (1887/88), 857–65; William Westgarth, "Australasian Public Finance," *Proceedings of the Royal Colonial Institute*, XX (1888/89), 230–52; Saul Samuel, "To the Editor of the *Economist*," *Economist*, XLIII (1885), 909; *idem*, "The Railways of New South Wales," *ibid.*, pp. 1504–6 and 1546; Robert Murray Smith, "Victorian Railways," *ibid.*, p. 1513; J. Langdon Parsons, "The Northern Territory of South Australia," *National Review*, III (1884), 78–88, a reply to criticisms by Major General Feilding; and Francis P. Labilliere, "The Contraction of England," with a denunciation of Goldwin Smith and Trollope on p. 479. Two complimentary texts at the secondary school level were J. F. V. Fitzgerald, late Colonial Secretary of Victoria, *Australia* (London, 1881), and K. E. Jung, formerly Inspector of Schools in South Australia, *Australia, the Country and Its Inhabitants* (London, 1884). Various additional aspects of Australian attitudes toward Britain in the nineteenth century are discussed in Henry L. Hall, *Australia and England: A Study in Imperial Relations* (London, 1934).

109. J. A. La Nauze, *Alfred Deakin* (Melbourne, 1965), p. 94.

successful free price system, in the evolutionary sense they were victims of climate, convict and mining origins, inadequate leadership, and destructive democratic institutions. The doctrine of evolution made a complex situation easier to comprehend—a dark and distant scene easier to imagine. By the 1880's most British commentators were ready to seize upon any fragment of evidence which seemed to confirm the evolutionary decline which they were certain was in progress. They noted indications of political and social decay, unhealthy exhilaration in markets, and even physiological deterioration among the population.

Defenders of the Australian economy responded with spirit to the charges of organic decline. They corrected misinformation, told of positive achievements in the colonies, and appealed for sympathy and understanding. It is significant, however, that in the main the defenders operated on a different plane of discourse from the critics. They replied to theory with facts; and the facts were not taken seriously enough to threaten the theory. Australia's bad reputation rested, in essence, on its failure to conform to models of social as well as economic development which had been constructed without reference to its own special experience or needs. Australia was bound to remain convicted of nonconformity so long as the models remained unchallenged. In the 1880's such a challenge was still some years away.

In the next chapter it will be seen how Australia's critics reacted during the 1890's to the strong corroborative evidence which seemed finally to banish all remaining doubts about their charges.

· 6 ·

Reaping the Whirlwind: Strikes and Depression

Critiques of the Australian economy in the second half of the nineteenth century prior to 1890 had a distinctly hollow ring. Observers might charge that the Australian economic and social systems were faulty and the people degraded and corrupt, but unquestionably the facts were ambiguous. Until the last decade of the century, the continent progressed rapidly, with only brief setbacks, and defenders were able to claim that the colonies could afford most mistakes they might make. In the 1890's, however, conditions changed dramatically; after an unprecedented boom in the 1880's the colonies experienced a disastrous collapse. In terms of the analogy introduced by Froude, the flowering of the aloe seemed, as predicted, to have been followed by its death. The aggregate gross domestic product of Australia in current pounds has been estimated at £133.8 million for 1880, £212.5 million for 1889, and £140.6 million for 1895.[1] This extraordinary fluctuation provided a legitimate subject for scrutiny and critique by almost anyone's standards. Interest among Britons in the economic difficulties was accentuated by mounting evidence that the colonies, rather than being chastened by their hardships, were continuing to pursue their radical social and economic policies.[2]

1. N. G. Butlin, *Australian Domestic Product, Investment and Foreign Borrowing 1861–1938/39* (Cambridge, 1962), pp. 6–7. These amounts in constant pounds are £133.5, £203.3, and £171.0 million. *Ibid.*, pp. 460–61.

2. Examples of descriptive accounts in British periodicals of Australian labor radicalism, land reform doctrine, and experiments with importation of non-white labor are A. J. Rose-Soley, "'New Australia': Communistic Work at the Antipodes," *Westminster Review*, CXL (1893), 523–37; A. J. Ogilvy, "The Malthusian Doctrine," *ibid.*, CXXXVI (1891), 289–97; H. W. Boyd Mackay, "Ruined Queensland: The Secret of Her Downfall," *ibid.*, CXLIV (1895), 152–59; Richard Tem-

Although most of the ideas expressed in the vigorous debates over the Australian economy in the 1890's had been anticipated in earlier years, the scope and intensity of the arguments in this decade had never been approached before. Criticism came from many types of commentator: economists, businessmen, opponents of organized labor who saw Australia as a symbol of market interference, disillusioned radicals, and a remarkable collection of miscellaneous writers, several of whom are examined in the next chapter, who turned attacks on the colonies almost into a career.

Economists and the *Economic Journal*

A significant entry into discussion of Australia during the 1890's was the main body of British economists, whose strength and self-confidence were currently on the increase with stimulus from their own association, the British Economic Association, a new publication, the *Economic Journal* (begun in 1891), and the leadership of Alfred Marshall, whose important *Principles of Economics* was published in 1890. Neither the Association nor the *Economic Journal* were the exclusive preserve of academic professionals; they both contained prominent members and contributors who were journalists, civil servants, politicians, labor leaders, and businessmen. But most of these persons were increasingly conscious of being practitioners of an advancing science.

Despite his own personal debt to Australia's economic success, Marshall sounded the signal note of concern about the colonies in the first edition of his *Principles*. Without giving any empirical evidence, he characterized Australian wage policy as holding out "specious promise of greater immediate comfort and ease to the workers," and he claimed that the eight-hour day had led to wage levels "much lower than they were before the hours were short-

---

ple, "Polynesian Labour Traffic," *National Review*, XIX (1892), 639–47, which includes discussion of additional contemporary literature on the topic. Advocates of federation in Australia took the trouble to comb the British press in 1890 for comments to show the unanimity of British opinion in favor of union. The collection of extracts, published as *United Australia* (Sydney, 1890), stood in sharp contrast to colonial hesitations over federation during the decade.

ened."[3] In the depths of the depression at the middle of the decade, Marshall was led to insert the following rash speculation in the third (1895) edition of the *Principles:* "it is not certain that the recent commercial troubles in Australia have not been in part caused by oversanguine estimates of the economic efficiency of short hours of labour."[4] By the end of the 1890's, he went even to the extent of arguing that the danger of Australia's economic heresy corrupting Britain itself constituted a case for establishing an economics tripos at Cambridge. He informed his university colleagues in 1902:

> . . . partly under English influence, some Australian colonies are making bold ventures, which hold out specious promise of greater immediate comfort and ease to the workers. But very little study of these schemes has been made of the same kind, or even by the same order of minds as are applied to judging a new design for a battleship with reference to the stability in bad weather: and yet the risks are much graver. Australasia has indeed a large reserve of borrowing power in her vast landed property: and should the proposed short cuts issue in some industrial decadence, the fall may be slight and temporary. But it is already being urged that England should move on similar lines: and a fall for her would be more serious.[5]

Marshall gave no indication of having undertaken a more serious analysis of data from the Australian economy than had most earlier critics. He argued from grounds of principle that such infringements of the free market economy as a maximum limit to hours of work must have negative results on economic efficiency, and he lent his great prestige to the mood of profound skepticism about the colonies.

The most interesting and yet disturbing feature of the Australian economy for most British economists, in addition to Alfred Marshall, was the colonial effort to regulate the aggregate wage

3. A. Marshall, *Principles of Economics*, ed. C. W. Guillebaud (London, 1961), I, 45 and 701. Marshall was able to attend Cambridge through a gift from an uncle who had prospered in Australia. A. C. Pigou, ed., *Memorials of Alfred Marshall* (London, 1925), pp. 11–12.

4. *Principles of Economics,* I, 701 n. Marshall qualified this suggestion in the fifth (1907) edition.

5. A. Marshall, "A Plea for the Creation of a Curriculum in Economics and Associated Branches of Political Science," reprinted in *Principles of Economics,* II, 167.

level. Potential problems with such an effort were thought to lie both in market disequilibria and in the unfavorable impact on incentives. The lead article in the first issue of the *Economic Journal* was an attempt by the historian of socialism, John Rae, to discern a "lesson for England" in the experience of "The Eight Hours Day in Victoria." Throughout the 1880's limitation of the number of hours worked had been one of the main and most publicized objectives of organized labor in Australia. Rae sought to assess the effects "of a reduction in the working day to eight hours on production, on wages, on the personal efficiency and character of the labouring class, or on the value of legislative intervention as a means of enforcement." [6] On the whole his conclusions were favorable to the legislation; he reported that morale and efficiency had been improved thereby and "nobody seems to be a shilling the worse." [7] An equally optimistic discussion was published a year later by the labor leader H. H. Champion.[8]

But Rae and Champion both wrote before full accounts of the major strikes and other labor disturbances of the 1890's had reached the *Economic Journal*. This information was provided later by the Sydney economist Arthur Duckworth, and it was profoundly disturbing.[9] Marshall's warning of the dangers in extending "specious promise" of impossible gains seemed to have been confirmed.

Australian tariffs as well as labor law came in for their fair share of the blame for the economic catastrophes of the 1890's. The Oxford economist L. L. Price reported that "students in the Old World . . . watched with something like dismay the unanimity [!] with which the peoples of the New have appeared to embrace a policy difficult to reconcile with an intelligent appreciation of the chief results of economic study." [10] C. F. Bastable, professor of Political Economy at Trinity College, Dublin, sug-

6. John Rae, "The Eight Hours Day in Victoria," *Economic Journal*, I (1891), 17.
7. *Ibid.*, p. 41, and *Economic Journal*, I (1891), 525–31.
8. H. H. Champion, "The Origin of the Eight Hours System at the Antipodes," *Economic Journal*, II (1892), 100–108.
9. Arthur Duckworth, "The Australian Strike, 1890," *Economic Journal*, II (1892), 425–41; *idem*, "The Broken Hill Strike," *ibid.*, III (1893), 148–54.
10. L. L. Price, Review, "*Industrial Freedom: A Study in Politics* by B. R. Wise," *Economic Journal*, II (1892), 676–81.

gested that the British government had shown "culpable neglect" in allowing the colonies to proceed along their wayward path in commercial policy.[11] Matthew Macfie, a regular commentator on colonial affairs, recounted for readers of the *Economic Journal* highlights in the conflict of principle between protectionist Victoria and free-trade New South Wales.[12] The statistician Robert Giffen, back from an inspection trip to scenes of protectionist crimes, concluded in 1898 that the colonial tariffs had failed even to achieve their declared objective of establishing domestic manufacturing industry.[13]

By the 1890's Australian public works policies had been under attack from British writers for nearly half a century, but even with the entrance of the economists, discussions of the subject still contained little dispassionate analysis, hard data, or consideration of alternative development policies for the new country. The criticism remained essentially that free enterprise produced most efficiently the goods which any economy required. Government could not help but produce items of second priority. Typically, in 1892 W. M. Acworth, the great authority on British railways, turned to Australia for an "object lesson" in government mismanagement. He gave little attention to such matters as the role of railways in Australian national development; he focused instead on the difficulties experienced by colonies in perfecting institutions to operate government lines.[14] On similar grounds Viscount Goschen, long a guardian of free enterprise and fiscal orthodoxy and a respected figure among economists, expressed grave doubt in 1895 that "a spirit of personal independence, of attachment to the principles of individual liberty, still holds good of our Australian kinsmen." He saw "the organization of in-

11. C. F. Bastable, Review, "*The Commercial Policy of the British Colonies and the McKinley Tariff* by Earl Grey," *Economic Journal,* II (1892), 682.

12. Matthew Macfie, "Australia Under Protection," *Economic Journal,* III (1893), 297–307. The controversy had been reviewed by another convinced free-trader, Sir Lyon Playfair, only a few years before. *Subjects of Social Welfare* (London, 1889), p. 171.

13. Robert Giffen, "Protection for Manufactures in New Countries," *Economic Journal,* VIII (1898), 3–16.

14. W. M. Acworth, "Government Railways in a Democratic State," *Economic Journal,* II (1892), 629–36; and "The State in Relation to Railways," in Thomas Mackay, ed., *A Policy of Free Exchange* (New York, 1894), 178–79.

dividuals into corporate bodies," presumably ranging in form from trade unions to government enterprises, as destroying the very fabric of the economy. This development, he said, "seems equally to have dethroned the principle of 'Laissez-faire,' and to be leading up to further encroachments on freedom of contract and the exercise of private rights." [15]

Of all the disturbing economic events which occurred in Australia during the 1890's, the financial crisis of 1893 was the most dramatic, and accordingly it received due attention from economists. Arthur Ellis, a journalist, provided the first chronicle of the crisis; he saw it simply as "the revenge of fate . . . wreaked on the Australian 'banking' system." [16] His confidence in the wisdom of British monetary institutions was complete; he could see that Australia's downfall was the result simply of her departure from the model afforded by the Old Country, and specifically her practice of making bank loans in some instances on real estate instead of on the time-honored commercial principle. Australia's "system had transgressed the traditions of banking as understood and practised in England, after a series of crises which can be traced back for a hundred years." [17]

Charles Gairdner presented a more detailed analysis of the "banking collapse" later in 1893—as he said, to identify "the general principles which it helps to illustrate." [18] Despite the well-known role of London bankers in Australian finance, Gairdner placed the burden of responsibility squarely upon the colonies rather than upon the mother country for "excessive borrowing" and for "an inherent defect in respect of the want of touch between the management and the remote Depositors." [19] Again, bank loans on real estate were severely condemned, and Gairdner indicated that he believed the correct objective of Australian banking should be security for the British depositor. As in the

15. Right Honourable Viscount Goschen, *Essays and Addresses on Economic Questions, 1865–1893* (London, 1905), p. 290.
16. Arthur Ellis, "The Australian Banking Crisis," *Economic Journal*, III (1893), 293.
17. *Ibid.*
18. Charles Gairdner, "The Lessons of the Australian Banking Collapse," *Economic Journal*, IV (1894), 114–19. The paper had been presented to the Economic Section of the British Association at its 1893 meeting.
19. *Ibid.*, p. 115.

case of so many other judgments of colonial economic actions, Gairdner did not accept Australia's long-term economic growth as a worthy or legitimate objective of colonial policy, particularly if this end might conflict with the private interests of British investors. Looking ahead Gairdner had only high moral principles to recommend as guides for future action. Australians "must remember, and educate the rising generation to understand, that Work and Thrift, applied to available materials, are the only sources of wealth." [20]

Despite this growth of interest among British professional economists during the colonies' hour of crisis in the 1890's, the outcome of the attention was disappointing. Criticisms continued to be based largely on hearsay and journalistic accounts rather than upon serious analysis. Stereotyped comments, now several decades old, were given greater authority by their distinguished new proponents. Above all, Australian economic policy continued to be judged by the professionals, as it had been by amateurs, first with regard to its probable effects on Great Britain's own economic interests, and second with reference to a set of economic and social models which had only limited relevance to the conditions and objectives of this new country. Judgments based on firm fact and with reference to Australia's own national goals were still for the future.

Businessmen and Financiers

The London financial community had remained ambivalent about Australian economic development from the earliest days of self-government at mid-century until the 1890's. On the one hand, financial writers applauded the rapid growth rate of the colonies, the large trade with Britain, and the unexploited field for investment. On the other hand, they expressed concern about unconventional public policies, the size of the debt, and the advanced stage of democracy. In the 1890's many financiers were able to simplify their position into unambiguous anger; they reported that their early fears had been better founded than their

20. *Ibid.*, p. 119.

optimism. Depressions, bank failures, and loss of British capital were, they said, what they had really anticipated all along. Rumors about the possibility of repudiation of colonial government securities caused especially strong shock waves to pass through the financial community.

The London *Economist* was, as usual, a leader of financial opinion on the economic problems of the colonies. As the skies darkened for Australia in the 1890's, the paper reported that the sad situation was all that should have been expected in light of the foolish economic policies which the paper had long decried, especially protection, unwillingness to consolidate politically into a federation, punitive taxes on the upper classes, inadequate controls over the public service, and excessive borrowing.[21] It is noteworthy that the *Economist*, like most other British observers, laid the blame for what it considered unjustified and speculative public investment in Australia upon the borrowers rather than the lenders. The so-called "Treasury view" was repeatedly applied to the colonies, that public expenditures detracted from and discouraged productive investment in the private sector. For example, in one typical report the *Economist* said: "The Government cannot, according to present accepted ideas, become a large employer of productive labour; and if by excessive construction and outlay of borrowed money it takes a large proportion of the community into its employ, and controls the supply of labour and the rates of wages in other directions, it is overstepping its functions, and doing mischief which, if carried too far, would tend to become permanent."[22]

When the worst of the financial crisis struck the colonies, the *Economist* took the position that a cessation of capital flows from

21. Representative discussions of Australian affairs at the beginning of the decade are "The Australasian Federation Conference," *Economist*, XLVIII (1890), 168–69; "Australasian Indebtedness and the Prospects of Federation," *ibid.*, pp. 235–36; "Victorian Affairs," *ibid.*, pp. 427–28; "Australasian Affairs," *ibid.*, pp. 519–20; "South Australian Views Upon Class Taxation," *ibid.*, pp. 552–53; "The Public Finances of Victoria," *ibid.*, pp. 692–93; "Australasian Affairs," *ibid.*, pp. 855–56; "Queensland Finance and Class Taxation," *ibid.*, pp. 1323–24; "Our Colonies in 1890," *ibid.*, pp. 1567–68; "The Distrust in Land Mortgage and Loan Companies," *ibid.*, XLIX (1891), 4–5; "Australasian Federation," *ibid.*, 460–62.

22. "The Influence of Government Employment in British Colonies," *Economist*, L (1892), 1183.

Britain, particularly for public works, was not only inevitable but salutary: "the present check to borrowing may be regarded as a good and invigorating tonic, however bitter its taste may be while it is being swallowed." [23] The collapse of the Melbourne land boom was described as a necessary purgative, and a variety of additional medical analogies were employed for their illustrative effect. Another statement was that the "great majority of the property institutions formed in Melbourne of late years are, in reality, cancerous growths upon the sound financial business of the colony." [24] Ironically, the colonies were roundly condemned for combining foreign borrowing with an excess of imports over exports; apparently, the critics did not recognize that these phenomena were simply two sides of the same coin. For example, in 1892 the colonies were told "with a decaying export trade and a rapidly expanding import trade, a day of reckoning could at the best be only postponed." [25] In 1892 the *Economist* was especially skeptical about a plan to make colonial bonds trustee securities in Britain.[26]

During 1893, the financial collapse in Australia was described through blow-by-blow accounts in almost every weekly issue of the *Economist.* Heavy moralizing followed each new report of failures, and the groping in the colonies for some means of dealing with the crisis such as an issue of government notes was portrayed as only one more indication of corruption and bad judgment. The following is a sample of the reports which came from the *Economist*'s "own correspondent" in Melbourne:

23. "Colonial Finance and the Market for Colonial Loans," *Economist,* XLIX (1891), 695; also "The Lesson of the Victorian Loan," *ibid.*, pp. 493–94; and "Australasian Debts as a Bar to Federation," *ibid.*, pp. 982–83.

24. "Melbourne Real Property Institutions and British Depositors," *Economist,* XLIX (1891), 1174; "The Liquidation of the Melbourne Land Boom," *ibid.*, pp. 1077–78; "Australasian Affairs," *ibid.*, L (1892), 9–11.

25. "The Financial Crisis in Melbourne," *ibid.*, p. 176; letters from correspondents throughout 1892 echo this critique; e.g., *ibid.*, pp. 380–82, 447–49, 631–32, 793–94, 1037–38, 1155–56, 1298–99, 1418–19, and 1579–81. See also "The Advantages and Disadvantages of a Public Works Policy," *ibid.*, p. 910; "The Financial Position of Victoria," *ibid.*, pp. 248–49; "A Change in the Market for Colonial Securities," *ibid.*, p. 537; "Dubious Colonial Statistics," *ibid.*, pp. 728–29, a critique of the economic statistics of the colonial statisticians Hayter and Coghlan; see below, Chap. 7.

26. "New South Wales Finance," L (1892), 1121–22.

> The development of the crisis has undoubtedly been impeded [sic] by the ostrich-like habit of the Melbourne people of thrusting their heads into a thicket of delusions rather than face the realities of the position. But in extenuation it has to be admitted that the Australian colonies have, to a considerable extent, been the spoiled children of fortune. Their crude ideas of statecraft have had the hasty eulogy of English writers like Dilke, who have regarded them as inspirations of genius; the British investor has lavishly poured into their laps enormous monetary resources, which they had not the skill and training to use aright. Australian banking, which if not incessantly watched by capable directors and managers, easily passes into Lawism, and thus becomes the most dangerous form of banking, and which, during the last eight years, has inflicted absolutely heavier losses on shareholders than have been experienced from banking failures in any other part of the world, has been misconceived and belauded in England.[27]

Australian flirtations with *crédit foncier* doctrine were condemned with the vehemence usually reserved for inconvertible government notes.[28]

The *Economist* was by no means the only forum for expression of criticism and concern about the Australian economy. A special meeting of the London Institute of Bankers in 1889, reported in the *Journal* of the Institute, brought forth a wide variety of opinions on the subject. A paper by H. F. Billinghurst, a council member of the Institute, opened the meeting and reviewed the disturbing growth of "colonial indebtedness." South Australia, the author said, "appears to have unduly anticipated the future," while in Queensland "Colonists have been trying to run before they can walk." [29] Because of the questionable economic policies pursued by the colonies, he concluded, colonial stocks should not be made eligible for purchase by trustees. In the discussion which followed, other bankers voiced their mounting fears, and representatives of the colonies attempted a defense.

27. "The Victorian Banking Crisis," *Economist*, LI (1893), 599.

28. E.g., *Economist*, LII (1894), 8–10, 110–11, 268–69, 389–90, 545–47, 669–70, 952–54, 1073–75, 1127–29, 1281–83, 1372–74, 1506–7; LIII (1895), 452–53, 618–19, 650, 748–49; 908–10, 1013–15, 1143–44, 1558–60, 1679–81. These selections include comment on the Victorian Banking Commission, said to be "composed of faddists and ignoramuses, qualified by the addition of a few men of experience." For the work of the Commission see my *Economic Enquiry in Australia*, pp. 161–62.

29. H. F. Billinghurst, "Colonial Indebtedness," *Journal of the Institute of Bankers*, X (1889), 135 and 136.

The generalist journals of the period were well supplied by financiers and their spokesmen with pleas for caution and retrenchment in the colonies. The hallmark of these commentaries is a single-minded concern with the immediate safety of securities. Such matters as long-run national goals, or the impact on dependent economies of sudden stops and starts in capital flows, were seldom given any attention.[30] William Broadfoot, a retired army officer turned journalist, was typical in admitting some negligence by Britain in allowing Australia to go her profligate way, like Job with the prodigal son, but he believed still that the cause of the transgression was the fundamental incompatibility of democratic institutions with sound business practices: "the colonies borrowed recklessly and spent their money lavishly, often rather with the view of present benefit to the democracy than on sound commercial principles." Rudyard Kipling offered a similar appraisal of colonial foolishness after a visit in 1891. "A hard land, it seemed to me, and made harder for themselves by the action of its inhabitants, who—it may have been the climate—always seemed a bit on edge." [31]

In a series of fifteen special letters from Australia to the London *Times,* Flora Shaw, later Lady Lugard, put effectively into words many of the assumptions which underlay critiques of Australia during the depression.[32] The colonies, she suggested, could be understood best if viewed as large development corporations rather than as fledgeling nation-states. Colonists were more anal-

30. E.g., Q, "The Borrowings of Australasia," *Investors' Review,* I (1892), 189–205.

31. William Broadfoot, "Australia and India: Their Financial Conditions and Mutual Relations," *Blackwood's Magazine,* CLIV (1893), 65; Rudyard Kipling, *Something of Myself* (New York, 1937), pp. 105–6.

32. The letters were published as follows: December 27, 1892, p. 10; January 7, 1893, p. 12; January 12, 1893, p. 12; January 31, 1893, p. 3; February 2, 1893, p. 6; February 9, 1893, p. 13; March 4, 1893, p. 5; March 30, 1893, p. 13; April 5, 1893, p. 13; April 8, 1893, p. 15; May 24, 1893, p. 3; July 14, 1893, p. 3; July 18, 1893, p. 3; July 26, 1893, p. 13, and August 2, 1893, p. 3. Miss Shaw's career is discussed in Mary Cumpston, "The Contribution to Ideas of Empire of Flora Shaw, Lady Lugard," *Australian Journal of Politics and History,* V (1959), 64–75. The first of Miss Shaw's letters moved the editor of *The Times* to an enthusiastic expression of interest. He described Australia as the only experiment in colonization undertaken without the complication of colored races. "A true parallel cannot be found in the history of the world, since the days of ADAM and NOAH, for the circumstances of the appropriation of Australia by the British Crown." December 27, 1892, p. 7.

ogous to employees than to citizens of distinct political entities, and the role of colonial governments was essentially that of managers and boards of directors. In explanation of her own function as an investigator from the Old Country, she wrote: "if the comparison of the colonies to big commercial enterprises is allowed to stand, investors in colonial stock take the position of debenture-holders who have a very large and legitimate interest in the matter." [33]

Miss Shaw's overall conclusion was that the colonists were not operating their development corporations as effectively as could fairly be expected. In almost every direction she could see potential fortunes which might be made but were going to waste. For example, after a few days on the Queensland coast she proclaimed that "vegetation runs riot over vast areas of fertile soil, and snakes and alligators [!] now disport themselves in solitude where a population as thick as the population of Egypt might subsist." Like so many other British travelers, Miss Shaw was specially impressed with possibilities afforded by the Queensland sugar industry. "It offers at the present moment a field for the employment of English labour, intelligence, and capital, such as is rarely presented by agricultural enterprise, and the opportunity appears to me to be one which ought not to be missed for want of knowledge of the existing conditions." [34] She was annoyed, however, by social and political policies—especially restrictions on immigration—which seemed needlessly to stand in the way of economic success: "commercial enterprise is being carried on under fluctuating political direction. The result can only be extravagance and mismanagement. . . ." [35] About Queensland in general she concluded, "the colony in its temporary phase of depression resembles a man with a nugget in his possession who should sit and starve for want of small change to buy a loaf." [36]

Miss Shaw condemned almost all aspects of public policy in the colonies. She deplored those public works which were not

33. "VII. New South Wales—Finance and Government," *The Times*, March 4, 1893, p. 5.
34. "Queensland: II," *The Times*, January 7, 1893, p. 12.
35. March 4, 1893, p. 5.
36. "The Mineral Wealth of Queensland," *The Times*, January 12, 1893, p. 12.

directly "remunerative," and she likened tariff protection to a prop which weakened that which it supported. She recounted the following parable from Melbourne. " 'In order to understand the present position of Victoria you have but to remember,' some one said to me the other day, 'the habitual attitude of the native-born Australian, who wherever he stands must lean against a post.' The more the financial situation is studied the more profoundly true the observation will appear." [37] Like so many of her predecessors, Miss Shaw viewed with alarm the growth of large cities and strong trade unions; she called for intensive land settlement; and she expressed impatience at delays in bringing about federation.

After her return from the colonies, Flora Shaw continued to write about them. She told the Royal Colonial Institute in 1893 that with effective use of "servile races" Australia's long-run prosperity could be assured. Ironically she was accused of painting too "rosy" a picture, and she replied in an address to the Scottish Geographical Society in 1894 that her optimism rested on the conviction that Australia had learned important lessons from the current crisis.[38]

The most vicious single attack on the colonies by a businessman came in the *National Review* from Harold Finch-Hatton, a former resident and propagandist for the colonies now living in London. Finch-Hatton denied categorically that the commercial institutions of the colonies such as the banks were to blame for the current troubles, except incidentally. The bank failures, he argued, were caused by the "sensation-mongering" of the British press and unreasoning panic among British investors, not by mismanagement. Rather, he continued, Australia's national sickness was of a more serious organic type. The economic classes had pitted themselves against each other in a suicidal conflict which would end only in catastrophe. The depression was crucial evidence that the lower classes of Australia, and especially those in New South Wales, had almost won their Pyrrhic victory. Through a variety of punitive measures, the democratically controlled legis-

37. "Victorian Finance," *The Times*, March 30, 1893, p. 13.
38. Flora Shaw, "The Australian Outlook," *Proceedings of the Royal Colonial Institute*, XXV (1893/94, 138–57); and "Australia," *Scottish Geographical Magazine*, X (1894), 169–84

latures had brought the pastoralists, upon whom the whole economy ultimately depended, to their knees:

There is an element in the financial situation of Australia of far wider scope and of more sinister import than even the present condition of the Banks, an element, indeed, which may be regarded as a deadly disease of which the banking crisis is to a great extent merely a symptom. I mean the legislation of the past nine years, which, in the case of New South Wales at least, has been continuously directed against the pastoral interest, and has been carried to a point where the pastoral tenants of the Crown known as squatters are brought face-to-face with irretrievable ruin.[39]

Finch-Hatton was opposed most of all to legislation which encouraged small-scale settlers or "free selectors"—"an impecunious tribe of jackals armed with manhood suffrage and letters-of-marque from the Government." Such legislation placed few yeoman farmers on the land and, incidentally, caused grievous harm to the large landholders. Australian land law as a reflection of its legislative authors, he said, was "in every way worthy of a body of men who have been well described as possessing the intellect of a turnip and the manners of a pig that roots it up." [40]

Events of the 1890's afforded businessmen and others in Britain an opportunity and an excuse to express vociferously ideas which they had nourished for years. The essence of the case was a political and social explanation of the economic collapse. Australia, they believed, illustrated clearly and for all to see that radical democracy untrammeled by responsible control was totally incompatible with economic success. "The Legislature has been left to be recruited from the lowest dregs of the community, and the squatters and what in the radical vernacular would be called

39. Harold Finch-Hatton, "The Collapse in Australia," *National Review*, XXI (1893), 439. Similar views to those of Finch-Hatton were expressed by W. F. Buchanan. He deplored "the insane class pressure as regards the introduction of emigrants, which has been strongly opposed by the working classes, who have been pandered to by leaders of our legislation, owing to their dependence on universal suffrage." *Australia to the Rescue: A Hundred Years' Progress in New South Wales* (London, 1890), p. 24. See also Baden Fletcher Smyth Baden-Powell, *In Savage Isles and Settled Lands* (London, 1892), pp. 58–59, 77–78, 91, and 128. Queensland opposition to the immigration of Kanaka labor was criticized by Gilbert Parker, "Australia for the White Man Again," *Nineteenth Century*, XLIX (1901), 829–33.

40. Finch-Hatton, *ibid.*, pp. 443–45.

'the classes' are reaping the whirlwind in the shape of extortion and spoliation."[41] The fact that Australian government, even through the troubled 1890's, remained controlled predominantly by the middle classes was not permitted to contradict a presupposition to the contrary.

Critics of Colonial Labor

The explanation offered most frequently for Australia's economic troubles during the 1890's was the character of her working class and the form of the legislation which regulated her labor market. At the beginning of the crisis Augustus Nash confidently diagnosed the unemployment as caused by exorbitant wage rates inherent to the economic system which left the unemployed "deprived of their dividend from the common wage fund." He said, "were the rate of wages regulated by supply and demand there would not be a sober and capable man out of work in any of the Australian colonies." The charges leveled at the laborers themselves included accusations that they were lazy, shiftless, and unwilling to provide a fair day's work for a fair day's pay. Edward H. Canney revived the old Social Darwinist speculations that Australian workers were congenitally unable to maintain a high level of production:

> You will see nothing like the number of tall, or well-made men—even in proportion to the population—in Australia, that you will in England.
>
> The explanation of this is, that, for the most part, it has not been the best of the race that have emigrated. . .
>
> Indeed, I have been told, on good authority, that, although the climate is doubtless advantageous in some ways, the race is degenerating. . . . Australia has been, and still is, to a certain extent, made the receptacle of our rubbish.[42]

41. Finch-Hatton, *ibid.*, pp. 444–45. More recent accounts of the growth of the Labor Party are Donald W. Rawson, *Labor in Vain?* (Melbourne, 1966); and R. A. Gollan, *Radical and Working Class Politics* (Melbourne, 1960).

42. Augustus Nash, "Democracy in New South Wales," *Fortnightly Review*, XLI (1887), 312–15; Edward H. Canney, *The Land of the Dawning* (London, 1894), pp. 55–56.

Jeannie Lockett, later a novelist, writing from Australia in 1889 told readers of the *Westminster Review* that workers had become so accustomed to ready employment on public works that they refused any longer to engage in the productive activities upon which the colonies in the long run depended. Instead of shifting out of the public sector into private enterprise, and especially agriculture, when public borrowing slackened, laborers fell back on union activity and various makeshift schemes designed to restrict the labor market even more. The effect on the economy of this behavior in recent years had been catastrophic:

> Instead of returning to the country in search of work, the unemployed collected together and marched through the streets. To look at them, they appeared merely a number of comfortably-dressed, able-bodied, and certainly not ill-fed men, marching gaily along, with banners waving and flags floating proudly on the breeze, and headed by a band playing inspiring, if somewhat martial, strains of music. . . . Yet, away from the metropolis, many thousands of broad acres were waiting to be tilled, and many of the natural resources of the colony remained underdeveloped, because of the scarcity and high price of labour. During this time the various labour organizations, in which Australia abounds, were busy adopting and putting into force rules for restricting the hours of daily labour, and for regulating the wages of labour, in order to prevent their falling below a certain minimum.

Another writer in the *Westminster* made the labor situation in Australia seem more comprehensible to general readers in Britain by reporting that despite severe unemployment domestic servants were still inexplicably difficult to find.[43]

Miss Lockett pictured the Australian maritime strike of 1890 as an inevitable confrontation between unrealistic aspirations of selfish and spoiled Australian workingmen and the harsh realities of a depressed labor market. Naturally, she pointed out, the market triumphed.[44] In a similar vein, A. Patchett Martin, an his-

43. Jeannie Lockett, "The Labour Question in Australia," *Westminster Review*, CXXXII (1889), 617–18. Miss Lockett had been more optimistic four years before in "Female Labour in Australia," *Nineteenth Century*, XVIII (1885), 651–56. C. J. Rowe, "Housekeeping Troubles in the Australian Colonies," *Westminster Review*, CXXXIV (1890), 509–14. Rowe was vigorously refuted by Mary Sanger Evans, the wife of an Australian clergyman, in "Domestic Servants in Australia: A Rejoinder," *ibid.*, CXXXVI (1891), 46–53.

44. Jeannie Lockett, "The Labour Battle in Australia," *Westminster Review*, CXXXV (1891), 134–46.

torian and a former colonist now living in Britain, saw in this strike destruction of "the priceless fabric of civilization which it has taken so many ages of man's ceaseless toil and noble endeavour to create." He gave as an additional cause of labor unrest the fact that "the Irish, or those of Irish origin, still form a very large proportion among that class of labour in Australia." [45]

Throughout the 1890's, British readers continued to be told that Australia was a hotbed of labor radicalism both in terms of organized militancy and legislative experimentation. The much publicized contribution by Australians to the London dock strikers in 1889 was long remembered,[46] and the pioneering role of the colonies with the eight-hour day was recalled with admiration by its advocates and anger by its critics.[47]

A noteworthy feature of the criticism of Australian labor during the 1890's was that it received support from several prominent British labor leaders. Not only were the achievements of Australian organized labor viewed with alarm by conservatives, but it became clear they caused deep concern also among some reformers and radicals. It is dangerous to generalize about things as diverse as the objectives and thought processes of British labor leaders in the 1890's. Nevertheless, it does appear that whereas English conservative thinkers saw Australia as confirmation of their fears about democracy and interference with the free market, radicals were filled with disappointment precisely because the colonies *did not* produce the condition of society which they had hoped and expected would follow manhood suffrage and drastic

45. A. Patchett Martin, "The Great Australian Strike," *National Review*, XVI (1890/91), 405 and 406.

46. C. W. Dilke in 1890 took pains to argue that this act was not designedly provocative but was merely a natural extension to Britain of close intercolonial relations among unions in Australia, who used their powers "upon the whole, with discretion and restraint." *Problems of Great Britain* (London, 1890), p. 519. Engels wrote to Kautsky that although the Australian gift "decided the victory" it was motivated by a desire only to "ward off a sudden mass importation of British workers." Henry Mayer, *Marx, Engels and Australia* (Melbourne, 1964), p. 138.

47. Charles Bradlaugh printed letters from the Australian political leaders Graham Berry, Arthur Blyth, and Saul Samuel in favor of regulated hours of work to support his own statement of the case. "Regulation by Statute of the Hours of Adult Labour," *Fortnightly Review*, XLVII (1890), 440–60. The extent to which the eight-hour day became the ultimate economic heresy for some writers can be seen in J. T. Blanchard, "The Eight Hours Question," *Westminster Review*, CXXXIX (1893), 526–53.

social reform. The revulsion of some British radical writers at the Australian economy of the 1890's seems almost as strong as that of the conservatives, but for diametrically opposite reasons.

The reservations of H. M. Hyndman in the 1870's about the concept of Australia as a workers' paradise have been noted above. In his autobiography, published in 1911, there is no indication that Hyndman experienced any change of view. Hyndman's impression was that Australia afforded a haven only for British people of the lower middle class with a small amount of capital and with the materialistic values of the *petit bourgeois*. The notion of equality among workers regardless of economic status had not by any means taken root.[48]

Henry Hyde Champion, leader of the 1889 London dock strike, brought back a particularly dark impression of the Australian economy from a visit to the colonies in 1890. He believed that the acquisitiveness and bad judgment of labor leaders had contributed to social and economic collapse and the loss of gains made in earlier years. He pictured the defeat of the maritime workers as inevitable because on the one hand labor could not win a "demand which the public holds to be arbitrary or unfair," and on the other hand the public had "no sympathy with methods forbidden by law." [49] Champion reflected disappointment akin to that of a naive political leader who discovers that his own party does not after all have a monopoly on wisdom when placed in power.

From the diary of a journey to Australia in 1898 by Beatrice and Sidney Webb, we gain valuable insights into the views toward Australia of these two founding Fabians and of visiting middle-class social reformers in general. The Webbs' impressions of Australia were distinctly unfavorable, and the explanation for their views is complex. To begin with, they were themselves insular in outlook, poor travelers, snobbish, and arrogant. What is

48. Henry Mayers Hyndman, *The Record of an Adventurous Life* (London, 1911), p. 122.

49. H. H. Champion, "The Crushing Defeat of Trade Unionism in Australia," *Nineteenth Century*, XXIX (1891), 236–37. Champion settled permanently in Australia later in the decade. The substantial impact within Australia of Champion's critical views is described in Jeannie Lockett, "The Labour Battle in Australia," *Westminster Review*, CXXXV (1891), 142.

more significant, however, is that like Hyndman and Champion they were naively disillusioned with what they saw. It appears that like so many other advocates of radical social change they had dealt too long with abstractions and with the particular conditions they sought to alter. They had not formulated realistically the nature of the new society they wished to create, nor had they studied actual social situations such as the Australian colonies which resembled in many ways what they prescribed. When the Webbs came face to face with what passed for the democratic ideal they had themselves advocated, they recoiled in horror. It was not only that they found the country and the people profoundly distasteful on personal and emotional grounds, they reacted also at a higher level of principle to the notion that here were the effects of their own most cherished reforms, especially wide participation in political affairs. The rough and coarse society which faced them seemed to cast doubt on the very legitimacy of their own efforts. Specific reactions of the Webbs to what they saw, particularly those of Beatrice, seem calculated above all to persuade themselves that somehow this could not be a valid social test case of democracy, as when she told her sister that "Australia is the most *un*democratic . . . nation in the world."[50] Certainly there is more than the customary xenophobia of the tourist in the following remarks, from Beatrice Webb:

> It [Sydney] is seemingly inhabited by a lower-middle class population suddenly enriched; aggressive in manners and blatant in dress. The loafer, very much out at elbows and carelessly insolent in bearing, is to be seen wandering through the streets or lounging in the public Domain. In this city there is neither homeliness nor splendour; only bad taste and cold indifference. . . .
>
> The rich people take no part and actually pride themselves on their contempt for public affairs; money-making and racing seem their only concern; such political ideas as they have resolve themselves into a hatred of "Trade Unions" and a strong desire to escape direct taxation. The working men seem also largely non-political and the most their political leaders can do is to propose the legislation of England or New Zealand; they have no ideas of their own. . . . The most depressing

50. A. G. Austin, ed., *The Webbs' Australian Diary 1898* (Melbourne, 1965), p. 17.

feature of New South Wales is the absence of education among the rich, and the bad manners of all classes. . . .

As for society in Australia, it is just a slice of Great Britain and differs only slightly from Glasgow, Manchester, Liverpool and the *suburbs* of London. Bad manners, ugly clothes, vigour and shrewdness characterise the settlements of Sydney, Melbourne and of bush stations, exactly as they characterise the lower and upper middle class folk of the old country. If anything the manners are worse, the dress more pretentious and glaring and lacking in taste, than with us!

And from Sidney Webb:

In short, in Queensland one finds at every turn, a most peculiar reminiscence of the bad manners, sullen insolence, and graspingness of the "man in possession." [51]

Ironically in the light of these views, Sidney Webb remarked in an interview after his return from abroad, "Australia sadly needs studying, as Mr. Bryce studied the American Commonwealth, and such a work would be of enormous value." [52] It was partly in response to this sentiment that several British commentators undertook the studies discussed in the next chapter.

51. *Ibid.*, pp. 22, 32, 108, and 40.
52. *Ibid.*, p. 113.

· 7 ·

The Heat of Battle: Attack and Counterattack

In retrospect the 1890's appear as the crucial watershed in British views of the Australian economy. Debate became so intense, and on the critical side so unreasonable, that the stage was set for significant change in the twentieth century. For this reason several writers and their work during this decade receive detailed attention in this chapter.

The Major Critics: Murray, Adams, Fairfield, the *Westminster Review*, Pearson, Fortescue, and Max O'Rell

A variety of British writers used the economic crises of the 1890's as an excuse and an opportunity for intensive and wide-ranging critical exposés of Australia. Their spirit of muckraking was strengthened by disclosures of political corruption as well as by evidence of some wild speculation in the colonies.[1] But the main thrust of the criticism continued to be directed less against single men and institutions than against the total social and economic system as the critics saw it. Models of proper behavior were set up as standards by which the colonies could be judged, and to a degree never seen before, the colonies were found wanting. Several critics became virtually professional skeptics of Australian affairs, and they receive attention in this chapter as a special phenomenon. One characteristic these writers had in common was that they all visited the colonies and were not pleased

1. Accounts of the colonial scandals are contained in Michael Cannon, *The Land Boomers* (Melbourne, 1966); and Margaret Kiddle, *Men of Yesterday* (Melbourne, 1962).

with what they saw. Economic collapse confirmed their darkest suspicions and gloomiest fears.

David Christie Murray, a novelist and foreign correspondent for English newspapers, toured Australia and New Zealand in 1889–91. He then contributed an extensive three-part indictment of "The Antipodeans" to the *Contemporary Review* which attracted the widespread attention of both friends and foes of Australia. Murray used the old parent-child analogy and pictured the colonies as simply not competent to manage their own affairs; they were, he said, like irresponsible adolescents intoxicated with their newfound powers and unwilling to accept advice from their elders and betters. "There is a stage of national hobbledehoyhood, and Australia has not yet grown out of it. Vanity, shyness, an intermingling of tenderness and contempt for outside opinion, a loud but uncertain proclamation of equality with the best, a determination to exact consideration before yielding it—all these are characteristics." Murray recited the familiar charges against Australia: that she discouraged immigration and settlement thereby excluding Britons from their imperial patrimony, that she built up luxurious cities through misguided economic policies and loans obtained from abroad, and that she carried democracy to excess. "There is one vote for one man, and about that fact almost the whole land is jubilant, though the practical good of it may as yet be a problem."[2] Even the criminals were more terrifying in Australia, he observed, because they ate a steady diet of meat. Murray expressed a marked personal preference, which some other British observers had also begun to voice, for the characteristics of New Zealand over those of Australia. "Australia enlisted, and still enlists, some classes of people for whom New Zealand has no charm, the pushing, eager men, who are in a hurry to be rich. New Zealand was largely peopled by English gentlemen and ladies. . . ."[3]

A more subtle and balanced appraisal of Australian development than that of Murray came from the poet and essayist Francis

2. David Christie Murray, "The Antipodeans," *Contemporary Review*, LX (1891), 299 and 303. The complete article is pp. 293–312, 450–68, 608–23.
3. *Ibid.*, pp. 308 and 611.

Adams in a series of articles in the *Fortnightly Review* (1891), republished with additions as a book entitled *The Australians* (1893).[4] Adams condemned in no uncertain terms the state of the discourse with the colonies: "A few Englishmen talking nonsense about England to Australians, a few Anglo-Australians talking nonsense about Australia to Englishmen, have now become something very like an organised self-advertising chorus of social cliques. . . ."[5] He argued convincingly that Britain failed to appreciate either the true character of Australian society or the aspirations of the people; this ignorance and insensitivity were manifest above all when the British government failed to annex territory of interest to the colonies in the New Guinea crisis of 1883 and when British writers tried repeatedly to persuade the colonies to accept free trade.[6] Like Murray, Adams found the analogy of parent and child useful in explaining imperial relations, and he saw Australia's adoption of protection as a form of adolescent rebellion against a thoughtless parent.[7]

Despite his good intentions to portray Australia in a new light, Adams drew a picture of Australian society which was almost as disquieting as those of the harshest critics. He was avowedly radical in sympathy and had supported social reform over much of his life, but he was uneasy about what he saw in Australia, his adopted home, where more than anywhere reform was in the wind. Two features of Australian development worried Adams, like the Webbs, above all: first, the growing power of monopolies and wealthy capitalists and, second, the pervasiveness of what he considered to be cultural philistinism. He attempted to explain these phenomena in terms of broad patterns of social change. He was clearly influenced by the theory of evolution and by the concept of natural selection in human society, a process which he

4. Adams, tubercular from childhood, visited Australia in the 1880's and became, in the judgment of one critic, "not the best but . . . the most significant poet we in Australia have had." Clive Turnbull, *Australian Lives* (Melbourne, 1965), pp. 97–125.

5. Francis Adams, *The Australians* (London, 1893), p. 2.

6. *Ibid.*, pp. 247–66. Adams described Lord Carrington, a former governor of New South Wales, as one of the few sensitive and effective interpreters of Australia to Great Britain. Adams dealt more fully with this subject in an article, "Two Australian Writers," *Fortnightly Review*, LII (1892), 352–65.

7. F. Adams, *The Australians*, pp. 247–53.

thought he observed in active operation in Australia. He carried the implications of the theory to considerable lengths and suggested that already among the colonies pronounced regional types had been determined by local conditions. The region which interested him most was "the interior," with its characteristic rough and ready inhabitant, the "bushman." He considered this person reminiscent of the American frontiersman—a human type which had included such distinguished specimens as Abraham Lincoln and U. S. Grant. Adams admired and respected the bushman, but he also expressed alarm at his behavior. He deplored the importation of so many American customs and the rejection of finer features of British culture—"native Australians . . . have too often the self-sufficiency that is begotten on self-confidence by ignorance. . . . They have the taint of cruelty."[8] Thinking perhaps of the bitter controversy which surrounded the depression, Adams prophesied that evolution was moving so rapidly in Australia that in a very short time the colonist would lose all sense of identity with his British forefathers and would be ruled by a dominant hatred rather than filial affection. "Matthew Arnold and a good many other clever people to the contrary notwithstanding, in two generations he is so far removed from the original Englishman that it is the clearest case of racial antipathy. It is tiger and lion—nay, it is cat and dog. Their instantaneous attraction is solely to one another's throats."[9] Such social prophecies as this boded ill both for tranquil social development and for schemes to increase imperial unity.

The extent to which by 1890 Australia and New Zealand had become identified as the fortress of socialism in the English-speaking world can be appreciated from the considerable attention the colonies received in a collection of essays in defense of economic freedom entitled *A Plea for Liberty*, edited by Thomas McKay (1891; second edition, 1892; with an introduction by Herbert Spencer). In this book, the colonies were honored with their own chapter, wherein Charles Fairfield described vividly the

8. F. Adams, "Social Life in Australia," *Fortnightly Review*, L (1891), 395.
9. F. Adams, "The Labour Movement in Australia," *Fortnightly Review*, L (1891), 187.

horrors of "State Socialism at the Antipodes." Fairfield wrote before the worst financial failures had occurred, and so he paid more attention to institutional matters than to events. Later, when the worst of the collapse came in 1893, his writing seemed to have that much more prescience and insight.[10]

In the same terms as Francis Adams, Fairfield complained of the biased and inaccurate descriptions of the Australian economy available in Britain. He claimed that the most unreliable and yet influential reporters were colonial government statisticians such as Coghlan and Hayter and a few imperial sentimentalists such as J. A. Froude, Baron Hübner, and Sir Charles Dilke, the latter with his new book *Problems of Greater Britain.* All these men supplied misinformation and misinterpretations which were in their own various self-interests. Fairfield's main thesis was that state enterprise and interference with the Australian economy rested on an informal conspiracy among several segments of the colonial community. Exploitation of the British investor was the objective. Manufacturers received as their payoff high tariffs; workers received trade union recognition, the eight-hour day, and free education; large landowners received protection from small-scale farmers; and social reformers received early closing legislation and local option.[11] The whole structure of the free market was distorted and rendered nearly ineffective by these strong pressures on all sides, and the edifice was prevented from crumbling only by the willingness of gullible British investors to continue pouring in capital. "While economists in Europe dispute the existence of a 'wage fund,' one becomes aware in Victoria of three such 'funds,' a ficticious 'wage fund,' an equally ficticious 'capital

10. *A Plea for Liberty* was reviewed enthusiastically in the *Economist,* XLIX (1891), 464. The wide impact of Fairfield's essay is described in J. W. Fortescue, "State Socialism and the Collapse in Australia," in Thomas MacKay, ed., *A Policy of Free Exchange* (New York, 1894), 114–15.

11. Fairfield regarded public education as "the most enticing" aspect of state socialism, yet also one of the most expensive and potentially destructive. He described Charles H. Pearson, Victorian Minister of Education, as the "Prosper Merimee" of the movement for public education, and the Melbourne economist W. E. Hearn as the most effective critic. Charles Fairfield, "State Socialism in the Antipodes," in Thomas MacKay, ed., *A Plea for Liberty* (London, 1892), pp. 152 and 162.

fund,' and finally a 'consumers' fund,' all miraculously supplied by the State and the foreign investor." [12]

Fairfield admitted that evolution of a new racial type might be a factor in Australian economic development, but he believed that the conspiratorial destruction of liberal institutions was a far more critical matter:

Special forces there are, slowly fashioning out of populations of British origin a new and distinct type of citizen, with special ideas. But deep speculations on the future evolution of races and nationalities are not requisite in order to understand the effect either of specific laws or of State Socialism grafted on to a community, transplanted it is true, yet bearing with it institutions copied closely from our own and based upon ideas and traditions with respect to civil and religious liberty, property, order, law, commerce, and economic conditions generally which have been the common property of all liberal thinkers and legislators in this country for the last fifty or sixty years.[13]

Fairfield objected to partial analysis of individual aspects of the Australian economy—tariffs, banks, land legislation, or public works. The continent provided, he said, the first full-blown example in the English-speaking world of "state socialism." Any inquiry as to a part of the problem missed the very essence of it. He asked for answers to fundamental questions; for example, anticipating the work of Charles H. Pearson two years later, "how State Socialism is affecting the national character, whether it is producing a nobler or baser type of man and woman in Australia." [14] Of equal significance, he said, was a second question of whether state socialism was an effective economic system in which to achieve rapid development. In his view the answer to this question was an unequivocal no:

While the "goal" or "ideal" of the economist and Free Trader, who finds before him boundless natural resources, may be roughly described as an "infinite" increase in the number of workers—never quite overtaking "infinite" increases in the demand for labour, production of exchangeable utilities and rise in wages—the goal or ideal of State

12. *Ibid.*, p. 145 n.
13. *Ibid.*, p. 125.
14. *Ibid.*, p. 134.

Socialists and Protectionists, so far as it can be ascertained from the speeches, writings, and actions of such persons in Australia, is one single worker earning all the wages paid in his own, rigidly protected and stationary, trade and producing an infinitesimal amount of exchangeable utilities.[15]

Fairfield did not hesitate to use straightforward language when summing up his view of the Australian economy as a whole: "State Socialism to-day in the Antipodes seems to me to preach to willing disciples the despicable gospel of shirking, laziness, mendicancy, and moral cowardice." [16]

Three articles in the *Westminster Review* in the early 1890's taken together constitute a fourth significant indictment of the Australian economy. Even though the articles may have been by three different hands, they had a distinct unity of viewpoint. In the first article, the familiar parable of the prodigal son was applied once again to the colonies. A typical passage said: "In Australia the air is full of the rumours of a United Australia, behind which looms the shadow of a desire to stand alone. The Australians are angry because the English investor has buttoned up his pocket, like the son who dashes off from his home because the father checks his extravagance. They cannot see that the lesson will be a salutary one." [17] In the second article, Matthew Macfie wrote of his "nearly seven years" in the colonies and sounded a slightly more optimistic note by picturing Western Australia as a final opportunity for Australians to take account of past errors and build a sound social system in their still relatively empty land.[18] The third article, signed "M," focused specifically on the causes of a recent decline in emigration to Australia. The conclusion this author reached was that the reasons lay with social and political failings of the colonies and the consequent decline in their at-

15. *Ibid.*, p. 142.
16. *Ibid.*, p. 172.
17. "The Colonial Government of Great Britain," *Westminster Review*, CXXXVII (1892), 9.
18. Matthew Macfie, " 'The Great West' of Australia," *Westminster Review*, CXXXVII (1892), 481–97. Macfie had taken a similar stand before the Royal Colonial Institute three years before in an address entitled "Aids to Australasian Development," *Proceedings of the Royal Colonial Institute*, XXI (1889/90), 53–72. Another signed article by Macfie was "Cultured Colonisation," *Westminster Review*, CXLII (1894), 673–80.

tractiveness to immigrants. Colonists had not made effective use of the bountiful resources available to them, and through such practices as protective tariffs and extravagant public works had caused a social deterioration which was known world wide:

> The practical effect of Protection is to foster, artificially, factory industries in the chief centres. To these the agricultural population, impatient of the monotony of rural life, are only too readily attracted in the hope of finding work at some trade, as well as an unlimited choice of amusements. The extension of public works with borrowed money—while Government loans flowed in freely from the London market—added to the chances of a floating population getting remunerative employment in the capitals. One section of disappointed persons who drift into the towns take to gambling on the turf—without exception the most prominent institution in the country—or sink down to the level of habitual drinking. Another section swells the crowd of unsuccessful office-seekers under the *regime* of State Socialism which exists.[19]

"M" concluded that the only hope for regeneration of Australia lay in massive settlement of the land by new immigrants yet unspoiled by the degenerate colonial society. He recommended as a stimulus to this development a land-grant railway on the North American model.

The comments upon Australia in the 1890's of the distinguished former colonist Charles H. Pearson were in some respects the most devastating indictment of all. Pearson had long been recognized as an admirer, defender, and leader of the new Australian states, and consequently criticism from him had the intimacy and special sting of words from a disillusioned lover.[20] Moreover, Pearson's critique was low-key and in sharp contrast to the violent denunciations of many of his contemporaries. His discussion of Australia was only part of a major treatise in which colonial conditions were highlighted against a worldwide panorama.

Pearson published his book entitled *National Life and Character: A Forecast* in London in 1893 as the last great work in an extraordinary life. He had come to Australia in 1864 as a young

19. "What Hinders Emigration to Australasia," *Westminster Review*, CXXXIX (1893), 405–6.

20. Pearson's defense of the colonies in 1867 has been mentioned above in Chapter 5.

man fresh from King's College, London, Oxford, Cambridge, and the invigorating society of such Victorian luminaries as F. D. Maurice, Henry Sidgwick, Henry Fawcett, Leslie Stephen, Henry Kingsley, George Goschen, M. E. Grant Duff, and Edward Dicey.[21] As a teacher, journalist, and legislator he entered vigorously into colonial controversies over such matters as higher education for women, tariff protection, and land taxation.[22] He made his reputation above all on the question of compulsory, state-supported, elementary education; in this field he implemented pioneering innovations as Victorian Minister of Education. Finally, he was a significant influence in the early lives of such Australian leaders as Alfred Deakin, Henry Bournes Higgins, and William Shiels.

The theme of *National Life and Character* was relatively simple. It had deep roots in the social and economic prognoses of the classical economists, especially John Stuart Mill, and in the sweeping pageants of nineteenth-century historians. Pearson pictured contemporary world affairs as dominated by a struggle between the white and colored races, the two brought into immediate conflict by the growth of population and the imminent settlement of the remaining vacant land areas, for "the races of the world are approaching a stationary condition as regards territorial limits between Aryan and others, what we call the higher being confined for practical purposes to a part of the Temperate Zone."[23] Under the stresses and strains of the struggle with "inferior" races, and faced with both land shortage and an end to emigration, white societies everywhere were destined to undergo profound change. In particular, Pearson predicted that they would adopt more and more extreme forms of democracy, would experience a decline in "original power, as genius is deprived of its noblest fields," and would suffer loss of the virtues normally associated with religion and family: "democracy is likely to find

21. An excellent biography of Pearson is John Tregenza, *Professor of Democracy* (Melbourne, 1968).

22. Pearson's views on property taxation in Australia attracted the attention of Emile de Laveleye and T. E. Cliffe Leslie. See Tregenza, p. 117, and my *Economic Enquiry in Australia*, pp. 107–9.

23. C. H. Pearson, *National Life and Character* (London, 1893), p. 261.

its consummation in State Socialism; and . . . certain notable influences, such as attachment to a Church, municipal feeling, and even family feeling, are likely to become less and less important as factors in the constitution of society."[24] Pearson did not deny that the society of the future might have certain material advantages, such as adequate subsistence for all. But at the same time, he had no doubt that it would bring a much lower quality of civilization: "the conditions of life will be more tolerable, though the sky above may be more gray."[25]

Pearson presented his prophecy in worldwide terms, and he used a range of historical examples stretching from classical Greece to the present day. Yet his references to Australia were the most prominent of all, especially as they illustrated conditions of social decline which he predicted for the world in general in the dark future. At the very beginning of the book Pearson said that the Antipodes would receive a large portion of his attention for two reasons: first, because this region of the world had been and would remain the frontier of conflict with the "inferior" races. The Australian continent was the last major unsettled land mass, and the white race was destined to test therein both its viability in a hot climate and its capacity to resist invading hordes:

> Twenty years' residence under the Southern Cross has forced me to consider a new side of this particular question: whether the capacity of European races to form new homes for themselves is not narrowly limited by climate, and by the circumstances of prior population. . . . The fear of Chinese immigration which the Australian democracy cherishes, and which Englishmen at home find it hard to understand, is, in fact, the instinct of self-preservation, quickened by experience. . . . We are guarding the last part of the world, in which the higher races can live and increase freely, for the higher civilisation.[26]

The second reason why Australia deserved special attention, Pearson said, was because its advanced democracy was a stage of society to which the white race as a whole was fast approaching as a result of internal and external population pressure. This argument for examining Australian social development was similar to

24. *Ibid.*, p. 261; see also pp. 26–27 and 84–85.
25. *Ibid.*, p. 28.
26. *Ibid.*, pp. 15–16.

that which other authors had proposed as early as the 1850's. But Pearson's case had much greater urgency than did that of his predecessors. The society which had grown up in Australia was of intense interest, he said, not simply as a shadow of Britain's distant future, but rather as a representation of conditions which faced the nation on the near horizon. On several grounds "State Socialism" in the colonies should give the mother country immediate and serious cause for reflection:

> Now the history of the English colonies in Australia and New Zealand is particularly instructive, because it shows what the English race naturally attempts when it is freed from the limitations of English tradition. The settlers of Victoria, and to a great extent of the other colonies, have been men who carried with them the English theory of government: to circumscribe the action of the State as much as possible; to free commerce and production from all legal restrictions; and to leave every man to shift for himself, with the faintest possible regard for those who fell by the way. Often against their own will the colonists have ended by a system of State centralisation that rivals whatever is attempted in the most bureaucratic countries of the Continent. . . . Planted in Australia, the Englishman, to whom St. Simon and Fourier are names of derision, if they are even names, is rapidly creating a State Socialism, which succeeds because it is all-embracing and able to compel obedience, and which surpasses its continental State models because it has been developed by the community for their own needs, and not by State departments for administrative purposes. Of course, it does not follow that even a race so highly gifted with political intelligence as the British is necessarily right in what it builds up. It may be that the brain and hand are more feeble than they were in the old time. Nevertheless, it is surely safe to say, that political experiments which half a dozen self-governing British communities are instinctively adopting, deserve attention as an indication of what we may expect in the future.[27]

Aspects of Australian economic policy which interested Pearson most in the context of his world forecast were those with which he himself had been involved closely as a public figure in the colonies: in particular, state control and regulation of land,[28] the growth of government employment and the national debt,[29] treat-

27. *Ibid.*, pp. 17–18.
28. *Ibid.*, pp. 19, 329.
29. *Ibid.*, pp. 21, 22, 97, 104, and 172.

ment of the Aborigines,[30] increase of waste and of materialism associated with the growth of cities,[31] immigration restriction both of the "inferior" races and of Englishmen too,[32] public education, and even extension of life expectancy.[33] Pearson was able to detect in the experience of Australia only a few hopeful exceptions to his grim prophecy for the white races, in particular the colonies' failure to build up standing armies.

It was simple for a reader of *National Life and Character* to put together a picture of Australia which, although moderate and temperate by the standards of the 1890's, was anything but flattering. The fact that Pearson described conditions and social institutions which he himself had helped to shape naturally improved his credibility. Pearson did not recommend any noteworthy reforms to retard the coming of the circumstances of his forecast. Rather, his attitude was of wistful submission to the inevitable. Like so many other immigrant British intellectuals, he had always espoused intercolonial federation as a solution to many of Australia's problems.[34] On the wider horizon of *National Life and Character*, however, he saw little to be gained from such international political consolidation as imperial federation.[35]

Pearson's book received wide acclaim from admirers as diverse as William Gladstone and Theodore Roosevelt. For many readers, he provided one of the few plausible explanations for such worrisome developments as growth of cities, the rise of the colored races, and an apparent trend toward "socialism." In addition, Pearson caught the mood of gloom and foreboding which pervaded the depressed 1890's.[36]

Reviewers who examined the economic aspects of Pearson's work generally were enthusiastic about it, and they raised questions mainly about the darkness of his pessimism.[37] L. L. Price in

30. *Ibid.*, p. 32.
31. *Ibid.*, pp. 142–46.
32. *Ibid.*, pp. 50, 105, 125–26, 221. This subject fascinated Pearson throughout his residence in Australia. See Tregenza, pp. 189–91.
33. Pearson, *National Life and Character*, pp. 213–15 and 322–24.
34. Tregenza, pp. 187, 194, and 220.
35. Pearson, *National Life and Character*, pp. 222–23.
36. See Tregenza, pp. 231–36.
37. E.g., Frederick Greenwood, "The Limbo of Progress," *Macmillan's Magazine*, LXVII (1893), 391–400; *Westminster Review*, CXXXIX (1893), 324–25.

the *Economic Journal* was one who did not fail to note carefully Pearson's message that many of the worst problems of the future were visible already in the colonies; in particular, the "tendency to invoke the interference of the state," "the steady influx into large cities," and "the ominous growth of public indebtedness." [38] In a similar vein the Indian civil servant Sir Alfred Lyall wrote:

> Buckle demonstrated from his library that the civilisation of Europe is due to the triumph of mental over physical laws. Mr. Pearson, who has sojourned long in another hemisphere, shows not only that beyond the temperate zone this advantage of mind over matter may be reversed, but also that when the expansion of the higher races is arrested by climatic conditions their progress will be checked and their whole civilisation may be placed in serious jeopardy.[39]

The Oxford philosopher and theologian Hastings Rashdall in the *Economic Review* was somewhat more skeptical about Pearson's prophecy; he suggested that the advance of civilization in North America tended to contradict some of Pearson's bleak prognoses. He said, "we cannot but suspect that Dr. Pearson has generalized too hastily from his Australian experiences." [40] The historian and civil servant S. N. Spencer Walpole in a long review article for the *Edinburgh Review* voiced a similar criticism; he believed that Pearson's portrayal of the yellow peril was valid, but he denied that socialism on the Australian model was likely to spread throughout the Anglo-Saxon world. "Mr. Pearson's Australian experiences have probably misled him in the second portion of his book; . . . there is no reason for thinking that socialism in older and thickly inhabited countries will necessarily take the form which it has assumed in Australasia. . . ." [41] It is significant that Rashdall, Walpole, and most other critical reviewers did not question Pearson's dreary portrayal of Australian society and its future but rather the notion that such dreadful conditions could ever come to pass in Great Britain.

In reply to critics who complained that he did not prophesy a

38. *Economic Journal*, III (1893), 483–87.
39. A. C. Lyall, "National Life and Character," *Nineteenth Century*, XXXIII (1893), 893.
40. H. Rashdall, *Economic Review*, III (1893), 448.
41. S. Walpole, "The Forecast of Mr. Pearson," *Edinburgh Review*, CLXXVIII (1893), 303.

sufficiently "prominent place" for Australia in the world's future, Pearson repeated the grounds for his concern. Soon, he said, the colonies might face a grim "alternative of leaving Northern Australia or of developing it by the coloured races." [42] In either case, whether from external attack or from internal absorption, they were in serious peril.

The most forceful and eclectic of all the critics of Australia during the 1890's was John William Fortescue, distinguished military historian and private secretary to Governor Sir William Jervois in New Zealand from 1886 to 1890.[43] Between 1891 and 1895, Fortescue wrote no less than five substantial articles, four of them for the *Nineteenth Century*, in which he repeated and extended virtually all of the criticisms of the colonies expressed to date. He also subjected to biting ridicule the most prominent colonial defenders. Undoubtedly, his writings received wide attention. Concerning his first article alone one of his most vigorous opponents conceded:

> Few magazine articles have attracted more attention than that written by the Hon. J. W. Fortescue in the April number of this Review, and entitled "The Seamy Side of Australia." Scarcely a journal but has made the article a subject of comment, and in commercial and social circles also it has been freely discussed. For one thing, this is the first systematic attack upon Australian credit to which the writer has had the courage to append his name; it brings together what other critics have said, and it translates their innuendo into plain and honest statement. It is evident also that the writer is fervent in his own belief; and when a man has thoroughly convinced himself he can usually arrest the attention of others.[44]

Fortescue's initial attack was prompted by a comparison of Governor Carrington's laudatory address to the Royal Colonial Institute entitled "Australia as I Saw It," with Charles Fairfield's exposé "State Socialism at the Antipodes." The former he called "one voice more in the chorus of admiration which lulls England

42. Charles H. Pearson, "An Answer to Some Critics," *Fortnightly Review*, LIV (1893), 159.

43. See *Dictionary of National Biography, 1931–1940* (London, 1949), pp. 286–87.

44. Howard Willoughby, "'The Seamy Side of Australia': A Reply from the Colonies," *Nineteenth Century*, XXX (1891), 292.

and colonies to rest in a fool's paradise." The latter he believed was the first genuine attempt to tell the truth about the colonies, and consequently it was "by far the most valuable contribution to colonial literature that has yet appeared." Fortescue himself set out to "call attention to the seamy side of the Australian colonies, of which Mr. Fairfield has kindly turned up one corner for us. There is, as we know, such a thing as cotton-backed satin, but the colonists take care to show us only the face of their goods." In Fortescue's eyes, the roughest seams behind the glossy Australian exterior were "colonial borrowing, protective tariffs, hindrances to emigration and to the growth of population, the labour question."[45] He wished to expose these matters to close public scrutiny.

Fortescue was no blind critic of the colonies; he knew well the defensive arguments which were employed, and he moved in advance to refute them. Above all, Fortescue understood that he had the current depression on his side. He admitted openly the plausibility in principle of the case for such developmental practices as state railways and other public works. But he called for judgment by results. He claimed that the actual effects of such policies had been political corruption and financial collapse. Widespread degeneration had followed "the concentration of a lamentably disproportionate number of the people, averaging more than one third, in the towns."[46]

Fortescue laid particular stress on climatic factors in the development of Australia. There was little doubt in his mind that "the Anglo-Saxon race does not thrive and cannot, at any rate, without physical deterioration, work within the torrid zone."[47] The disastrous result for the British Empire of tropical conditions in Australia had been that the relatively few debilitated whites who lived there had become insistent on excluding non-white labor which might be effective in these latitudes: "the Australians are prepared, not to say determined, to leave a vast extent of their

45. J. W. Fortescue, "The Seamy Side of Australia," *Nineteenth Century*, XXIX (1891), 524.
46. *Ibid.*, p. 529.
47. *Ibid.*, p. 531. Fortescue cited the writings of Sir Anthony Musgrave as evidence for this assertion.

territory untouched and unprofitable sooner than admit another race that can turn it to account; in other words, to cancel a considerable portion of the assets on the security of which they have borrowed and are borrowing millions of money."[48] It may be seen from this statement that Fortescue, like Flora Shaw and others, viewed Australia not as a new nation with legitimate national aspirations, but rather as a giant British investment which was being badly managed. He treated depression in the colonies not as a broad economic problem with worldwide origins but as conclusive evidence of administrative incompetence and the need for Great Britain to restore discipline in its dependencies.

Fortescue presented the core of his criticism of Australia in his first article in 1891. His later publications consisted largely of answers to colonial defenders who had replied to his charges, and of summaries of other contemporary indictments. In response to Howard Willoughby, an Australian journalist, he developed the familiar parent-child analogy to illustrate how the lender-borrower relationship had gone wrong in the colonies. He complained that Britain, like other rich and doting fathers, had permitted Australia too long to indulge in childish fantasies. The colonial economies were like spoiled children "playing at" raising poultry. "The father supplies land, buildings, labour, stock, and food; he buys the eggs and chickens at something over the market price, and the children reckon the proceeds of the sale as net profit. Often as I have witnessed this little drama, I never dreamed that it could be exalted to the dignity of a serious financial operation."[49]

The writings of Francis Adams stimulated Fortescue to relate a wide range of colonial habits and customs, stretching from "mental characteristics" to "the abominable corrupt pronunciation" and "the influence of climate on race." First of all, he concluded, a hot climate made men lazy. "I cannot but think myself that the Australian climate, by disinclining men to hard work, has very greatly favoured the system, or rather theory of administration which has brought the four Eastern provinces almost to bank-

48. *Ibid.*, p. 535.
49. J. W. Fortescue, "Guileless Australia," *Nineteenth Century*, XXX (1891), 433.

ruptcy. The legal enforcement of an eight-hours day in Australia was recently defended to an English audience on the ground that the climate made it imperative." Second, he said, climate made Australians instinctively selfish with their natural resources, especially in the northern region:

It cannot be denied that the Australian animosity against coloured races is perfectly natural. It is generally attributed exclusively to the working man's prejudice against cheap labour—and indeed it is doubtful whether the antipathy has any other conscious motive; but it is more than probable that there is an unconscious and instinctive dread of any race which is more at home in a hot climate than the Anglo-Saxon.[50]

Understandably, Fortescue presented the financial collapse of 1893 as a predictable result of the conditions he had been describing for two years. With his customary fondness for analogy, he compared the current catastrophe to the experience of France with John Law: "the Australian bubble has burst; banks have fallen like autumn leaves; and across the flaming advertisement of 'boundless resources,' 'millions of realised wealth,' 'matchless prosperity' and the like, wherewith the Australian Governments used to feed our fancy and fill their treasuries, are pasted the fateful words 'moratorium,' and 'forced paper currency.' "[51] Fortescue denounced the Australian statisticians as tools of the propagandists, especially the Tasmanian R. M. Johnston, whom he recognized as a formidable adversary and accused of writing "a clever parody (disguised with rare humour as an attack upon myself) of the methods of Messrs. Coghlan and Hayter."[52]

Fortescue's most thorough attack on Australia came in 1894 as an essay, "State Socialism and the Collapse in Australia." By this date the main influence upon Fortescue had become Charles H. Pearson's "Forecast." He wrote, "we cannot sufficiently admire the practical courage and candour wherewith he has given it

50. J. W. Fortescue, "The Influence of Climate on Race," *Nineteenth Century*, XXXIII (1893), 868 and 869. Fortescue developed this thesis for other parts of the Empire as well, e.g., "Jamaica and Mauritius," *National Review*, XVIII (1892), 536–55.

51. J. W. Fortescue, "The New South Sea Bubble," *Nineteenth Century*, XXXIV (1893), 22.

52. *Ibid.*, p. 32.

utterance." He agreed with Pearson that in Australia the state had gained an aura almost of mystical religion "promising great good" and demanding "proportional sacrifices." J. A. Froude had made a pilgrimage to Australia in the same way as the wise men to the Holy Land, but with less satisfactory results. "Mr. Froude journeyed to Australia to see the wonderful things that were there; for the fame thereof had reached his ears in his own country. And he saw the ministers of the State, and communed with them; he saw their work also and blessed it. And his blessing is a curse unto Australia unto this day." [53] The religion of state socialism had led Australians to expect a future which could never come to pass—full employment and steadily rising incomes, in fact "universal prosperity and universal contentment." To these unreasonable expectations had been added a willingness to take long chances because "Australia is from the nature of the case a gambling country." The result of this combination was inevitable disaster. "Surely a people which throws itself in despair into the arms of an helpless abstraction; which fears the bare idea of the worst going to the wall; which shrinks from the laws of nature and tries to evade, instead of obeying and subduing them—surely such a people will never win battles." [54] Like the other major critics, Fortescue stopped his attacks by the middle of the 1890's when it began to look as if Australia might, after all, win its battles.

The most lighthearted, if not the least venomous, of the major critics of Australia writing in England was Paul Blouet, a Frenchman who used the pseudonym Max O'Rell to write a popular indictment of the British Empire entitled *John Bull and Co.: The Great Colonial Branches of the Firm.* Blouet's contempt was for Anglo-Saxons as a race, but he found the qualities he most dis-

53. J. W. Fortescue, "State Socialism and the Collapse in Australia," in MacKay, *A Policy of Free Exchange,* pp. 109 and 113. Other contributors to this volume also mentioned Australia in passing. For example, William Maitland remarked that the financial transgressions of the colonies had, at least, diminished their attractiveness to other imperial powers and thereby reduced the burden of their defense. "If our Colonies have done nothing else by incurring the enormous load of debt which now weighs them down, they have at least discovered a new protection against annexation . . . the surplus population of this and other countries will prefer the United States as a field of emigration." *Ibid.,* p. 81.

54. *Ibid.,* pp. 125 and 139–40. Fortescue explained once again the reasons for Australia's gambling propensities: gold, an uncertain climate, and a steady inflow of "undisciplined" and "discontented" immigrants (pp. 126–31).

liked accentuated in the colonies, and above all, in Australia, which he visited in 1893. Most of the criticisms Blouet made of Australia were clichés by the mid-1890's: excessive urbanization, cultural desolation, bumptiousness, drunkenness, biological degeneration, and political corruption. But he added a few novelties, such as an attack on the Antipodean practice of outdoor lovemaking, and he packaged the whole in a form that reached a wide audience.[55]

Colonial Defenders: Foreign and Domestic

The vigorous criticism of the Australian colonies during the 1890's brought forth an equally energetic response. Although it cannot be claimed that the defenders were successful in refuting to the satisfaction of many British readers the wide range of charges lodged against the colonies, at least they made strenuous efforts in that direction. Moreover, the defensive statements described in this section appear to have had two side effects: first, to their readers, Australia began to assume a new role as a distinct entity within the Empire with its own national views and with spokesmen capable of voicing them. Second, among Australians themselves the need for defense against external verbal attack contributed to the growth of national feeling in the crucial decade before Federation. The defenders of the colonies may be divided roughly into two groups: those who were essentially British in their orientation and those who had firm roots in the colonies.

Defense of the colonial economies during the 1890's from within Britain itself rested upon two different bases. The first was an open-minded new interest in social and economic experimentation which was far wider and more urgent than that exhibited at an earlier period by a few travelers such as Dilke and Trollope. A wide range of British economists reacted critically to doctrinaire condemnation of the colonial economies merely because they were different from British models, and strong appeals were made for study of facts before judgments were made. In particular, the

55. The copy consulted of *John Bull and Co.* (London, 1894) indicates "twentieth thousand."

heterodox *Economic Review,* a periodical founded by the Oxford University Branch of the Christian Social Union in 1891, the same year as the establishment of the *Economic Journal,* opened its pages to sympathetic coverage of Australian institutions and events. In 1893 and 1894, "village settlements" which had been established in Victoria as antidepression measures were described by their initiator Horace F. Tucker and by a complimentary observer, H. C. Hancock.[56] Also in 1894, George M. Lester gave a sober assessment of radical sentiment in Queensland; he urged support for true "social reformers" in the colony and said that blanket condemnation of change merely strengthened the hand of the destructive "socialists."[57] In 1895, Lester described in detail the course of the shearers' strike to illustrate once again the merit of the moderate position.[58]

The position of almost all writers on the colonies in the *Economic Review* was that economic institutions should not be criticized until after they had been thoroughly examined and evaluated. This was partly due to an attachment to the historical method, and partly to sympathy on moral grounds for policies and practices which were often condemned merely on the basis of appeals to orthodox economic theory. Typically the blanket denunciation of "Socialism" by the Australian politician Sir Henry Wrixon was rejected by the economist Sidney Ball on the ground that it was undocumented and unconvincing.[59] In the same spirit, the journal published a sympathetic account of social legislation in New Zealand by a former colonist, William Warrand Carlile.[60]

The second source of inspiration for defense of the Australian

56. Horace F. Tucker, "Village Settlements in Victoria," *Economic Review,* III (1893), 514–20; H. C. Hancock, "The 'Tucker Village Settlements' in Victoria," *ibid.,* IV (1894), 253–55. Hancock reported that Tucker aimed "to steer carefully between cut-throat competition and the absolute subordination of individuality" (p. 254).

57. George M. L. Lester, "Wage-earners in Western Queensland," *Economic Review,* IV (1894), 345–52.

58. G. M. L. Lester, "The Shearers' Strike of 1894 in Western Queensland," *Economic Review,* V (1895), 392–97.

59. S. Ball, *Economic Review,* VII (1897), 263–73. Ball, six years earlier, had roundly condemned Thomas MacKay's book *A Plea for Liberty,* in which Charles Fairfield's denunciation of Australia had appeared. *Economic Review,* I (1891), 327–47.

60. W. W. Carlile, "Democracy in New Zealand," *Economic Review,* IX (1899), 298–310.

economy by British observers was a mounting sentiment of imperial solidarity which made critiques of one part of the Empire seem attacks on the whole. Typically, the old free-trade imperialist George Baden-Powell rallied behind a sympathetic interpretation of Australia's troubles. He had not himself visited the colonies for many years, but he recalled their special circumstances and needs for such eccentric economic institutions as developmental public works. In refutation of Fortescue's description of Australia's "seamy side," Baden-Powell gave a glowing account of the "satin side."[61] Similarly, Charles Dilke, mellowed by a quarter century of experience and a host of personal vicissitudes, brought forth a second book on the Empire which contained far fewer doubts about the organic soundness of the colonial societies than had been expressed in the first.[62] A eulogistic report in 1893 by the imperialist Lord Meath of a recent trip to Australia may be compared with the typical xenophobic accounts of twenty or thirty years before.[63]

Predictably, the Royal Colonial Institute provided a hospitable forum for imperialist defenders of the colonies, both domestic and from overseas.[64] The most significant statement to this body came from Lord Carrington, former governor of New South Wales, at a meeting with the Prince of Wales in the chair.[65] The tone of the address was slightly patronizing and condescending, but it was clear that the speaker was at least sympathetic to overall Aus-

61. George Baden-Powell, "The Credit of Australasia," *Fortnightly Review*, L (1891), 3–12.

62. C. Dilke, *Problems of Greater Britain* (London, 1890). Part II dealt with Australasia. One reviewer at least took note of the favorable new light which Dilke cast upon Australia. W. J. Courthope, "Problems of Greater Britain," *National Review*, XV (1890), 433–45. Another favorable review is *Westminster Review*, CXXXIV (1890), 349–54. The complexities of Dilke's later life are described in Roy Jenkins, *Sir Charles Dilke, a Victorian Tragedy* (London: Fontana Books, 1968). Dilke expressed optimism about Australian federation in "The Commonwealth of Australia," *Forum*, XI (1891), 379–97.

63. Meath, "A Britisher's Impressions of America and Australasia," *Nineteenth Century*, XXXIII (1893), 493–514.

64. As the turbulent 1890's were just beginning John Dennistoun Wood of Melbourne reminded the Institute of Australia's imperial loyalty with an execrable poem entitled "The Briton's Land: A Lay of Imperial Unity," *Journal of the Royal Colonial Institute*, XXII (1890/91), 3–5.

65. Francis Adams commented upon this address and another by Lord Carrington in Bristol. At the presentation of the latter, "For this first time the English public heard something very like an enunciation of the general views of the Australian public." *The Australians* (London, 1893), p. 266.

tralian national objectives. Carrington's theme was an elaboration of the old argument that young Australia was essentially childlike and should be treated accordingly. Evidently, however, he subscribed to principles of progressive education when dealing with Australia rather than to the strong discipline recommended by so many of his countrymen: he urged Britain to be patient and, above all, to follow the reverse of the rule "spare the rod, spoil the child." He advised his English audience to "tend her with love and kindness, draw her to you, let her feel respect for you, but leave her to find out her own way as far as possible." [66] Carrington was unusually optimistic about the prospects for Australia's maturation and federation among the colonies.

Imperialists wrote often during the troubled 1890's of the homes for emigrants, the strategic bases, the loyal friends, and the substantial trade (approaching one quarter of the total with all possessions) provided to Great Britain by Australia. These accounts, as much as the sympathetic arguments, gave weight to the case for more understanding treatment of the colonies.[67]

Although native defenders of the colonial economies were obviously self-interested, they were also more vigorous and compelling than their British counterparts. The natives fall into three categories: official public figures, former colonists now resident in Britain, and miscellaneous private citizens responding to criticism from the colonies themselves.

The public figures were under direct obligation by virtue of their positions as visiting legislators, agents-general, or other public servants to present the homeland in its best light; and they

66. Lord Carrington, "Australia as I Saw It," *Journal of the Royal Colonial Institute,* XXII (1890/91), 169.

67. See for example, a work by the principal of Illawarra College, New South Wales, Maurice H. Hervey, *The Trade Policy of New South Wales* (London, 1892); Kenric B. Murray, "Mr. Chamberlain and Colonial Commerce," *Economic Journal,* VII (1897), 21–33; and R. E. Macnaghten, "Emigration: A Plea for State Aid," *Economic Review,* VIII (1898), 58–76; Lord Brassey, "Imperial Federation," *Nineteenth Century,* XXX (1891), 480–89; *idem,* "The Diamond Jubilee in Victoria," *ibid.,* XLII (1897), 353–61; *idem,* "Recent Social and Political Progress in Victoria," *Proceedings of the Royal Colonial Institute,* XXIX (1897/98), 282–93; Walter Frewen Lord, "Protection and the Empire," *Nineteenth Century,* XXXIII (1893), 1062–74; James Long, "Can the Empire Feed Its People?" *ibid.,* XXXIX (1896), 16–27; Arthur Silva White, "Australia as a Strategic Base," *ibid.,* XXXIX (1896), 457–64.

often had the added stimulus of colonial bonds for sale. Nevertheless, the energy, self-confidence, and ability with which some of these colonists undertook the task constituted a new feature of imperial relations. From the plethora of statements by colonial officials, it is worth mentioning a few examples. The New Zealander, Sir Julius Vogel, attempted in an interesting way to show how the Australian colonies had become adjusted to a rapid rate of economic growth sustained from abroad with the result that a departure from this rate caused serious trouble. Sudden cessation of the inflows either of capital or of immigrant labor, he said, placed unbearable strains on a wide range of economic institutions such as banks and loan companies. Booms and failures in the colonies were not the results of political irresponsibility or moral decay as charged; rather they were predictable "reactions" to fluctuations in external stimuli by dependent economies geared to rapid growth. In considering reform, it would have to be remembered that if the colonies were more stable they might also become stagnant.[68]

Sir Edward Braddon from Tasmania presented to the Royal Colonial Institute one of the most elaborate defenses against what he termed "atrabilious and unwarrantable onslaughts upon Australasian manners, morals, and money." He addressed himself especially to the attacks of Fortescue, Fairfield, and Murray, and he refuted their specific charges one by one. His main complaint about the critical literature as a whole was that the authors had not gathered sufficient evidence to provide respectable foundations for their condemnations. He reported a recent comment from Lord Jersey, a former Governor of New South Wales, as follows: "it would seem as if Australia had become the happy hunting-ground of the scribbling globe-trotter. When I open my morning paper I almost expect to read that some new volunteer has opened fire." [69]

68. Julius Vogel, "The Bank Panic in Australia," *Fortnightly Review*, LIII (1893), 753–61.

69. Sir Edward Braddon, "Australasia: A Vindication," *Journal of the Royal Colonial Institute*, XXIII (1891/92), 76. An earlier address to the Institute by Braddon, before the worst attacks on Australia began, was entitled "Tasmania: Its Resources and Prospects," *ibid.*, XX (1888/89), 319–43.

T. J. Byrnes, young native-born Attorney General of Queensland and later premier, accused a British audience in 1897 of gross ingratitude. Australia, he said, had accepted the burden of an experiment which was crucial to the future of all the white race—the development of new homes in the tropics. Despite what was said, he insisted, the experiment had been a success:

> The mining, public works, the mechanical trades, and labour generally throughout the tropical country are carried on solely by white men, and but a small fraction of the population consists of coloured men who are engaged exclusively in field operations. I have every faith eventually in the acclimatisation of our race in the tropics, and in the improvement of machinery and the methods of production, that we shall be able successfully to solve this problem. However, in the meantime, instead of being the targets for unmerited attacks, we ought to be rather protected by all persons who desire to see the bounds of civilisation grow wider and wider, and the tropical parts of the world brought to their highest stage of development.[70]

An indication of the growing self-confidence of some Australian official spokesmen when confronted by attackers is the speed with which the New South Wales premier, Sir George Dibbs, responded to slurs upon his colony, and specifically upon his statistician Timothy Coghlan in the London *Economist.* Dibbs denied that Coghlan had published exaggerated statistics of the extent of Australian wealth, as this newspaper had claimed. He concluded angrily: "You charge us with extravagance in living. We may be so according to Old World notions, but at least we earn a good deal more than the money we spend, as I hope to prove before I return to New South Wales." [71]

A most persuasive defense of the Australian economy came from Robert Mackenzie Johnston, the Tasmanian government statistician, in an article for the *Nineteenth Century.* Johnston was an able and perceptive amateur economist who held a leading

70. T. J. Byrnes, *The Resources of Queensland* (London, 1897), pp. 11–12.

71. G. Dibbs, "Dubious Colonial Statistics: To the Editor of the Economist," *Economist,* L (1892), 764–65. Coghlan and Henry Hayter had both been attacked in an article entitled "Dubious Colonial Statistics," *ibid.,* pp. 728–29. An example of economic propaganda prepared by the statisticians, presumably for the London audience, is H. H. Hayter, *Facts Relating to the Colony of Victoria (Having Special Reference to Its Financial Position)* (Melbourne, 1891).

position among colonial statisticians.[72] His approach to the task of answering critics was to explain economic activity in the colonies as a process above all of national development. He differed totally from J. W. Fortescue, who saw the colonies merely as pools of British investment.

Johnston argued that observers in the mother country were conditioned both by experience and by self-interest to misunderstand colonial growth. In particular, Englishmen had come so to identify their own government activity with warfare and other economically unproductive efforts that they could not visualize government elsewhere providing the very sinews of an economy as it did in Australia:

> In the self-governing colonies of Australasia, the scope of general government—owing to the peculiar condition of lands thinly populated with vast undeveloped areas—embraces many functions which it would be impossible to resign to local bodies or to private enterprise as in older countries. . . .
>
> In the colonies . . . the major part of the so-called *public debt* is as much a commercial asset as the capital invested in railways and tramways in England, and with the exception of about one or two percent. the remainder is represented by public works of a permanent character, whose value, as wealth-producing auxiliaries, enormously exceeds the nominal debt standing against them.[73]

Johnston believed that railways were central to colonial development and that their net worth to the community could not be estimated from their direct revenues alone:

> The principal additions to the wealth of the country due to railways are derived as follows:
>
> (1) By the saving of time and cost of transit. (2) By giving commercial value to vast natural products hitherto lacking value, owing to lack of cheap means of transit. (3) By the impetus given to the creation of fresh wealth in areas formerly unproductive.[74]

British observers were so certain about what policies were correct for Australia, Johnston said, that they often jumped to false conclusions on the basis of inadequate evidence. A fluctuation in

72. See my *Economic Enquiry in Australia* (Durham, 1966), pp. 480–84.
73. R. M. Johnston, "The Attack on the Credit of Australasia," *Nineteenth Century*, XXXI (1892), 607 and 611.
74. *Ibid.*, p. 616.

a single variable, such as the price of urban land, or several bank failures were cited confidently by the critics as evidence of total collapse. In reality, "To gauge the material and social condition of any country with accuracy is a matter involving many difficulties, even to those who are skilled in making such estimates." [75] British commentators also applied a dual standard to the colonies. When they condemned such phenomena as the growth of cities, they neglected to point out that this development in particular had taken place in Britain for centuries in conjunction with rising standards of living. "The relative increase in the ratio of the urban population is a natural consequence. To deplore, therefore, the increasing ratios of urban centres of industry, is to deplore the higher advance made in modern civilisation." [76] Johnston suggested even that misrepresentation of the Australian economy was at times a machination of "that powerful class of speculators who have been well though severely described by Schaeffle as that 'Whole unclean brigand aristocracy of the Bourse'." [77]

During the crisis years of the 1890's, the unofficial defenders of Australia, except for a few exceptions, were not as effective as were their official counterparts. At the beginning of the most serious trouble the redoubtable old warrior William Westgarth sallied forth, followed by colleagues in the Royal Colonial Institute.[78] With a similar defensive purpose, A. Patchett Martin published a collection of his essays on Australia in which he condemned the criticism contained in Froude's *Oceana* and Finch-Hatton's *Advance Australia*.[79] Edward A. Petherick used the disarming device of laying the main criticisms of the colonies openly on the table for his readers so that he could evaluate them one by one. He printed a letter from "an investor in Australian securities" which summarized two of the main arguments: first, that Australia departed unwisely from Old Country models; and second,

75. *Ibid.*, p. 606.
76. *Ibid.*, p. 619.
77. *Ibid.*, p. 606.
78. E.g., William Westgarth, "Australasian Public Finance," *Proceedings of the Royal Colonial Institute*, XX (1888–89), 230–52.
79. A. Patchett Martin, *Australia and the Empire* (Edinburgh, 1889), pp. 34, 40–41, 78, 83–84, and 88–90. Martin was a friend of Alfred Deakin in his youth and moved to London in 1882. J. A. La Nauze, *Alfred Deakin* (Melbourne, 1965), I, 21.

that large-scale national borrowing was as iniquitous as excessive personal debt:

My opinion is that young and energetic communities like the Australian Colonies, isolated as they are in many respects from European influences, and unencumbered by any burdens of former generations, should not have been in their present circumstances; they ought to have profited, politically and economically, by the experience of older countries. Your several governments are now on their trial and must be prepared to give an account of their stewardships. They have been selling part of their estates in order to live, and borrowing, or mortgaging revenue, to pay for improvements.[80]

Petherick replied to these criticisms that foreign borrowing had led to impressive economic growth; the unique economic conditions in Australia had dictated distinct economic policies and institutions.

From the colonies directly after suitable delays for the return mail, came replies to most of the specific attacks described in this chapter.[81] But there were not as yet private defenders of the stature of Johnston or Vogel.

The Image in Sharp Relief

The 1890's were years of serious crisis for Australia in the evolution of its image abroad as well as in its internal development. Main themes in discussions of the colonies did not change markedly from earlier years, but criticism of the growth process and of social and economic institutions reached a peak with the appearance on the scene of several strong and effective spokesmen. At the same time, in response to this attack, competent defenders came forth and the factors which soon would bring about a sharp improvement in the colonial image began to take effect.

80. Edward A. Petherick, *The Australian Colonies in 1896* (London, 1897), p. 6.

81. E.g., Howard Willoughby, "'The Seamy Side of Australia': A Reply from the Colonies," *Nineteenth Century,* XXX (1891), 292–302; and Norwood Young, "Australasia and British Money," *Contemporary Review,* LXV (1894), 257–70; John D. Fitzgerald, "Mr. H. H. Champion on the Australian Strike," *Nineteenth Century,* XXIX (1891), 445–53; R. G. C. Hamilton, "Lending Money to Australia," *ibid.,* XXXII (1892), 194–202; R. Newton, "Facts About Queensland," *Westminster Review,* CXLV (1896), 568–74.

The intensity of debate during the 1890's helped to highlight main features of it. Above all was the continuing influence on the debaters of models taken from social and economic theory. By some observers Australia was judged for conformity to principles which were thought appropriate for Britain herself: in particular rules concerning free trade, free markets, free migration, and a limited role for the state in the economy. By others Australia was viewed still in an older Mercantilist mode as an imperial possession with responsibilities primarily to British capitalists. Finally, a variety of miscellaneous metaphors were applied to Australia such as those of parent and child, and the evolutionary struggle for survival. Most British observers of the Australian scene hoped to portray, understand, or condemn complex circumstances in this far-off land by the use of analogy and superficial application of theory rather than empirical analysis. Defenders of Australia, answering theory with facts, were still on a different plane of discourse from the critics. For Australia's image to change it was necessary either for the Australian facts to discredit the theory or for the theory to move onward. Both of these developments occurred in the twentieth century.

·8·

Return to Respectability

Late in the 1890's and during the early years of the twentieth century the stereotype in Britain of Australia as the fount of political error and the seat of economic unorthodoxy began gradually to disappear. In this chapter the change of attitude and the developments which lay behind it are examined.

A Better British Press

A number of factors help to explain the improved tone of writings about the Australian economy. The first was the course of events in several different spheres. Economically the colonies moved rapidly out of deep depression into a sustained boom. From a level of £189.8 million in 1900, Australian gross domestic product rose to an estimated £220 million in 1903/4, and to £412.1 million by 1913/14.[1] In contrast to the crisis years of the early 1890's, by the first decade of the twentieth century it had become difficult to criticize an Australian economy which clearly now was a robust success rather than a near disaster. *The Economist* began to note this change of direction by 1896; and instead of the incessant black predictions of a few years before, the paper reported bank reconstructions and exciting mining opportunities in Western Australia.[2] Throughout the years before World War I

1. N. G. Butlin, *Australian Domestic Product, Investment and Foreign Borrowing, 1861–1938/39* (Cambridge, 1962), pp. 6–7. In constant 1910/11 pounds the figures are 212.9, 243.2, and 355.8. *Ibid.*, pp. 460–61. See also Colin Forster, ed., *Australian Economic Development in the Twentieth Century* (London, 1970).

2. E.g., *Economist*, LIV (1896), 46, 133–34, 199, 358–60, 456–57, 481–83, 652–53, 895–97, 1528–30; LV (1897), 159–60, 777–78, 1529–30, 1667–68; LVI (1898), 1179–80. For other optimistic comments see T. M. Donovan, "Industrial Expansion in Queensland," *Westminster Review*, CLXVII (1897), 254–59; Oli-

the *Economist* continued to carry regular descriptions of what it considered to be Australia's policy transgressions; but increasingly these accounts were merely reportorial rather than moralistic or philosophical in tone and they were balanced with accounts of economic progress.[3]

A large study entitled *Australasian Democracy* written in 1896 by a visitor, H. de R. Walker, illustrated the changing views. Walker believed that the series of catastrophes through which Australia had just passed was the result of a combination of internal and external factors: within the country gold had nurtured such radical notions as trade unions and government intervention in the economy; in addition, temporary economic success had attracted an excessive flow of capital which led to unrealistic speculation.[4] The financial and labor crises, however, had modified the radical and collectivist tendencies of the colonies, had taught lessons, had restored balance, and now had given way to prosperity.

Within the British economy during the twentieth century a different view of empire served also to change the light in which Australian affairs were viewed. Economic writers came to assume that although a friendly and mutually profitable relationship with the Dominions should be preserved, this relationship could never again be critical to the welfare of Great Britain. The shift in viewpoint cannot be explained in detail here, but in essence it involved rejection, or at least serious questioning, of all the arguments for territorial dependencies which had flourished in the nineteenth century. First of all, after Chamberlain's failure to obtain imperial

phant Smeaton, "Colonial Expansion," *ibid.*, CXLVII (1897), 455–62; and A Colonial Contributor, "Progress of the Australasian Colonies," *Journal of the Royal Statistical Society*, LXIII (1900), 657–67.

3. E.g., *Economist*, LIX (1901), 319–21 and 1208–9; LX (1902), 848–50; LXII (1904), 1380–81; LXIII (1905), 1074–76; LXIX (1909), 20–22; LXXII (1911), 443; LXXVI (1913), 1086–87.

4. Henry de R. Walker, *Australasian Democracy* (London, 1897), esp. Chap. 10, entitled "Salient Features of the Australasian Democracy." Another visitor a year later reported that he could find no remaining "evidences of stagnation or depression in the general aspects of the people." Joseph Coats, *Notes on Sea and Land* (Glasgow, 1898), p. 157. William Johnson Galloway, M.P., reached a similar conclusion in *Advanced Australia* (London, 1899), as did E. C. Buley in *Australian Life in Town and Country* (London, 1905). Two syrupy accounts of visits early in the new century were William Cuff, *Sunny Memories of Australasia* (London, 1904); and J. G. Greenhough, *Towards the Sunrising* (London, 1902).

preference, the notion of a secure imperial trading area became improbable. Second and third, the old long-run Malthusian and Ricardian nemeses of population pressure and natural resource shortage were submerged beneath short-run economic difficulties, including crises surrounding war and evidence of a declining domestic birthrate.[5] At least by the early 1920's Sir William Beveridge and others were proclaiming that unemployment was no indication of overpopulation or other secular problems for which emigration could be a solution.[6] But even for those who continued to accept the old notions, the growing autonomy of the Dominions clearly reduced the reliability of any contribution they might make to the solution of Britain's resource problems. As one disgruntled *Edinburgh Reviewer* remarked in 1909 "it is impossible to assume that either Australia or Canada will permanently be willing to be regarded as an outlet for the surplus population of Great Britain." [7] Fourth, Hobson in a preliminary and incomplete fashion in the 1890's and then Keynes definitively in the 1930's pointed out that the key to maintaining adequate effective demand and opportunites for investment lay in internal reform rather than external expansion. Finally, the notion which had flourished from the middle of the nineteenth century, that Britain had a humane responsibility to assist new nations along the paths of economic wisdom and righteousness, was dealt a mortal blow by the South African War.

The importance of this shift in opinion for views on Australia was that writers now could see the Antipodes with a new detachment, if not disinterest, almost as they would regard, say, Latin American nations. Errors of policy in Australia were still errors, but they were no longer body blows to the motherland.

5. James W. Barclay, "Malthusianism and the Declining Birth Rate," *Nineteenth Century,* LIX (1906), 80–89; James A. Rigby, "The Diminishing Birth-Rate: Is it a National Danger?," *ibid.,* LXXV (1914), 434–45; Edwin Cannan, "The Changed Outlook in Regard to Population, 1831–1931," *Report of the British Association for the Advancement of Science,* C (1931), 110–21; James Davenport Whelpley, "The Fallacy of an Imperial Food Supply," *Fortnightly Review,* XCIV (1913), 1100–11.

6. Sir William H. Beveridge, "Population and Unemployment," *Report of the British Association for the Advancement of Science,* XCIII (1923), 138–61.

7. "The Economics of Empire," *Edinburgh Review,* CCIX (1909), 399.

On the political side, Australian Federation in 1900 robbed critics of a favorite charge that the colonists reveled in masochistic fragmentation of their economic system. During the first half of the 1890's, British commentators remained doubtful whether colonial muleheadedness would ever make way for federation; but by the second half of the decade the federal writing was clearly on the wall.[8] Robert Giffen hailed Australian Federation as a triumph for free trade principles, and Alfred Marshall looked back upon it in 1919 as a wise act which had reduced the trade of the colonies theretofore subject to restriction "by more than a third." [9] James Bryce, from a detailed examination of the history and structure of the new federal constitution, found it to be "the high-water mark of popular government. It is penetrated by the spirit of democracy." Moreover, he thought, the new nation was the product of enlightened economic reasoning on the part of all segments of the population:

> one perceives through the whole instrument that dominant factor of our age, the ever-present and all-pervading influence of economic forces, of industrial production, of commerce, of finance. The increased and increasing importance of these influences in the life of the modern world, stimulated as they have been by the amazing progress of scien-

8. E.g., "Australasian Federation Conference," *Economist,* XLVIII (1890), 168–69. In 1895 the journalist Edward Salmon angrily told readers of the *Fortnightly Review* that "The chances are very strong that federation would have saved Australia from the maëlstrom." "Australian Federation: Its Progress and Its Prospects," LVIII (1895), 67. Four years later these same readers were informed by another author that federation was about to become a reality because of the preponderance for the first time of native-born Australians. "And out of the squalor of his surroundings has come the desire for Federation. . . . Coincidentally with the passing of the squatter, the British-born Australian generally has slipped into the background." Harold G. Parsons, "Australian Federation—from the Inside," *Fortnightly Review,* LXVI (1899), 614. Other optimistic reports are Edward Wilson, Letter to the editor, *National Review,* XXV (1895), 420; E. N. C. Braddon, "The Federation Movement in Australasia," *Nineteenth Century,* XL (1896), 156–72; Lord Brassey, "Australian Federation," *ibid.,* XLV (1899), 548–57; A. G. Berry, "The New Commonwealth," *ibid.,* XLVIII (1900), 219–25; W. Harrison Moore, "Constitution Making in Australia," *National Review,* XXXI (1898), 269–79; and B. R. Wise, "The Commonwealth of Australia," *ibid.,* XXXIII (1899), 823–44. A more equivocal report on Queensland was T. M. Donovan, "Queensland Politics and Federation," *Westminster Review,* CLII (1899), 155–65.

9. Sir Robert Giffen, "Protectionist Victories and Free Trade Successes," *Economic Inquiries and Studies* (London, 1904), II, 178–88, an address delivered in 1897; *idem,* "The Relative Growth of the Component Parts of the Empire," *Proceedings of the Royal Colonial Institute,* XXX (1898/99), 136–57; Alfred Marshall, *Industry and Trade* (London, 1919), pp. 24 and 160–61.

tific discovery, finds a fuller expression in this Constitution than in any other yet framed.[10]

The fact that the building of the new Australian nation could be carried on in conjunction with loyal participation in the South African War and continued feelings of friendship and imperial patriotism seemed to most British observers to confirm their most optimistic expectations about Federation.[11] A decline in Australia's trade with Britain as a proportion of her total trade was seen only as a small warning light on the horizon.[12]

A final strand in the course of events which helps to explain the change in British mood was the evidence that Australian radicalism no longer seemed to keep ahead of the times and that the economy and polity of the colonies had not suffered mortally from their former extreme heresies. Public works and welfare measures, payment of legislators, wage and price regulation, direct taxation, and even tariff protection were far less startling to Englishmen in the early years of the twentieth century than they had been in the 1860's and 1870's. Not only were they old hat in Australia by then, but they all were either implemented or viewed as active possibilities for Britain itself.

At least as important as the shift in the pattern of events for improvement of Australia's economic image was a change in the character and force of the main British interpreters. Beginning in

10. James Bryce, "The Constitution of the Commonwealth of Australia," in *Studies in History and Jurisprudence* (New York, 1901), p. 448. See also Hutcheson Macaulay Posnett, "The Federal Constitution of Australia," *Fortnightly Review*, LXIX (1901), 969–88; and Arthur P. Poley, *The Federal Systems of the United States and the British Empire* (London, 1913), pp. 279–367.

11. This message was given often in the periodicals of the time. E.g., W. H. Fitchett, "The Australian View of the South African Crisis," *National Review*, XXXIII (1899), 992–99; A. Patchett Martin, "An Australian's Reflections on the War," *ibid.*, XXXV (1900), 122–27; and Edward Jenks, "The Making of Australasia," *Contemporary Review*, CIII (1913), 525–34; Percy F. Rowland, *The New Nation* (London, 1903); *idem*, "The Literature of the Australian Commonwealth," *Nineteenth Century*, LI (1902), 655–70; *idem*, "The Beginnings of an Australian National Character," *ibid.*, LII (1902), 400–11; *idem*, "Australian Federation," *Macmillan's Magazine*, LXXXIV (1901), 151–60; J. W. Kirwin, "The Australian Labour Party," *Nineteenth Century*, LVIII (1905), 827–37; R. E. Macnaghten, "Tasmania's Halcyon Isle," *Pall Mall Magazine*, XXXIII (1904), 83–96.

12. Thomas H. Haynes, "An Analysis of Australian Imports of Merchandise from the United Kingdom and Foreign Countries," *Journal of the Royal Statistical Society*, LXIX (1906), 200–211; and S. Rosenbaum, "The Trade of the British Empire," *ibid.*, LXXVI (1912/13), 739–65.

the second half of the 1890's, at least three distinct but not mutually exclusive categories of sympathetic commentator began to make themselves heard with new vigor: ardent imperialists, social reformers, and economists.

Advocates of Empire

The first category of commentator had predecessors throughout the second half of the nineteenth century in the spokesmen for various forms of imperial union or federation, but its numbers reached a peak, ironically, just as the death knell of empire was sounding. Australians themselves were active in the early years of the imperial federation movement, in which they joined missionaries from other parts of the Empire in stressing loyalty to the Crown and the importance of the colonies for Britain's well-being.[13] A succession of British travelers to the colonies beginning in the late 1890's expressed the strengthened imperialist viewpoint. But for their wider belief in the virtues of empire, one suspects they might have exhibited a condescension and skepticism of social and economic policies similar to that of their predecessors.[14] Most imperialists portrayed Australian federation as

13. For discussion of Australia's role in the imperial federation movement see Charles S. Blackton, "Australian Nationality and Nationalism: The Imperial Federationist Interlude, 1885–1901," *Historical Studies: Australia and New Zealand,* VII (1955/57), 1–16; and Charles Grimshaw, "Australian Nationalism and the Imperial Connection 1900–1914," *Australian Journal of Politics and History,* III (1957/58), 161–82. One of the first full-blown plans for imperial federation came from an Australian, H. Mortimer-Franklyn. See his *The Unit of Imperial Federation: A Solution of the Problem* (London, 1887). F. P. de Labilliere, an Australian living in Britain, provided a full case for imperial federation in a volume entitled *Federal Britain; or, Unity and Federation of the Empire* (London, 1894). B. R. Wise presented arguments for a version of imperial preference to Australia in "Australia and Preferential Trade," *National Review,* XLIII (1904), 146–59. A book-length expression of warm imperial feeling was Alfred Buchanan, *The Real Australia* (London, 1907). Even a Canadian, J. Castell Hopkins, testified to Australia's sound imperial faith. *Links of Union Between Canada and Australia* (Toronto, 1890). A cautious assessment of Australia's attitude toward imperial union was John Douglas, "Imperial Federation from an Australian Point of View," *Nineteenth Century,* XVI (1884), 853–68.

14. E.g., John Lowles, Conservative M.P. and advocate of Imperial Federation, reported after a tour of Australia that colonial enthusiasm for empire was high. He emphasized that closer links with the colonies would make possible a lessening of British "dependence as at present upon foreign countries for so large a portion of our food supply." *Proceedings of the Royal Colonial Institute,* XXVIII (1896/97), 4–30. James Francis Hogan, an Australian who had lived for seven years in London and supported the notion of imperial solidarity, returned to Australia in

only the first move toward a wider imperial unity, and some were able even to praise Australian tariffs as an important precedent for imperial preference.[15] Others, such as Lionel Curtis, founder of the Round Table, argued that the secret of the Empire transformed into a new "Commonwealth" would be mutual toleration. Therein trade and migration would remain important, but economic policies such as tariffs and immigration restriction should be domestic affairs of the constituent nations not to be determined or even judged by other members of the Commonwealth.[16] All of these arguments helped Australia to slip out of the old charge against it of commercial heresy.

The former colonist and ardent imperialist John Henniker Heaton became known in Britain as the "member for Australia" and from his seat in Parliament represented colonial interests almost as much as his constituency of Canterbury. He wished to strengthen all the bonds of empire and especially facilities for communication; he believed that the "number of letters forwarded and received" was "a true index of the degree of civilization," and as postmaster-general he is remembered as the father of imperial penny postage.[17] Undoubtedly the outpourings of im-

---

1896 to investigate the charges of the previous few years, particularly those of Max O'Rell (Paul Blouet). Like most imperialists he was not averse while defending the colonies to urging upon them a larger measure of social conservatism. For example, he said: "Australia has been frequently described in the London Press as 'the laboratory of the Empire,' but the practical consideration for Australians is that care, caution, and consistent sanity are more necessary in a laboratory than anywhere else, if disastrous explosions and other unpleasant possibilities are to be averted." *The Sister Dominions: Through Canada to Australia by the New Imperial Highway* (London, 1896), p. 230.

15. E.g., Richard Jebb, *Studies in Colonial Nationalism* (London, 1905), pp. 61, 191–92, and 267. Jebb's book led him to an important friendship with Alfred Deakin. See J. A. La Nauze, *Alfred Deakin* (Melbourne, 1965), p. 353. Two examples of mildly imperialist accounts of colonial history, which emphasized the successful experience of practically all the colonies and stressed "the fortitude of the race" even in Australia, are William Parr Greswell, *The Growth and Administration of the British Colonies, 1837–1897* (London, 1898); and Matthew Macfie, et al., *Australasia*, The British Empire Series No. IV (London, 1900).

16. Lionel Curtis, *The Problem of the Commonwealth* (London, 1915), pp. 47–64; Thomas Hodgkin, "Southward Ho!" *Contemporary Review*, XCVIII (1910), 213–29.

17. J. Henniker Heaton, "Postal and Telegraphic Progress Under Queen Victoria," *Fortnightly Review*, LXI (1897), 839–49; *idem*, "The Imperial Conference and Our Imperial Communications," *Nineteenth Century*, LXX (1911), 265–78. See also Mrs. Adrian Porter, *The Life and Letters of Sir John Henniker Heaton* (London, 1916), esp. pp. 4–5, 10–11, 158–66. Heaton is reported to have informed Thomas Carlyle about events in Australia. In one interview "Carlyle

perialists such as Heaton were not to every Englishman's taste, but at the same time they probably contributed to a more favorable attitude toward Australia.

Sir Charles Dilke's second book on the colonies, *Problems of Greater Britain* (1890), was both a bellwether and a significant work of transition in the new mood of imperialism. Much had happened to Dilke as well as to Australia in the quarter century since the first *Greater Britain,* and the second work in contrast to the first was written with assistance and without recent experience on the spot. The change in attitude is marked. In 1890 Dilke revealed a new defensiveness about colonial affairs, and he voiced an optimism about economic matters which was only barely evident in the earlier work. In particular, he stressed now the inherent conservatism of the colonists. He was concerned still about the relative failure of small-scale land settlement, but he was satisfied that the result of disproportionate urbanization would not be extreme radicalism.[18] In Victoria, where the danger was greatest,

> While democracy and State-socialism have completely triumphed, the conservatism of those who have much to lose has been quieted by the practical proof that their interests are safer in Victoria than they are in many older countries, that socialism in the French and English sense is less developed in Victoria than even in the United States, and that a considerable body of small proprietors, and of house-owning workmen, have become sturdy supporters of the present order of society.[19]

Dilke complained about the frequent misrepresentation of the colonies by British commentators, and he found a long list of colonial practices and institutions upon which he could heap praise: for example, the quality of public administration, the consumption level of imports from Britain, the monetary system, graduated death duties, the high level of legislative morality, widespread

---

spoke much of Australia and asked repeatedly about the youth of Australia: what were the young men doing—what were they reading? Did they work?" *Ibid.,* p. 151.

18. *Problems of Greater Britain* (London, 1890), pp. 167–68, and 492, 511–14.

19. *Ibid.,* p. 112, and also pp. 507–8. Dilke outlined cultural benefits of large cities and concluded that the "effect must be a quickening of the national pulse." P. 497.

observance of law and order, the large number of distinguished legislators, and the equitable treatment of labor.[20]

Dilke suggested that an entirely different set of criteria should be employed for judging the role of government in a colonial economy from that in an older country. "It was no doubt the early circumstances of the young country . . . which forced upon the people of New South Wales, as on the people of the other Australian colonies, the principle of the Government entering upon tasks which in England and in the United States would be left to the enterprise of private individuals or to corporate bodies." [21] He seems to have lost all his old fears about the likelihood of racial decline brought on by climate and the stain of convict blood. Comparing the newer and more tropical colonies of Queensland and Western Australia with the original settlements he said, "The English race shows as much vitality in the younger colony as in the older one." [22] Dilke believed still in 1890 as he had in the 1860's that Britain could see her own future in the present state of the colonies, but now the picture he saw was a happier one.[23]

Dilke wrote his second book just before the cataclysm of the early 1890's, and his prophecies about uninterrupted progress and industrial peace seemed ironic very soon after publication.[24] Yet the book was read throughout the turbulent years as well as into the twentieth century, and his optimistic tone was reiterated by others before the nineteenth century ended.

An extensive descriptive work in the new mood of sympathy toward Australia as an important part of the Empire was *Life and Progress in Australasia* by Michael Davitt, an Irish political leader and member of Parliament. Davitt's tour of seven months through the colonies covered much of the same ground and many of the same subjects as the journeys of Dilke, Trollope, and Froude. But Davitt's report was markedly different from the earlier works in tone, in interpretation of events, and in overall attitude. The patronizing look of condescension was replaced by genuine admira-

20. *Ibid.*, pp. 113, 118, 121, 145–48, 150, 164, 171, 486–88, 495, 501.
21. *Ibid.*, p. 165.
22. *Ibid.*, p. 222, and also, pp. 189, 192, 226 and 696.
23. *Ibid.*, pp. 490–94, 522.
24. E.g., *ibid.*, p. 489.

tion and respect. It is true that Davitt did attribute colonial achievements more to the free operation of Irish genius in an hospitable environment and to the economic and political power of organized labor than to unique colonial conditions.[25] But still, it was a bright picture that he painted instead of the customary gloomy one.

The causes of and attempts to ameliorate the depression of the 1890's interested Davitt above all. He was not a simple apologist for all colonial policies before or during the crisis, but he did bring a degree of balance to his comments which was almost unknown among British observers to date. He repeated the familiar criticism of the colonists for building "overcrowded centres," but at the same time he condemned London investors for "overcapitalising" urban sectors of the economy. He denied categorically that basic character faults in the Australians were any part of the explanation for depression. Drunkenness, he said, was less of a social problem than it was in Britain,[26] and because the founding convicts were merely unfortunate products of a corrupt environment, they bore no special mark of Cain.[27] Gold, rather than leading to national degeneracy, had been a major boon as "an economic recruiting agency for land settlement." [28]

Davitt devoted attention to novel public institutions in Australia which, on the whole, he applauded. Throughout New South Wales he saw "a steady application of progressive ideas observable in the laws and government of the colony," and in specific fields such as care of the destitute he reported progress over the Old Country.[29] He described the Murray River labor settlements as "a standing evidence of the enlightened spirit in which South Australia has tried to solve the problem of the unemployed, while the recent establishment of a State Bank, on the Credit Foncier plan, exhibits the courageously practical nature of the colony's statesmanship in its resolve to make government not a mere tax-

25. M. Davitt, *Life and Progress in Australasia* (London, 1898), pp. 52–54, and 222.
26. *Ibid.*, pp. 29 and 121.
27. *Ibid.*, pp. 194–95.
28. *Ibid.*, p. 31.
29. *Ibid.*, pp. 48 and 241.

collecting machine, but a real factor in the actual industrial life of the country as well." [30] Davitt suggested that the labor legislation of Victoria might be a model for the world. "It is the first attempt that has been made in modern times to make a minimum wage a legal obligation upon employers, and the working of such a law will be watched with the keenest interest by everyone interested in the progress of Labour legislation." [31]

Davitt held an unusually optimistic view of the evolutionary process in Australia. He agreed that physiological as well as social change was taking place, but he discerned it to be clearly on an upward path. The following description is in sharp contrast to the comments of most earlier travelers which have been discussed above:

> Here, undoubtedly, there is a marked advance for the better, so far as physique is concerned, and in both sexes too. I would go so far as to say that the Australian, born of British or Irish parents, is the best physically developed man of either of these races. This will, I think, be acknowledged by all who have travelled in the colonies, and by those who saw the Australian contingents in London during the "jubilee" celebration of this year. The dry and healthful climate, the influence upon the atmosphere of the limitless eucalypti forests, over which the winds are eternally blowing; the outdoor life and labour of those who live and work beyond the confines of the very few large cities, and are engaged in agricultural, pastoral, and mining industries; all go, I think, to explain the vigorous frame, manliness of bearing, and stamp of independence characteristic of the average Australian.[32]

He reached an equally optimistic conclusion with regard to mental development:

> Speaking of the Australian people as I observed them—in their universities, colleges, and schools; in their homes; in their conversation and general demeanour; their information and intelligence, in the relatively large number of their newspapers; and in their manifest zeal for the intellectual development of their children—I would say that they favourably compare in general educational equipment and average culture with similar populations in any part of the English-speaking world.[33]

30. *Ibid.*, p. 60; and see also pp. 80–109.
31. *Ibid.*, p. 147.
32. *Ibid.*, p. 118.
33. *Ibid.*, pp. 123–24.

As one who was becoming increasingly skeptical of Britain's own imperial ambitions, Davitt attributed some of the high moral tone he discerned in Australian public life to the absence of foreign designs. "All the colony's energies are devoted to the betterment of its population and the general progress of the country. The saying which attributes happiness to the country that has no history might more appropriately be applied to countries having no conquering or 'civilizing' mission to rule, or ruin, other nations." [34]

A series of fourteen unsigned articles on "Australian Ideals" in *The Times* from July to October 1908 took as a major theme that the new nationalism of Australia was both worthy of special attention in Britain and consistent with continued imperial sentiment.[35] British observers were criticized for ignorance of the colonies and for failing to recognize that Australia was no longer Britain overseas but a genuine new country with a national character and problems all its own. "We have a settled habit of regarding the Colonies merely as political and commercial organisms." [36] The colonists themselves were blamed for helping to foster skeptical attitudes toward their homeland through exaggerated self-criticism and unnecessary stress on the presence in Australia of bitter class divisions. The basic principle students of Australia must accept, the Correspondent emphasized, was that her national policies were and should be aimed to achieve her own national objectives. Some actions by the new nation might seem unnecessarily selfish and immature, but this was only to be expected:

> Australians have reached the first stage of national consciousness distinguished by ethnologists; they feel themselves a chosen people, different from and superior to any other race . . . the natural materialism of a young country eager for development is in complete possession of the field, and Australians, awakened to the potentialities

34. *Ibid.*, p. 214.

35. The "Special Correspondent" who wrote the articles was presumably Arthur W. Jose. See J. A. La Nauze, *Alfred Deakin* (Melbourne, 1965), p. 354. They appeared in the following issues of *The Times:* July 4, 11, 18, and 25; August 1, 8, 15, 22, and 29; September 5, 12, 19, and 26; and October 3.

36. "The Background of News," *The Times*, July 11, 1908, p. 8. The Correspondent attacked Keir Hardie for remarking during a visit to Australia a year before that "colonial loyalty was merely a surface sentiment." "Political Theory and Popular Sentiment," *The Times*, July 4, 1908, p. 8.

of their own life and land, are almost exclusively concerned with themselves.[37]

Despite the nation's immaturity, the Correspondent was quick to point out, prospects for extreme radicalism had almost disappeared in Australia, and hopes for cordial relations with Britain were bright.

A second remarkable, and almost bizarre, series of weekly letters from Australia appeared in the London *Morning Post* from 1900 until 1914, contributed anonymously by Alfred Deakin even during his terms as cabinet member and prime minister. This series, like that in *The Times,* capitalized on the new interest in the wider Commonwealth stage which made possible detailed comment even on localized political events and economic conditions.[38] Professor La Nauze writes of this period in general: "it is likely that never before or since were English newspaper readers as copiously supplied with authoritative comment on Australia as they were for some years after 1905. Whether they eagerly took advantage of their privileges may be doubted." [39] This situation can be contrasted with the 1890's, when readers of *The Times* had letters from Flora Shaw.

One more significant indicator of the new light in which members of the British elite, at least, had come to see Australia is the report of an official visit to the Pacific in 1909 by Sir Charles Lucas, Assistant Under Secretary of State for the Colonies and a distinguished scholar. The most noteworthy feature of the report was its humility. Lucas stated clearly in a fashion almost unknown

37. "The Growth of an Australian Sentiment," *The Times,* July 25, 1908, p. 6.

38. J. A. La Nauze, *Alfred Deakin* (Melbourne, 1965), pp. 199–200 and 347–61. Professor La Nauze writes that Deakin's purpose in the letters was "to present to English readers material which should help them to realize that the Australian colonies had grown into a nation, and allow them to interpret spasmodic news of political crises and difficulties in the light of the special conditions and problems of youthful nationalism in its vast and peculiar geographical setting" (p. 352). One of the *Morning Post* letters which dealt with economic aspects of federation has been republished by La Nauze, with comments, as " 'The Chariot Wheels of the Central Government': Deakin's Prophecy of 1902," *Economic Record,* XXVIII (1952), 235–44. Others are contained in J. A. La Nauze, ed., *Federated Australia: Selections from Letters to the Morning Post, 1900–1910, by Alfred Deakin* (Melbourne, 1968).

39. La Nauze, *Alfred Deakin,* p. 349. A series of letters in the London *Standard* which used such novel terms to describe Australia as "land of delight" and "sane socialism" was republished as Frank T. Bullen, *Advance Australasia* (London, 1907). Another series from the Walsall *Advertiser* was S. B. Sheway, *Australasia: Impressions of a Colonial Tour* (Walsall, 1910).

to writers in the nineteenth century that he did not feel qualified after only a few months of travel to pronounce on Australian affairs. He took an optimistic view that the principal reason for much past ill feeling between Britain and her dominions was misinformation based on bad reporting and inadequate communications. There was no valid reason for continued antipathy, he thought, except failure of each party to understand the other. He rejected such long-standing calumnies against the Australians as that their cities were too large and that they were walking examples of racial decline:

> Indeed, any small difference which may arise between the British type in England and the British type in Australia I should attribute largely to the fact that in Australia few Englishmen are living in large spaces, and in England many Englishmen are living in a small area.
>
> Each province of the Empire must, in the course of generations, develop its own type of the British race, and this, it seems to me, will be to the great advantage of the whole. . . .[40]

Lucas's main reform proposal was for reduced costs of transportation and communication within the Empire, and not for any institutional change in Dominion status or stronger discipline by British investors. This, he confidently believed, would improve understanding and sympathy, generate friendships at all social levels, and strengthen imperial bonds. By 1909 this one influential observer at least had no doubt that increased British contact with Australian society would produce admiration and respect rather than the traditional suspicion and distaste. The demonstrated loyalty and willingness to sacrifice of Australia during World War I added converts to Lucas's opinion.[41]

The impression should not be left that criticism of the Australian economy ceased with dramatic suddenness at the end of

40. "Note on a Visit to Australia, New Zealand, and Fiji in 1909, by Sir Charles Lucas, K.C.M.G., C.B., Assistant Under Secretary of State for the Colonies," Cd. 5100, *Accounts and Papers,* 1910, LXV, 682. Lucas said further: "For my own part I could not, and cannot, detect any difference between Australians, New Zealanders, and home-bred Englishmen as wide as those which exist between men from Lancashire, Yorkshire, and Devon" (p. 684).

41. B. R. Wise, "The Reorganisation of the Empire: An Australian View," *Nineteenth Century,* LXXIX (1916), 717–24; Everard Cotes, "The Australasian Tour of the Prince of Wales," *ibid.,* LXXXVIII (1920), 967–78. A volume of essays designed to "assist the reader to appreciate the significance of this Greater Britain in the Southern World" just before World War I was James Colwell, ed., *A Century in the Pacific* (London, 1914).

the depression of the 1890's. Echoes of the old critiques could be heard throughout the years before World War I. The single topic which continued to bother the imperialists most was Australia's development policy in the north. Japanese prowess in the Russo-Japanese war seemed, more than ever, to establish the need for aggressive settlement policies to ward off "the yellow peril." Australia's seeming indifference to this problem, or at least her continued resistance to non-British immigration and plantation agriculture, were often discussed and deplored.[42] Australians and their friends in Britain replied to these critiques with explanation of their hopes for a "white Australia," sometimes citing Pearson's *National Life and Character* as defense.[43] Professor J. W. Gregory of Glasgow University reported optimistically in 1910 that the prospects were good for expanding the sugar industry of Queensland with white labor alone.[44] In the 1920's, continuing to play the role of a twentieth-century Roderick Murchison, Gregory urged Australians to bestir themselves and settle the north with white men before colored men took it from them.[45]

42. The *Nineteenth Century,* in particular, kept up a steady stream of complaint. John Douglas, "Asia and Australasia," *Nineteenth Century,* LII (1902), 43–54; Guy H. Scholefield, "The White Peril in Australasia," *ibid.,* LVIII (1905), 198–203; J. A. Hogue, "The Outlook from Australia," *ibid.,* LXXII (1912), 1–10; C. H. Young, "Australia and the Empire," *ibid.,* LXXXVI (1919), 483–92; C. Freeman Murray, "Australia for the White Man," *ibid.,* LXXXIX (1921), 417–27; M. L. MacCallum, "Australia's Territories," *ibid.,* XCVI (1924), 123–36; L. St. Clare Grondona, "A Straight Talk to Australia," *ibid.,* CXXIV (1938), 430–33. Alfred Stead, "Japan and the Policy of a White Australia," *Monthly Review,* July 1904, pp. 84–104. One visitor early in the twentieth century was led even to write a lengthy indictment in reaction to "so much adulation lately of Australia, Australian institutions, and the Australian people by writers with axes to grind and English politicians with party ends to serve." She attacked the quality of political life, social customs, culture, and the appearance of Australian women, which she illustrated with an unflattering diagram. Valerie Desmond, *The Awful Australian* (Sydney, 1911). Some of the same sentiment was expressed by C. E. Jacomb in *"God's Own Country": An Appreciation of Australia* (London, 1914).

43. Oswald P. Law and W. T. Gill, "A White Australia: What it Means," *Nineteenth Century,* LV (1904), 146–54; Meredith Atkinson, "The Washington Conference: Australia's Position," *ibid.,* XC (1921), 941–49.

44. J. W. Gregory, "White Labour in Tropical Agriculture: A Great Australian Experiment," *Nineteenth Century,* LXVII (1910), 368–80. See also *idem, The Dead Heart of Australia* (London, 1906), and *Australia* (Cambridge, 1916), esp. p. 149. A similar but later report was George H. Frodsham, "Tropical Australia: A Great Colonising Experiment," *ibid.,* LXXIV (1913), 333–40.

45. J. W. Gregory, "Inter-Racial Problems and White Colonization in the Tropics," *Report of the British Association for the Advancement of Science,* XCIV (1924), 125–47; and *The Menace of Colour* (London, 1925).

British imperialists were probably encouraged in their admiration for the overall performance of the Australian economy during the early years of the century by attentions from prominent foreign commentators. In particular, Mark Twain while *Following the Equator* reported that to him many Australian qualities and institutions seemed superior not only to those of Britain but also to those of America.[46] In a more restricted area Henry Demerest Lloyd, the prominent American economic reformer, described the labor legislation of Australia and New Zealand in glowing terms as "a substitute for a French Revolution."[47] The French immigrant Paul Wenz helped through his writings to build the image of the Australian workingman as an heroic and virile figure.[48]

Sympathy for Social Reform

One distinct factor in Australia's return to economic respectability was a shift in attitude among British writers and politicians which brought their ideas more into line with long-standing Australian public policy. Late in the 1890's, in sharp contrast to the previous four decades, writings in Britain on Australian experiments with social and economic legislation began to exhibit sympathetic curiosity rather than mere condemnation on grounds of the universality of laisser-faire principles. The evolution of British attitudes toward the economic role of the state is beyond the scope of this study, but clearly it affected significantly views of Australia without any effort on Australia's own part.[49]

46. Mark Twain, *Following the Equator* (New York, 1897), pp. 129, 136, and 225. Pierre Leroy-Beaulieu was less complimentary in his *Les Nouvelles Sociétés anglo-saxonnes* (Paris, 1901). See also André Siegfried, *Democracy in New Zealand* (1904; English trans., London, 1914); C. H. Northcott, *Australian Social Development* (New York, 1918); Robert Schachner, *Die soziale Frage in Australien und Neuseeland* (Jena, 1911).

47. Henry Demarest Lloyd, *Newest England: Notes of a Democratic Traveller in New Zealand, with Some Australian Comparisons* (New York, 1902), and also *A Country Without Strikes* (New York, 1900). A very critical review article describing the latter is by Alice Henry in *Westminster Review*, CLIX (1903), 24–28. Tom Mann claimed that a reading of this book caused him to visit Australia. *From Single Tax to Syndicalism* (London, 1913), p. 29.

48. See Werner P. Friederich, *Australia in Western Imaginative Prose Writings, 1600–1960* (Chapel Hill, 1967), Chap. 7.

49. On the development of British social philosophy during this period, see in particular Melvin Richter, *The Politics of Conscience: T. H. Green and His Age*

A second factor in the softening of views toward Australian social policy was an apparent slowdown in the rate of legislative innovation in Australia itself. The old atmosphere of radical experimentation had thinned, both in the new country and in the eyes of observers. Significantly, a scathing indictment of Australian social and economic legislation as inadequate and insufficient came from the British radical leader Tom Mann, writing from Melbourne in 1904. Mann was furious that Australian labor leaders seemed willing to tolerate and to work within a capitalist system; Mann's indignation rested on the same assessment of Australian radicalism as did the growing sympathy of persons nearer the middle of the political road.[50]

It was noted in Chapters 6 and 7 above that early in the 1890's a few British social reformers were conscious of and interested in Australian experiments with innovative legislation.[51] After Federation this interest spread wide and deep into official and professional quarters. Several spheres of economic policy in particular received attention. For example, Agnes Frances Dodd, a writer on economic developments in the Empire, informed readers of the *Economic Journal* in 1904 that experiments with "Taxation of Land Values in Australasia" should be of interest to Englishmen because they had been "on the whole . . . successful." [52] Five years later an extensive report prepared for Parliament on "Taxation of Land, &c." featured the experiences of the colonies and contained both official documents and testimony from such authorities as T. A. Coghlan and William Pember Reeves.[53] British readers at various times were informed about Australian public ownership, bimetallism, direct taxation, primary education, wom-

---

(Cambridge, Mass., 1964). On the relationship between economics and policy, see Donald Winch, *Economics and Policy: A Historical Study* (New York, 1969).

50. Tom Mann, "The Political and Industrial Situation in Australia," *Nineteenth Century*, LVI (1904), 475–91. See also *idem*, *From Single Tax to Syndicalism* (London, 1913), pp. 29–61.

51. E.g., Charles Bradlaugh, "Regulation by Statute of the Hours of Adult Labour," *Fortnightly Review*, XLVII (1890), 440–60; and contributions on Australia to the *Economic Review* discussed above in Chap. 7.

52. *Economic Journal*, XIV (1904), 401–12. Australian land policy was described first in detail to British readers in W. Epps, *The Land Systems of Australasia* (London, 1894).

53. Cd. 4750 and Cd. 4845, *Accounts and Papers*, 1909, LXXI, esp. pp. 431–50.

en's rights, price regulation, old-age pensions, child-welfare legislation, and in general the moderate nature of all these programs.[54] Even on the subject of tariffs, where in the nineteenth century economists were almost unanimous about Australia's folly, an open mind became not uncommon.[55]

The one aspect of Australian public policy in which there was by a wide margin the greatest interest was labor legislation. An excess of enthusiasm for the Australian models of labor boards and other devices by such early observers as the radical thinkers Charles Bradlaugh, Michael Davitt, and John Garrett Leigh may help to explain the sharpness of some critiques which followed.[56]

54. F. A. Keating, "The Economic Problem: An Australian Appeal," *National Review*, XXX (1897/98), 561–66; A. G. Burke and G. L. Spencer, "Children's Courts in Victoria," *Economic Review*, XXIII (1913), 295–300; "Australia: Report of the Royal Commission on Old-Age Pensions," Cd. 3341, *Accounts and Papers*, 1907, LVI; George H. Frodsham, "Primary Education in Australia," *Nineteenth Century*, LV (1904), 219–28; Vida Goldstein, "The Political Woman in Australia," *ibid.*, LVI (1904), 105–12; *idem*, "Socialism of To-day—An Australian View," *ibid.*, LXII (1907), 406–16; Charles K. MacKellar, "The Neglected Child in New South Wales," *ibid.*, LXXII (1912), 953–63; Jessie Ackermann, *Australia from a Woman's Point of View* (London, 1913), Chaps. 21–24; C. G. Wade, "Nationalisation in Australia," *Fortnightly Review*, CVI (1919), 381–94; *idem*, "Price Fixing by Law," *ibid.*, 692–704; *idem*, "Price-Fixing with Special Reference to Australian Experience," *Report of the British Association for the Advancement of Science*, LXXXVII (1919), 246–47. Timothy Coghlan's testimony before the Select Committee on Income Tax, 1905–6, was said to have been influential. Sir Charles Dilke, "Presidential Address," *Journal of the Royal Statistical Society*, LXX (1907), 559; and Sir Bernard Mallet, "Obituary: Sir Timothy Coghlan," *ibid.*, LXXXIX (1926), 785.

55. E.g., C. F. Bickerdike, "Review of *The New Australian Tariff* (The Tariff Commission, 1907)," *Economic Journal*, XVIII (1908), 92–93; and "Trade with Australia: Board of Trade. Commercial Intelligence Committee. Report upon the Conditions and Prospects of British Trade in Australia, by the Advisory Committee on Commercial Intelligence of the Board of Trade; Based upon Information Collected by their Commissioner Mr. R. J. Jeffray," Cd. 3639, *Accounts and Papers*, 1907, LVI. One enthusiastic advocate of Australian tariffs reported as background that "An Australian Parliament seeks the ideal system of government with the spirit in which navigators sought the North-west Passage." Frank Fox, "The New Protection," *National Review*, LVIII (1911/12), 471. Examples of twentieth-century restatements of nineteenth-century free-trade refrains were C. H. Chomley, "Free Trade New South Wales and Protected Victoria," *Contemporary Review*, LXXXV (1904), 172–85; H. Morgan-Browne, "Australia's Plea for Preference," *ibid.*, XCII (1907), 43–54; and Edward Pulsford, "A Lesson from Australia," *Nineteenth Century*, LXV (1909), 471–79.

56. Charles Bradlaugh, "Regulation by Statute . . ."; Michael Davitt, *Life and Progress in Australasia* (London, 1898), p. 147; John Hoatson, "Anti-Sweating and Factory Legislation in Victoria," *Westminster Review*, CLIV (1900), 398–412; John Garrett Leigh, "The Australian Arbitration Act," *Economic Review*, XII (1902), 212–13; Hartley Williams, "Anti-Sweating Legislation," *Westminster Review*, CLXIX (1908), 167–71. B. R. Wise explained his own contribution to labor legislation in "The Industrial Arbitration Act of New South Wales," *National Review*, XXXIX (1902), 880–96, and in his *The Commonwealth of Australia*

In any event, the subject remained highly controversial. The future British prime minister, Ramsay MacDonald, after a visit to Australia, complained to a meeting of the British Association in 1907 of "the altogether overdrawn praise given to Australasian labour legislation by some writers," and he argued that conditions in Britain were sufficiently different from those in the colony to prevent any simple transfer of these models.[57] Ironically, in view of opinions a few years before, MacDonald believed that Australian legislation was too conservative. It attempted to provide palliatives for a social and economic system which needed fundamental reform. "The Australasian experiments but touch the soiled hem of the garment." [58] Concerning the Australian machinery for averting "sweating" MacDonald stated unequivocally: "Wages Boards misdirect our energies and create a cumbersome industrial machinery, which may look well, but which will not work; only an attack in detail upon the several causes of sweating can have a permanent and beneficial effect upon our industrial condition and upon the victims of its shortcomings." [59]

In hopes of answering through impartial study the question of whether Australia's labor law should be brought to Britain, Ernest Aves, a collaborator of Charles Booth in his London Study, was despatched to Australia and New Zealand by the Home Secretary as a special commissioner of inquiry. He spent more than six months, and in 1908 submitted a detailed report of one hundred and twenty-five pages "On the Wages Boards and Industrial Conciliation and Arbitration Acts of Australia and New Zealand." Aves brought a great deal of information back to the debate over labor legislation, but he did not settle it. In fact, he kept a suitably judicious and impartial distance above the most controversial

(London, 1909). A favorable commentary just before World War I was J. H. Harley, "Labour Legislation and the Australian Elections," *Contemporary Review*, CIV (1913), 86–93. On this subject see also O. de R. Foenander, *Industrial Conciliation and Arbitration in Australia* (Sydney, 1959); *idem, Solving Labour Problems in Australia* (Melbourne, 1941); and *idem, Towards Industrial Peace in Australia* (Melbourne, 1937).

57. J. Ramsay MacDonald, "The Labour Legislation of the Australasian States," *Report of the British Association for the Advancement of Science*, LXXVII (1907), 596.

58. J. Ramsay MacDonald, "Arbitration Courts and Wages Boards in Australasia," *Contemporary Review*, XCIII (1908), 325.

59. J. Ramsay MacDonald, "Sweating and Wages Boards," *Nineteenth Century*, LXIV (1908), 748–62.

aspects of the subject where no final answers could reasonably be offered. On most important questions he was satisfied to transmit the facts he had gathered and to describe the differences of opinion he had encountered. He pointed out that while few doubted the worthy intent of the legislation the aggregate effects remained uncertain: "A fair wage and the maintenance of industrial peace are great objectives, and it is from the desire to secure and maintain these that much of the industrial legislation of Australasia has sprung. The question that is most important, and most difficult to answer, is as to the point, if any, at which the plant of this fair origin is in danger of casting, not a protecting, but a harmful shade." [60] He concluded that it was impossible to judge unequivocally the aggregate merits or ill effects of the Antipodean approach. On the positive side were the benefits of industrial peace, worker security, and protection of weaker groups. On the negative side stood the well-known economic costs of interfering with a free market: distortions, "inequities," and inflexibility during bad times. On balance, the net gain or loss of any particular scheme seemed to depend upon the circumstances in which it operated: "Although advantages and defects of one system or another, or of both, may thus be pointed out, their real significance will always be contingent upon some definite application, either social and personal or industrial, so multitudinous are the differences in character and temperament as well as in trades which the organic unity of industrial life conceals. Thus, the suitability or unsuitability of a system of industrial settlement will depend largely upon the particular circumstances under which, and because of which it is utilised." [61]

Ernest Aves' inconclusive report did not silence the doubt among many British observers about Australian labor legislation. Professional academics, in particular, continued to express skepticism and to argue that it was incumbent upon the advocates of this market intervention to demonstrate convincingly that the economic gain exceeded the cost. Even the two prominent economists L. L. Price and W. J. Ashley, both sympathetic to innovative

60. [E. Aves] "Report from the Secretary of State for the Home Department on the Wages Boards and Industrial Conciliation and Arbitration Acts of Australia and New Zealand by Ernest Aves," Cd. 4167, *Accounts and Papers,* LXXI, 327.

61. *Ibid.,* p. 438.

institutions and policies, concluded after reading Aves' report that the experience of Australia and New Zealand should "give pause to those who advocate the imitation of the particular expedient in our country."[62] H. E. Egerton, first Beit Professor of Colonial History at Oxford, described Australian arbitration court judges as "benevolent deities doling out distributive justice to the different classes of the community," and he feared that the effects must be inflation and continued high tariffs.[63] Sidney Low, the journalist and ardent imperialist, concluded in 1912 that at the very least the current state of social flux in Britain dictated a continuing interest in colonial models: "since recent events have compelled us with a rush to jettison large blocks of our own remaining cargo of *laissez-faire* . . . we can hardly pay too close attention to the experiments which have been conducted in the great sociological and legislative laboratories of the Antipodes."[64] Even though British economists in fact seldom did see fit to make additional on-the-spot studies of the labor law they deplored, they kept informed of works by economists from other nations who did—in the same secondhand way that preachers keep apprised of sin.[65] Almost all serious discussions in Britain of government interference in the labor market came routinely to contain some mention of Australia, favorable or not.[66] Typically, G. F. Shove, fellow of

62. L. L. Price, *Economic Journal,* XVIII (1908), 598. W. J. Ashley, "Wages Boards and Home Workers," *National Review,* LII (1908/09), 636–49. See also A. St. Ledger, *Australian Socialism* (London, 1909); Pollio, "Strikes and the Australian Remedy," *National Review,* LIX (1912), 296–303; P. Airey, "The 'Australian Remedy'," *ibid.,* pp. 1030–35; E. Lyttelton, "Wages Boards," *Contemporary Review,* XCV (1909), 227–38; Mary Theresa Rankin, *Arbitration and Conciliation in Australasia* (London, 1916).

63. H. E. Egerton, "The Australasian Precedent in Social Legislation: An Example or a Warning?" *Economic Review,* XXIV (1914), 162–69.

64. Sidney Low, "Anti-Strike Legislation in Australasia," *Fortnightly Review,* XCI (1912), 585.

65. For example, see reviews of Robert Schachner, *Australien in Politik, Wirtschaft, Kultur* (Jena, 1909), *Economic Journal,* XIX (1909), 583–85; and National Industrial Conference Board, *Arbitration and Wage-Fixing in Australia* (Boston, 1918), *ibid.,* XXIX (1919), 219–26. Other works by foreign observers included Victor S. Clark, *The Labour Movement in Australasia* (New York, 1906); Albert Métin, *Le Socialisme sans doctrines* (Paris, 1901); and Paul Collier, *Minimum Wage Legislation in Australasia* (Albany, N.Y., 1915). See also my *Economic Enquiry,* p. 382 n.

66. E.g., W. L. Hichens, "The Principles by Which Wages Are Determined," *Report of the British Association for the Advancement of Science,* LXXXIX (1921), 95–109; F. Y. Edgeworth, "Equal Pay to Men and Women for Equal

King's College, Cambridge, drew British attention in 1925 to the work of the Queensland Economic Commission on the basic wage because of the grim lessons it contained. "For English economists, the main interest of the Report lies in the confirmation by experience, as there recorded, of some accepted generalisations about the difficulties of applying the living-wage principle." [67]

Professional Economists Relent

Whereas in the 1890's the attitude of most British professional economists toward Australia was that of the priest to the unrepentant sinner, in the twentieth century a change took place toward sympathy and admiration, or at least tolerance.

The views of Alfred Marshall illustrate this change. He removed the harsher comments on Australia from later editions of the *Principles,* and while he remained uneasy about urbanization and certain aspects of Australian labor policy, he was optimistic and congratulatory about the country's economic progress. He wrote in *Industry and Trade:*

> Australia is leading the way bravely in the great endeavour to bring the labouring population as a whole up to a high level of culture and physical enjoyment. It appears indeed that her procedure involves certain forms of restrictions which might prove fatal to a country whose natural resources are on less generous a scale than hers; and the rate of increase of her population is somewhat slow. This retardation, partly due to the predominance of urban conditions, has been caused in great measure by her geographical peculiarities. . . . the splendid energies of her people may be trusted to develop the natural resources of their great country in spite of difficulties.[68]

Other professional economists revealed similar changes of view. Henry Sidgwick gave an optimistic turn to the nineteenth-century notion that Britain could see her own future in Australia: "Our own colonies may teach us valuable lessons of experience as to

---

Work," *ibid.,* XC (1922), 106–32; Henry Clay, "The Public Regulation of Wages in Great Britain," *ibid.,* IIIC (1929), 119–37.

67. G. F. Shove, *Economic Journal,* XXXV (1925), 500.

68. Alfred Marshall, *Industry and Trade* (London, 1923), pp. 160–61. Marshall continued to record the Melbourne land boom as one of the most spectacular examples of sudden and rapid inflation. *Ibid.,* p. 265.

the working of that representative democracy which appears to be our destiny, but which is more completely established there than here."[69] The change in attitude was coincidental also with more favorable comments about policies in which Australia had been a pioneer. S. J. Chapman in his presidential address to the economics section of the British Association in 1909 explained that worker pressure for shorter working hours—an area of reform where the Australian eight-hour day was the most conspicuous success—was only natural and proper. Such a suggestion, in some circles at least, would have been the rankest heresy twenty years before.[70] Even A. C. Pigou, Marshall's successor at Cambridge, when looking for means of averting the "wide-reaching industrial disputes" which he expected at the end of World War I, observed, "Many examples of such machinery are available in the legislation of our colonies in Australasia, South Africa, and Canada."[71]

Among professional economists, the Australian economy had minor champions in the founders of economic history in Great Britain. In general these men objected to facile application of economic theory to the complex problems of distant countries. William James Ashley, as president of the economics section of the British Association in 1907, stated unequivocally that economic science as it then stood could afford but slight guidance to Australia—"it is evident that the lonely figure of the 'marginal shepherd' would give little help in settling, let us say, the Australian shearers' strike."[72] William Cunningham went one step further and suggested that colonies not only found poor advice in the metropolis, they presented "a clear field for the working out of new ideas" which might help to reveal the "philosophical principles as to the manner in which communities ought to develop."[73]

69. Henry Sidgwick, *The Development of European Polity* (London, 1903), p. 6.

70. S. J. Chapman, in *Report of the British Association for the Advancement of Science*, LXXIX (1909), 539–53; and *idem*, "Methods of Industrial Peace," *ibid.*, LXXXII (1912), 546–47.

71. A. C. Pigou, "Labour Problems After the War," *Contemporary Review*, CX (1916), 334–45.

72. W. J. Ashley, "The Present Position of Political Economy," *Economic Journal*, XVII (1907), 479.

73. W. Cunningham, "Unconscious Assumptions in Economics," *Report of the British Association for the Advancement of Science*, LXXV (1905), 471 and 472. Cunningham expressed sympathy for aspects of Australian social policy in *The*

R. H. Inglis Palgrave in 1904 reminded those British readers who might be inclined to regard the young dominions with contempt that with respect to Britain's own prosperity, "Had it not been for our Colonies our plight would have been a sorry one indeed." [74]

The British Association for the Advancement of Science held its annual meeting in Australia in 1914, and the proceedings of Section F, "Economic Science and Statistics," symbolized the newfound professional sympathy for the Australian economy. The president of the Section, Professor E. C. K. Gonner, began his address by stressing the value of comparative studies of "economic development," and he emphasized the special problems younger nations faced in their "dependence" on older lands. He recognized the economic costs of those interventionist policies which for years had concerned British economists, but he saw that, in the alternative of the completely free market, "Two considerations may come into sharp conflict: on the one hand, the rapid production of wealth may be assisted; on the other hand, serious effects in respect of economic progress, nationality, and orderly growth may be experienced." [75] Gonner expressed sympathy for the active role of government in Australia, and he called upon his fellow economists to conduct "careful investigation and detailed inquiry" before offering their condemnations. In the meetings of Section F the British visitors were exposed to results of research in progress by the new generation of native Australian economists and statisticians.

Domestic Defenders

Probably the most important single element in the rehabilitation of Australia's economic reputation was the appearance on the literary scene of prominent and persuasive domestic exponents of colonial policies. It must have seemed to British observers in the nineteenth century that most of the distinguished

Growth of English Industry and Commerce in Modern Times (London, 1903), p. 879.

74. R. H. I. Palgrave, "Colonial Friends and Foreign Rivals," *National Review*, LXII (1903/04), 1000.

75. E. C. K. Gonner, in *Report of the British Association for the Advancement of Science*, LXXXIV (1914), 456.

Australian intellectuals, such as Charles H. Pearson or B. R. Wise, were in opposition to their own national policies, or at least the economic philosophy which lay behind them. Their successors in the twentieth century, while by no means uncritical of details, seemed more often to be in fundamental agreement with the broad goals of the new nation. Australian politicians as well as economists, most notably Alfred Deakin, were more plausible and convincing in the twentieth century, but they are, in the main, outside the scope of this study.[76]

By far the most effective spokesman for Australian economic policies during the early years of the twentieth century was the New Zealand statesman and scholar William Pember Reeves. In a long succession of journal articles, public addresses, and a classic two-volume study, *State Experiments in Australia and New Zealand* (1902), Reeves described with sympathy and understanding practices which usually before in Britain had received little more than scorn and vituperation. Several characteristics of Reeves' work gave it special influence among economists.[77] First, he was thoroughly familiar with his material. While resident in New Zealand he had been both the principal theorist behind and main political advocate of many of the policies which he described. Second, he had close links with prominent British intellectuals, notably the Fabians, and he bore their imprimatur. After serving as agent-general for New Zealand, he became director of the London School of Economics. Third, he could speak the language of economists, and he could hold their attention. He did not talk like a propagandist, and he was willing to admit that there were problems with much reform legislation. He gained a reputation as a committed moderate who deserved an audience. For example, Alfred Marshall wrote to J. N. Keynes in 1900 that he had read "some dozen articles" by Reeves "in various journals," and he added: "I have got the impression that he is so faithful to his 'Fabian' cause, that he can not see any facts which tell against it.

76. E.g., see John La Nauze, *Alfred Deakin* (Melbourne, 1965), *passim.* A contemporary account of Britain's "discovery" of Alfred Deakin is Richard Hain, "Alfred Deakin," *Fortnightly Review,* LXXXII (1907), 101–8.

77. An excellent interpretive biography of Reeves is by Keith Sinclair, *William Pember Reeves, New Zealand Fabian* (Oxford, 1965).

But with this exception, I should think he is a good authority." [78] The fourth characteristic of Reeves' work was the remarkable energy with which he presented his case: he wrote extensively for the *National Review*, the *Economic Journal*, the *Economist*, the *Statist*, and *The Times*, and he addressed such bodies as the British Association, the Political Economy Club and the Royal Colonial Institute.[79] In many of his writings, Reeves' main focus was New Zealand, but for his readers and listeners the well-known colonial economic heresy was the main subject of interest, and few anyway could draw clear distinctions among parts of the Antipodes.

The second especially effective native exponent of the Australian economy resident in Britain was the statistician Timothy Coghlan, who arrived as agent-general for New South Wales in 1905. Coghlan's writings were well known as early as the 1880's when he began to assume the mantle of senior statistician from the Victorian Henry Hayter. By the turn of the century, Coghlan's various official publications, such as *The Wealth and Progress of New South Wales* and *Statistics of the Seven Colonies of Australasia*, were used widely as primary sources by most general writers. To give only one citation to illustrate Coghlan's high

78. Alfred Marshall to J. N. Keynes, 28 March 1900, Keynes Papers, Marshall Library, Cambridge University.

79. See Sinclair, *William Pember Reeves*, pp. 247–48, 256, and 321. Samples of Reeves' contributions to the literature of economics are "The Australian Labour Ministry," *Independent Review*, June 1904, pp. 108–23; "The Working of Compulsory Arbitration in Labour Disputes," *National Review*, XXX (1897/98), 360–70; "Criticisms of Australasian Democracy," *ibid.*, XXXI (1898), 587–601, defense against French and American critics; "Colonial Governments as Money-Lenders," *ibid.*, XXXVI (1900/01), 579–91; "The Exclusion of Aliens and Undesirables from Australia and New Zealand," *ibid.*, XXXVIII (1901/02), 596–615; "Protective Tariffs in Australia and New Zealand," *Economic Journal*, IX (1899), 36–44; "The Minimum Wage Law in Victoria and South Australia," *ibid.*, XI (1901), 334–44; "Mr. Wise's Industrial Arbitration Act," *ibid.*, XII (1902), 320–26; "Land Taxes in Australasia," *ibid.*, XXI (1911), 513–26; "Colonial Governments as Money-Lenders," *Report of the British Association for the Advancement of Science*, LXX (1900), 848–49; "Presidential Address: Land Taxes in Australasia," *ibid.*, LXXXI (1911), 450–58. A report is printed of a talk by Reeves to the Political Economy Club, in 1912, on "compulsory arbitration." He joined the club in 1908. See *Political Economy Club, Minutes of Proceedings, 1899–1920 Roll of Members and Questions Discussed, 1821–1920*, VI (London, 1921), 169 and 366. Favorable reviews of *State Experiments* in the two principal economics journals are by Edward Jenks in *Economic Journal*, XIII (1903), 215–19; and by Sidney Ball in *Economic Review*, XIII (1903), 295–315. Ball saw Reeves' material as having a significant "bearing on problems in our country."

reputation, Pember Reeves himself acknowledged in the preface to *State Experiments* that Coghlan "has the first place as a general authority." [80] Coghlan's monumental four-volume *Labour and Industry in Australia* (1918) became immediately an authoritative account of economic events leading up to Federation. The nearly twenty-five hundred pages were enough to daunt the staunchest of readers, but at least the detailed chronicle was there to dignify and make respectable the developments. Coghlan did not by any means whitewash those incidents and activities in the 1890's which for many years had drawn unfavorable attention. In fact, a reviewer in the *Economic Journal* drew a moral from the work which would have been acceptable even to Fortescue or Fairfield. He said: "It is well always to bear in mind the old adage about fools and angels; but there is one conclusion which he who runs may draw from the facts of history. Again and again there is borne in upon us the sense of the folly of man and of the bounty of Nature." Yet this writer, unlike the Cassandras of the preceding century, ended on a bright note: "The reader's last thought will perhaps be the good fortune that has attended the country at more than one crisis of its history. This may have helped to breed the optimism which seems indigenous to the soil and race." [81] Coghlan had not changed Australia's story completely, but he had placed it in new perspective and, where necessary, had purged it of egregious error.

Several minor Australian exponents of the new national economy also wrote for the British audience in the years around World War I. Arthur Duckworth, a Sydney businessman and enthusiastic amateur economist, kept up a flow of reports on events for the *Economic Journal.* In his writings Duckworth was mindful of the bitter early criticisms of Australia; in 1912, for example, he

80. Coghlan's work is discussed in my *Economic Enquiry in Australia* (Durham, 1966), and in E. C. Fry, "Labour and Industry in Australia," *Historical Studies,* XIV (1970), 430–39. Another general writer who depended heavily on Coghlan was William Parr Greswell; see his *The Growth and Administration of the British Colonies, 1837–1897* (London, 1898). Sir Charles Dilke paid high tribute to Coghlan and the contributions of Australian statisticians generally in his presidential address to the Royal Statistical Society in 1907. *Journal of the Royal Statistical Society,* LXX (1907), 553–81.

81. H. E. Egerton, "Review of *Labour and Industry in Australia* by T. A. Coghlan," *Economic Journal,* XXIX (1919), 234 and 238.

surveyed recent vital statistics to show that contrary to some claims "the British race settled in Australia" had not shown "signs of decreasing vigour and vitality." [82] Two writers dealt repeatedly with the Australian economy for the *Economic Review,* a journal which continued to be sympathetic toward a positive economic role for the state. Percy F. Rowland, in the same tradition as Davitt and Reeves, described Australian social philosophy as "conservative socialism" practiced in a true egalitarian fashion whereby "every politician constitutes himself every other politician's valet." [83] R. E. Macnaghten explained and defended such specific policies as construction of a new capital city and continuance of tariff protection.[84] Descriptive papers by Australian economists to the meeting in Australia of the British Association in 1914 were made available to a wider audience through publication in several British journals.[85] In 1915, relatively unnoticed because of the war, R. C. Mills published in London his doctoral thesis, *The Colonization of Australia, 1829–1842,* which demonstrated that native-born Australians were capable of making specialized contributions to their own economic history as well as to an understanding of recent events. As the war ended, Sir Charles Wade set out to bring Coghlan's work up to date with a volume of lectures entitled *Australia, Problems, and Prospects.*[86]

82. A. Duckworth, "White Australia: A Study of Australian Vital Statistics," *Economic Journal,* XXII (1912), 421–35. Duckworth was less optimistic about the Australian economy in the 1920's; see "Australian Notes," *ibid.,* XXXV (1925), 502–5; and "Australian Notes," *ibid.,* XXXVI (1926), 130–33. On Duckworth's career as an economist see S. J. Butlin, "Arthur Duckworth," *ibid.,* LIV (1944), 443–45, and my *Economic Enquiry in Australia, passim.*

83. Percy F. Rowland, "Political Life in Australia," *Economic Review,* XII (1902), 257–67. A proud description by Rowland of the economic potential of the new nation was "The Economic Resources and Prospects of the Australian Commonwealth," *ibid.,* 172–84. Rowland had been a student at Oxford of Hastings Rashdall, one of the editors of the *Economic Review.* He collected the various articles which grew out of a visit to Australia in a book, *The New Nation* (London, 1903).

84. R. E. Macnaghten, "Australia's Opportunity," *Economic Review,* XIII (1903), 280–94; "Is Free Trade a Fallacy?" *ibid.,* XIV (1904), 23–38; "A Study in Exports and Imports," *ibid.,* XV (1905), 184–202.

85. Papers which were published in the *Economic Journal,* XXV (1915), were G. S. Beeby, "The Artificial Regulation of Wages in Australia," pp. 321–28; F. A. A. Russell, "Industrial Arbitration in New South Wales," pp. 329–46; and F. W. Eggleston, "The Australian Democracy and Its Economic Problems," pp. 347–59.

86. Sir Charles G. Wade, *Australia, Problems and Prospects* (Oxford, 1919).

A Brighter Image at Last

By World War I the Australian economy was for the first time perceived by British observers in warm hues and was described with admiration. Two developments help to explain the change. First, the models of social theory by which Australia had for long been judged had evolved to make accepted standards closer to the general perception of Australia's performance. Notions had altered both about the best means of designing and regulating a modern industrial economy and about the handling of a disintegrating empire. Second, the information from which mental pictures were constructed improved in quality and amount. More and more data about Australia came from "friendly" sources such as imperialists, sympathetic students of social reform, and colonists who had gained steadily in self-confidence and effectiveness as communicators. A generally healthy economy after 1900 and the fact of Federation provided the necessary background for positive reports. In essence, the image of Australia was brighter because of new raw material and because of new filters through which this material was seen and given meaning.

· 9 ·

"The Utopia of Practical Economists"

After World War I a marked difference from earlier years was the lower level of interest in Australian affairs in Britain. In the generalist quarterlies, monthlies, and weeklies the Australian social and economic systems ceased to attract much serious attention. The country might still on occasion excite anger or praise, but it was no longer the puzzle it was thought to be in the nineteenth century. Except for a few moments of special crisis Australia could no longer command center stage. This chapter covers a time period much longer than its predecessors—from World War I until the present day—because the material on which it is based is both thinner and more repetitive.

The Nineteen-Twenties: A Short Reprise

In the unsettled years after World War I, desultory skirmishing went on between the newly effective defenders of the Australian economy and the remaining critics. In some respects this period resembled a minor relapse into the dark days of the 1890's. Most of the old charges against Australians were revived, about their social policies and about their national character.

In the 1920's the *Edinburgh Review*, edited by the doctrinaire free-trader Harold Cox, and the *National Review* both contained occasional attacks on Australian economic policy from a Tasmanian, F. A. W. Gisborne, who equaled Fortescue or Fairfield thirty years before in the intensity of his criticism.[1] Some other

1. Gisborne wrote about most aspects of the economy. For example, he said that defenders of Australia's selective immigration policy had "exhausted the whole vocabulary of cant in defending their faith." "The Future of Tropical Australia," *Edinburgh Review*, CCXXXVIII (1923), 49, and "Australia's Vital

commentators, noting the restiveness of Western Australia, observed that even the federal structure was in danger.[2] Still others wrote about what they saw as continued selfishness in land policy, labor radicalism, and the possibility of open class warfare, especially in Queensland.[3] But in their comments none went beyond what were by then old refrains.

During the 1920's Frederic Benham, the last distinguished representative of British academic economists deeply skeptical of

---

Problem," *National Review*, LXXIX (1922), 255–67. He had treated the subject as early as 1909 in "The Monroe Doctrine of Australia," *Chambers' Journal*, Jan. 1909, pp. 61–64. He described Australian protection as "self-flagellation": "For some years past she has been vigorously belabouring herself with a four-thonged scourge, possibly for the good of her soul, but unquestionably not for that of her corporate body." "Protection in Australia," *Edinburgh Review*, CCXXXIX (1924), 162. He saw the Australian system of industrial arbitration as the product of "the pernicious designs of a small body of active and determined men, who are undoubtedly trying to introduce the plague of Bolshevism into the Commonwealth . . . an end should be made of a system of compulsory arbitration, which in its operation not only conflicts most disastrously with the requirements of reason and economics, but violates the basic principles of freedom and justice." "Arbitration in Australia," *Edinburgh Review*, CCXLI (1925), 246–47, and "The Recoil of the 'Living Wage' in Australia," *National Review*, LXXVII (1921), 848–61. He predicted disaster from a national debt which was "far too heavy" and "costs of government and taxation" which were "excessive." "Australia's Economic Troubles," *Edinburgh Review*, CCXLVII (1928), 134–44. He described land policy in the Northern Territories as "An Australian Comedy," *National Review*, LXXXVI (1920/21), 131–40. In 1928 he warned of the danger of a Communist take-over. "Reds and Pinks in Australia," *National Review*, XCII (1928/29), 219–34. F. W. Eggleston reported in the same spirit in 1929 that the "lesson of Australian experience is that political remedies cannot be relied on to cure economic evils." "Australian Experiments in State Socialism," *Edinburgh Review*, CCL (1929), 271.

2. M. L. MacCallum, "Constitutional Issues in Australia," *Nineteenth Century*, XCI (1922), 278–87.

3. W., "Queensland and the Australian Labour Movement," *Fortnightly Review*, CVI (1919), 616–23. A new expression of the old allegation that Australia selfishly was misusing lands which rightfully were imperial property, was the volume by Fleetwood Chidell, *Australia—White or Yellow?* (London, 1926). A general indictment of a supposed Australian "Bolshevism" was "Australia After the War," *National Review*, LXXIV (1919/20), 135–40. Other critiques were P. Airey, "Arbitration in Extremis: An Australian Study," *National Review*, LXXIV (1919/20), 704–09; James Edmond, "A Great Australian Failure," *National Review*, LXXXI (1923), 296–311, on the growth of cities; James Edmond, "Some Australian Complications," *National Review*, XCII (1928/29), 900–907. J. B. Bryce concluded that with respect to the role of government in the economy "the results so far obtained do not encourage the extension of the experiments tried." *Modern Democracies* (New York, 1921), p. 259. Queensland, with a succession of labor governments, was a favorite object of attack in the 1920's. E.g., C. P. Kininmonth, "Labour Government in Queensland," *Contemporary Review*, CXXIX (1926), 628–36. Professor J. W. Gregory continued to chide Australian economists for their conservatism in estimating the continent's capacity to absorb immigrants. "Capacity of Australia for Immigration," *Contemporary Review*, CXXXVI (1929), 476–82.

Australia, came on the scene. He went out to teach in Sydney University in 1923 from the London School of Economics, where he had studied under Edwin Cannan and, according to Professor S. J. Butlin, arrived "a self-confident, occasionally even brash young man" who "irritated politician and business man alike, volunteering Tariff Board evidence with a sturdy free-trade foundation."[4] Until his departure in 1931 Benham defended stoutly strict observance of free market principles in numerous journal articles and in his book *The Prosperity of Australia* (London, 1928).[5]

Two Australians, Hal Colebatch, former agent-general for Western Australia, and E. C. Dyason, both replied vigorously in early issues of the *Economic Record,* the journal of the Australian economists, to what they took to be misrepresentation of Australian economic conditions by English commentators. Dyason complained of the "hundreds of pregnant warnings" which had been issued regularly for almost seventy-five years, despite the unblemished record of payment on Australian government securities. A difference in Dyason's reply from those of his predecessors was that now he could present substantial data about Australia's national income and prospects for growth.[6]

Among visitors during the 1920's, one of the most sympathetic and perceptive was the future prime minister Anthony Eden. His principal observation was that such Australian economic policies as tariff protection and immigration restriction were rooted in complex social and political soil. British commentators on these policies were likely to produce little more than facile critiques. Eden was particularly impressed by the capacity of the Australian federal system to resolve conflicting pressures and support a viable nation state. He wrote:

4. S. J. Butlin, "Frederic Benham: 1900–62," *Economic Record,* XXXVIII (1962), 386–88.

5. Another work in the same free-trade tradition was Nancy Windett, *Australia as Producer and Trader, 1920–1932* (London, 1933), esp. Chap. 2.

6. Both Colebatch and Dyason were angered by a pamphlet entitled *Australian Finance* (1936) by S. R. Cooke and E. H. Davenport. Hal Colebatch, "Australian Credit as Viewed from London," *Economic Record,* III (1927), 217–27; and E. C. Dyason, "The Australian Public Debt," *ibid.,* 161–74. Dyason was taken to task by the Australian businessman Sir Lennon Raws for suggesting that strict commercial tests need not be applied to public investment. W. L. Raws, "Australian Loan Expenditure," *Economic Record,* IV (1928), 209–26.

The task of government in Australia is in vivid contrast to that task at home. The problems are of another texture and upon another plane. The government upon a democratic basis of a continent of so vast an area and of so sparse a population, where reign varied conditions of climate and of occupation, is beset with difficulties which the closely herded countries of Europe are spared, and which their inhabitants must find it a difficult task to visualise. The problems of administration are proportionately greater. The adaptability of home-bred institutions is here on its trial; the test has been well met.[7]

After World War I there came forward the greatest Australian international publicist of them all, Douglas Berry Copland, a New Zealander and professor of economics first at the University of Tasmania and then at the University of Melbourne. In 1920 Copland began a stream of economic analysis and description of conditions in Australia and New Zealand in books, articles, and notes for professional journals. His style was confident and his prescriptions for reform were closely in accord with the conventions of the time on matters of the greatest controversy, especially money, banking, public finance, and international trade. The message Copland was able to put across to British economists more effectively than anyone before him was that Australia's economic policies and practices were different from those of Great Britain because, at least in part, the problems, conditions, and objectives were not the same. Moreover, Copland showed that these policies and practices could be supported enthusiastically by an observer who was trained in scientific economics and was neither blind nor narrowly self-interested.[8]

7. Anthony Eden, *Places in the Sun* (London, 1926), pp. 101–2. Another complimentary account is L. St. Clare Grondona, *The Kangaroo Keeps on Talking* (London, 1924).

8. Copland's contributions on Australian topics to the *Economic Journal* alone included "Currency Inflation and Price Movements in Australia," XXX (1920), 484–509; "The Economic Situation in Australia, 1918–23," XXXIV (1924), 32–51; "Some Problems of Taxation in Australia," XXXIV (1924), 387–97; "The Commonwealth Bank of Australia," XXXV (1925), 145–48; "Notes on Australian Exchange," XXXV (1925), 645–49; "Financial Relations of the States and the Commonwealth of Australia," XXXVII (1927), 590–96; "The Australian Problem," XL (1930), 638–49; "Readjustment in Australia," XLI (1931), 534–49; "New Zealand's Economic Difficulties and Expert Opinion," XLII (1932), 371–79; "Australian Banking Policy in the Crisis," XLII (1932), 583–87; "Problems of Federal Finance in Australia," XLV (1935), 280–85; "Some Problems of Australian Banking," XLVII (1937), 686–96. A special issue of the *Economic Record* entitled "Essays in Honour of Sir Douglas Copland," contains memoirs and a bibliography of Copland's writings. XXXVI (1960), 1–178.

Copland's most important asset with a British audience was his professional respectability. Unlike even Coghlan or Reeves he had never been a senior public servant and therefore could not be accused of employee bias when discussing national policy. In addition, he was an active organizer of the other Australian economists and in 1924–25 was instrumental in founding both a local Economic Society and the first domestic professional journal, the *Economic Record.*[9] Copland was not loath to criticize as well as to defend. During the postwar inflation he followed most respectable economists in other countries in calling for "a restriction of the Australian note issue." [10] Yet shortly afterward he took special pride in reporting both on the Australian advance toward true central banking and on various imaginative experiments with federal economic arrangements.[11]

In 1929, together with L. F. Giblin, J. B. Brigden, E. C. Dyason, and C. H. Wickens, Copland issued a "report from the economists" on *The Australian Tariff* which, although not satisfying all doubters, gave Australian protection its first reasoned appraisal and was greeted as an important contribution to the literature of international trade.[12] *The Australian Tariff* probably did not convert many British economists to the virtues of protection, but it did at least examine the question in terms which they found reasonable, and it showed that there were measurable "national benefits" to place against the well-known costs. Copland and his colleagues stressed among the positive results of the tariff its ability to provide an increased volume of industrial employment. Englishmen might disagree that this achievement was worth the sacrifice of forgone primary production and consumer satisfaction, but as an insular people who had been conscious throughout their existence of external threat, they could appreciate the Australian

9. See S. J. Butlin, "The Hundredth *Record*," *Economic Record*, XLII (1966), 508–19.

10. "Currency Inflation and Price Movements in Australia," p. 509.

11. "The Commonwealth Bank of Australia" and "Financial Relations of the States and the Commonwealth of Australia."

12. A skeptical review of the tariff report in the *Economic Journal* was by Arnold Plant, XL (1930), 284–87. Frederic C. Benham had stated his opposition to Australian tariff, taxation, and wage policy on grounds of economic distortions in his book *The Prosperity of Australia* (London, 1928). He expressed continuing doubts in *Economic Journal*, XLIV (1934), 135. The report and other works by Copland are discussed in my *Economic Enquiry in Australia*, esp. pp. 35–39.

desire for population growth and the yearning for a balanced and viable nation-state. No longer could Australian tariffs be pictured simply as eccentric heresy and pursuit of a pied piper's tune.

Douglas Copland's works were not the only writings read in Britain which pictured the Australian economy in a favorable light during the 1920's, but among economists they had the greatest impact.[13]

One of Copland's special projects, the *Economic Record,* began publication in 1925 and helped to improve the image of the Australian economy among academic economists abroad. One example may illustrate the journal's effect. In 1925 the Yale geographer Ellsworth Huntington published a book entitled *West of the Pacific* in which he reflected on a seven-week visit to Australia. The method and conclusions of this work were remarkably like several of the nineteenth century travelers' accounts. However, the work received a reception very different from those predecessors. Now Australia had a body of professional social scientists ready to examine skeptically the conclusions of outsiders—even eminent ones—and where necessary meet them head on.

In contrast to the earlier visitors, Huntington was complimentary about most aspects of Australian life; however, like them, he made loose statistical extrapolations and facile applications of the theory of evolution in order to reach what appeared to be preconceived conclusions. He listed various Australian national characteristics which he regarded as unusual, and he attributed them to natural selection both through the immigration process and as a result of environmental conditioning. He discussed the notorious proclivities for city life, sport, and government control of the economy, emulation of Britain, cultural homogeneity, and unreasonable optimism about the future.[14] Throughout the work Huntington stressed the role of genetics in Australian history. "Many of

13. Other works in a positive vein were J. R. Collins, *The Public Debts of Australia* (London, 1929); Kenneth T. Henderson, "Migration: An Australian View," *Contemporary Review*, CXXXV (1929), 491–97; Julius L. F. Vogel, "The Fiscal Policy of Our Overseas Dominions," *Fortnightly Review*, CXVIII (1925), 113–21.

14. E. Huntington, *West of the Pacific* (New York, 1925), pp. 309, 315, 328, and 372.

the peculiarities of Australia seem to be largely explained by natural selection."[15] In general, he concluded that the selection process had produced good citizens who were healthy, contented, and strong. His main worry was that the climate in the tropical regions would lead to degeneration and the appearance of poor white "crackers."[16] In his terminology as well as in his analysis Huntington betrayed the transference to Australia of his New England view of the American South. In the following comments on the Queenslanders he might have been writing about the Mississipians or Carolinians:

> Although their parents or grandparents were highly selected, and hence able to cope with the climate, the children, according to a fundamental biological law, tend to return to the average condition of their race. Hence, although inheriting a certain degree of fitness for a tropical climate, they presumably are not so well fitted as their parents. Moreover, they lack the advantage of the vigor that comes from a childhood spent in a bracing climate.[17]

Ultimately, Huntington thought, the Queenslanders might adapt satisfactorily to their environment, but for the next few generations at least the situation was not encouraging.[18]

Huntington's book started a heated international controversy from which he did not emerge unscathed. Both the Commonwealth Statistician, C. H. Wickens, and R. W. Cilento, a physician whose data Huntington had used, reported that the evidence simply did not prove his case. Huntington's critics did not propose counterhypotheses for the application of evolutionary theory to Australian society; they simply denied the legitimacy of his particular conclusions.[19] Such critiques as these of one distinguished foreign commentator on Australian society served notice

15. *Ibid.*, pp. 369 and 370.
16. *Ibid.*, pp. 351, 353, 374, 385 and 390.
17. *Ibid.*, p. 380.
18. *Ibid.*, pp. 385 and 390.
19. C. H. Wickens, "Vitality of White Races in Low Latitudes," *Economic Record,* III (1927), 117–26; *idem,* "Dr. Huntington and Low Latitudes," *ibid.*, VI (1930), 123–27; R. W. Cilento, "Rejoinder to Professor Huntington," *ibid.*, pp. 127–32; *idem,* "The White Settlement of Tropical Australia," in P. D. Phillips and G. L. Wood, *The Peopling of Australia* (Melbourne, 1930), pp. 222–45. Huntington's reply to his critics was "Natural Selection and Climate in Northern Australia," *Economic Record,* V (1929), 185–201.

to others that in future they would be required to defend their views thoroughly.[20]

The Second Great Depression: Echoes from the Past

In the late 1920's the second Great Depression hit Australia with a vengeance. At the mercy of fluctuations in capital flows and foreign demand for raw materials, Australian gross domestic product fell from £798.5 million in 1927–28 to £533.4 million in 1931–32 (in 1910/11 constant £ from 423.7 to 386.9).[21] Soon after the first signs of serious trouble in 1929 an "Economic Mission" was dispatched from the Bank of England to inspect the situation and to offer advice. The somber missionary appeared to Australians like an avenging nemesis, with the long shadow before him of the 1890's and a name that still brings a chill to Australian bones, Sir Otto Niemeyer. The tone and general outline of Sir Otto's assessment were remarkably similar to those of his predecessors forty years before. He looked for the roots of the current crisis as much in the character and moral condition of the Australian people as in the contemporary world situation, and he postulated an imposing list of character faults. Most fundamental, he thought, was the "natural optimism of the Australians," which, he implied, degenerated in critical conditions into simple fecklessness. "So long as it is generally believed in Australia that there is an unlimited market abroad for Australian goods, and that something will turn up, it will be difficult to face the realities of the situation." [22] Manifestations of Australian financial irresponsibility,

20. An example of a more modest critique of inaccuracy abroad was a review by E. O. G. Shann of C. R. Fay's *Imperial Economy and Its Place in the Formation of Economic Doctrine, 1600–1932* in *Economic Record*, XI (1935), 129–33.

21. Noel Butlin, *Australian Domestic Product, Investment and Foreign Borrowing, 1861–1938/39* (Cambridge, 1962), pp. 6–7 and 460–61. Various documents relevant to the depression are reproduced in L. J. Louis and Ian Turner, *The Depression of the 1930's* (Sydney, 1968). See also C. B. Schedvin, *Australia and the Great Depression* (Sydney, 1970).

22. "Sir Otto Niemeyer's Statement" at the Melbourne Conference of July and August 1930, reprinted in *Banker's Magazine*, CXXX (1930), 759–66; and in E. O. G. Shann and D. B. Copland, *The Crisis in Australian Finance, 1929 to 1931* (Australia, 1931), pp. 18–19, and *Report of the British Economic Mission* (Canberra, 1929). William Pember Reeves in 1930 reported that Niemeyer had "a good head where money matters are concerned and his verdict will undoubtedly carry weight in London." Keith Sinclair, *William Pember Reeves, New*

he declared, were her continuing proclivity for tariffs and her "considerable unfunded and maturing debts both internally and externally; in addition to which she has on her hands a very large programme of loan works for which no financial provision has been made."[23] Finally, Niemeyer accused the Australians of the sin with which they had been charged so often before—living beyond their means. "There is also evidence to show that the standard of living in Australia has reached a point which is economically beyond the capacity of the country to bear without a considerable reduction of costs resulting in increased per capita output."[24]

Responses to the report of the British Economic Mission varied. Some Australians, as in the 1890's, listed and described the country's long-run accomplishments in the hope of counterbalancing the criticism.[25] But again, as in the 1920's, Douglas Copland and the other professional economists were ready to put events in better perspective. To a British audience Copland emphasized that external forces—dislocations in international trade and factor flows—were the major determinants of Australia's fate. In contrast to Niemeyer and the commentators of the 1890's who blamed internal policies above all for the misfortunes of depression, he argued that Australia, as a dependent economy, was only partially master in its own house.[26] Copland did not claim that Australia was totally blameless in arranging its own affairs, nor did he advocate laissez-faire to combat current problems. Rather, he thought Australia should attempt to deal with the onset of depression in the same way as other nations, with clear recognition of the worldwide phenomenon and of its own special conditions.

Zealand Fabian (Oxford, 1965), p. 344. D. O. Malcolm, another member of the "British Economic Mission" voiced his concerns about Australian protection, arbitration, and inattention to staple industries in "Impressions of Australia," *National Review*, XCIV (1929/30), 65–72.

23. "Sir Otto Niemeyer's Statement," p. 21.

24. *Ibid.*, p. 27.

25. E.g., Arthur Jose, "Peopling the Empire," *Edinburgh Review*, CCL (1929), 242–56; *idem*, *Australia: Human and Economic* (London, 1932); J. R. Collins, *The Public Debts of Australia* (London, 1929, published in part in *The Times*, April 13 and 15, 1929); Pytheas, "An Australian Looks at England," *National Review*, XCV (1930), 490–98.

26. D. B. Copland, "The Australian Problem," *Economic Journal*, XL (1930), 638–49.

He himself advocated a set of Draconian measures to combat the crisis, with drastic monetary policy the crucial tool. Copland summarized his recommendations as follows: "(a) real wages should be reduced by 10 percent; (b) an increase in the exchange rate to a discount of 20 percent should be made; (c) an easing of the credit situation by the purchase of Government securities through the Central Bank; (d) the balancing of the budgets through a reduction in Government expenditures and an increase in taxation; (e) some restoration of overseas borrowing to ease the burdens of crisis." [27]

The Australian economists were successful in obtaining a hearing from the political leaders. Copland joined Professors Giblin, Melville, and Shann, and the under-treasurers of every state except New South Wales, in forming an advisory committee to the Australian Loan Council.[28] Their recommendations were referred by the Council to a conference of state premiers, and Copland was able to report triumphantly in 1931 that "To a large extent the policy followed by Australia has been on these lines" the economists had proposed, now in a form called the Premiers' Plan. At this point the Australian economy reached a pinnacle of respectability with British economists it had not ever approached at any time in the preceding century. Without attempting to judge here whether or not the measures which the Australian economists proposed were best for the country, it can be reported that many prominent economists elsewhere thought that they were and became aware that their professional colleagues in Australia had had a powerful hand in the policy formulation and implementation.[29] W. R. Hancock was quick to point out to admiring Englishmen that Australia's pioneering antidepression

27. D. B. Copland, "Readjustment in Australia," *Economic Journal,* XLI (1931), 535–36.

28. These events are described in detail in F. A. Bland and R. C. Mills, "Financial Reconstruction: An Examination of the Plan Adopted at the Premiers' Conference, 1931," *Economic Record,* VII (1931), 161–76; and E. R. Walker, *Australia in the World Depression* (London, 1933). Relevant documents are contained in E. O. G. Shann and D. B. Copland, *The Battle of The Plans* (Sydney, 1931).

29. Australian policy in the crisis, and the role of economists in it, were described to Americans in a special issue of the *Annals of the American Academy of Political and Social Science,* No. 158 (1931), edited by Copland, entitled "An Economic Survey of Australia."

measures were, after all, only the most recent case in which the colonies had shown the way to the motherland.[30]

When in 1932 J. M. Keynes himself was commissioned by the Melbourne *Herald* "to write on the economic problems confronting this country, dealing particularly with the Premiers' Plan and the report of the Experts' Committee" he concluded that, if anything, Australia's plans might be too drastic in their effect.[31] Having moved by this time well along the road to his *General Theory*, with its relative emphasis on fiscal over monetary policy, Keynes was skeptical about the desirability of such painful monetary and price level adjustments as those proposed by Copland and his colleagues. He wrote:

> I sympathise intensely with the general method of approach which underlies the new proposals of the economists. I am sure that the Premiers' Plan last year saved the economic structure of Australia. I am not prepared to dispute that another dose of the same medicine may be necessary. But there are some aspects of the Experts' Report which cause me hesitation. I am fearful lest a degree of readjustment should be attempted which is impracticable in the environment of present world conditions. . . .
>
> It is a serious mistake, in my judgment, for any country to attempt a complete adjustment to the present level of wholesale prices, whether measured in gold or in sterling. The long continuance of this level of prices is not a practical working hypothesis. It is one of the things like the end of the world, against which, though it is possible, it is not sensible to insure.[32]

Thus, to the "Expert" Australian economists who called for sharp reductions in prices and pursuit of fiscal orthodoxy, Keynes preached moderation and remembrance that the true objective of economic policy should be recovery and not observance of any particular practices no matter how sacred. He continued:

> If, therefore, I were an Australian economist advising Mr. Lyons today, I should be decidedly moderate in my view. I should recommend him to ride his difficult and suffering steed with as light a rein as he dare. I should not press for heroic measures. It is a time to chas-

30. W. R. Hancock, "England and Australia: A Study in Democratic Development," *Nineteenth Century*, CXIV (1933), 29–50.

31. J. M. Keynes, in the Melbourne *Herald*, June 27, 1932. The article is reprinted in L. J. Louis and Ian Turner, *The Depression of the 1930's*, pp. 217–23.

32. *Ibid.*

tise gently. Moreover, I should have sufficient confidence to take this line, precisely because Australia has done so much already, and has been relatively so successful in her programme of necessary adjustment—if only, in spite of disappointments, she could, by comparison with the state of others, know it!

There is more chance of improving the profitableness of business by fostering enterprise and by such measures as public works than by a further pressure on money-wages or further forcing of exports. The problems of the Budget and of Unemployment are more pressing than that of the Balance of Trade.[33]

It was certainly a novelty for Australia to be charged in this way with an excess of economic virtue rather than with a total absence thereof. Keynes was able to report that even in the trough of depression, because of her proven economic responsibility "Australia's credit is rising rapidly in the estimation of the London market." He ended his article by assuring Australian readers: "The acuteness of your domestic political struggle has at least had the advantage of throwing into the limelight the quality of the intentions and principle of the Commonwealth Government, which London, though undemonstrative, profoundly appreciates." Australians, in this testament, found that they were accused only of failing to keep up to date fully with John Maynard Keynes and his fast-moving ideas.

Through the 1930's Copland continued to describe proudly to his British audience the sustained pressure kept up by wise economists on government in Australia. As evidence of their success he cited the creation of an effective central bank and the establishment of a Commonwealth Grants Commission to ease "problems of federal finance." On the latter body the respected economist L. F. Giblin sat.[34] In 1937 Copland pictured the Report of a Royal Commission to Inquire into the Monetary and Banking System in Australia as yet one more confirmation of the decision by Australian governments to tread firmly the paths of economic righteousness and to accept advice from their academic advisors.[35]

33. *Ibid.*

34. D. B. Copland, "Australian Banking Policy in the Crisis," pp. 583–87; *idem*, "Problems of Federal Finance in Australia," pp. 280–85. Copland even disputed the criticisms of an English author in the preface to her own book. Nancy Windett, *Australia as Producer and Trader, 1920–1932* (London, 1933), pp. ix–xiii.

35. D. B. Copland, "Some Problems of Australian Banking," pp. 686–96.

What is most significant is that Copland's message was received abroad and taken to heart.

The praise for Australia's performance in the depression of the 1930's became often as extravagant as the condemnation of the 1890's. The *National Review*, a periodical which through the 1920's had contained stinging indictments of the Australian economy, reported in 1933:

> in whatever political adventures Australia indulges, she will always emerge that much saner for the trial, purged by the rejection of undesirable or unworkable experiments, and tenaciously clinging to any new maxims which prove successful. Australia is, fundamentally, a nation governed by common sense, ready to accept new ideas and methods, but equally ready to throw out any false gods of slipshod economics.[36]

Geoffrey Ellis announced in 1934 that "Australia faces the world to-day: of good credit and ready to begin again." [37] R. G. Hawtrey found Australian policy "appropriate" and "judicious," and he noted proudly that "Australia anticipated the United States in seeking guidance from a brain trust to deal with the depression." [38] Herbert Heaton, an Englishman who had recently re-emigrated from Australia to the United States, wrote in similar vein: "She had her brain trust nearly two years before the term was coined in America; she tackled the necessary deflation with greater courage, skill, and rough justice than did any other country, and reached a realistic currency and credit policy more quickly than did most lands." [39]

By the middle of the 1930's, despite a few setbacks brought on

36. X.Y.Z., "Australia Re-discovered," *National Review*, C (1933), 511–12. Another commentator, Kenneth Henderson, reported in 1932 that "Australians seem to have behaved as an intelligent people whose social and political ideas were sharply denied and shocked to the core by the facts of the sudden crisis." "Australian Characteristics," *Contemporary Review*, CLXII (1932), 59.

37. G. Ellis, "Australia—Prospect and Retrospect," *Nineteenth Century*, CXV (1934), 499; also J. D. L. Hood, "The Australian Elections," *ibid.*, CXVI (1934), 239–46; and H. Campbell Jones, "Australia's Recovery," *Fortnightly Review*, CXXXIV (1933), 567–75.

38. R. G. Hawtrey, "Australian Policy in the Depression," *Economic Record*, X (1934), 1.

39. Herbert Heaton, *The British Way to Recovery: Plans and Policies in Great Britain, Australia, and Canada* (Minneapolis, 1934), p. 144. Another account published in the United States was David M. Dow, *Australia Advances* (New York and London, 1938), esp. Chaps. 5 and 6.

by such incidents as the repudiation threats of Premier Lang in New South Wales, Australia had lost almost completely her former image as an economic heretic. By radicals and conservatives, and even by historians, she was viewed as an honored pioneer of social reform now settled into responsible maturity. By economists she was seen enviously as the land where "the plans of the Economic Men have been put into practice." [40] When a volume in 1937 described recent events in Australia, the reviewer for the *Economic Journal* commented: "Readers of the *Economic Journal* will be gratified by the important part played by economists, which should be a lesson to us all." [41] A prominent Indian economist, B. P. Adarkar, was almost lyrical in his comments. He said:

> The most attractive feature of Australian public life that strikes an outside observer is the thoroughly scientific spirit in which social problems are being approached and dealt with and the unity of purpose with which Governments and experts have been working together with a view to their solution. For this reason, Australia is rightly called the Utopia of practical economists, and is in direct contrast with many countries in the modern world, where the mere economist is derided as a man who cannot make up his mind about anything, and the "expert" has almost become a joke in high political circles. The Commonwealth has been the pioneer in the rationalization of economic life in many fields, in wage fixation, in tariff-making, in monetary management, and lastly, in Federal finance; and its experience has no doubt been extremely useful to statesmen and students in many lands.[42]

The economic historian C. R. Fay expressed the new viewpoint succinctly when he congratulated the authors of a study of Australian land policy in 1939 for their "good fortune to live in a country where economists occasionally are heeded." [43]

But for this marked change of reputation there would surely have been noticeable stirrings in the honoree's tomb when Doug-

40. A. F. W. Plumptre, review of *Australia in the World Crisis, 1929–1933*, by Douglas Copland, *Economic Journal*, XLV (1935), 131–33. There were still exceptions to the plaudits, for example, Paul Staal, *A Foreigner Looks at Australia* (London, 1936).

41. R. L. Hall, review of *Economic Planning in Australia, 1929–36*, by W. R. Maclaurin, *Economic Journal*, XLVIII (1938), 119–21.

42. B. P. Adarkar, "Federal Finance in Australia," *Economic Record*, XII (1937), 1.

43. C. R. Fay, in *Economic Journal*, IL (1939), 767.

las Copland, the Australian economist par excellence, delivered the Marshall Lectures at Cambridge University in 1933.[44]

Caution and Respect

By the middle of the 1930's the improved reputation of the Australian economy had two discernible effects. First, domestic writers on the economy became more self-confident in correcting foreigners who discussed Australia without sufficient care or information.[45] Toward the end of the decade they became impatient even with the laudatory clichés about their performance in the depression. An Australian reviewer of an American work in which the customary tributes were paid to that "group of economists who miraculously spoke with one voice and were listened to" remarked: "Australia's recovery was not quite the neat and ordered thing that Mr. Maclaurin and other economic writers have pictured it to be."[46]

The second and related effect of Australia's improved reputation was that commentators from abroad became more cautious in their remarks. The single strand of criticism which remained untouched was that against the slow rate of population growth. The judicious tone of a volume of interpretive essays about the Australian economy by a group of expatriates and former residents published in 1939 may be contrasted with the characteristically scathing attacks of their predecessors forty-five years before.[47]

After World War II, only occasional faint refrains were heard of earlier British declamations against the Australian economy. Occasionally a visitor such as the historian Arnold Toynbee would express wonderment at the empty north, but outsiders seldom any longer preached the necessity of closer settlement with the confidence of old.[48] At least partly in the old tradition Professor James

44. Published as *Australia in the World Crisis, 1929–1933* (London, 1934).

45. E.g., George Berrie, "The Case for Australia," *Contemporary Review,* CL (1936), 333–40.

46. Hugh Adam, "Review of *Economic Planning in Australia, 1929–36,* by W. R. Maclaurin," *Economic Record,* XIII (1937), 278–79.

47. J. C. G. Kevin, ed., *Some Australians Take Stock* (London, 1939); and Sydney Upton, *Australia's Empty Spaces* (London, 1938).

48. Arnold J. Toynbee, *East to West: A Journey Round the World* (New York, 1958), pp. 31–34. A volume of "letters home" from two British academic em-

Meade in 1956 recommended what would have amounted to fundamental social reconstruction as a solution to a current balance-of-payments problem. He called for, among other things, "a monetary and budgetary disinflationary policy . . . settlement of wage problems . . . to the rate at which the productivity of Australian labour is rising . . . some fiscal arrangements for obtaining desired effects upon the distribution of income without having to rely on import restrictions as the only practicable method of affecting the incomes of rich landowners." [49] Professor W. B. Reddaway, who had lived in Australia in the 1930's, was more cautious in his comments on the Australian economy in the Giblin Memorial Lecture in 1965.[50] He was careful also in his review of the Vernon Report in 1966 to confine himself largely to questions which Australians should ask themselves rather than to restatements of "all-too-familiar half-baked ideas which they may have had to debunk many times." [51]

A bibliography of articles on the Australian economy published outside Australia over the period 1946–1962 confirms the impression that British writers, whether from timidity or lack of interest, paid relatively little attention to the Australian economy in the years after World War II.[52] A high proportion of the articles were by Australian professional economists explaining the workings of their economy to readers abroad. Douglas Copland is still prominently represented, with twelve entries in such diverse journals as the *Banker, Lloyd's Bank Review, International Labour Review, Economics and Commerce, Canadian Journal of Economics and Political Science, India Quarterly, Oxford Economic Papers,* and

---

igrants in 1963 had a tone of unpatronizing enthusiasm almost never heard in earlier years. Elizabeth and Derek Tribe, *Postmark Australia, the Land and Its People Through English Eyes* (Melbourne, 1963).

49. James Meade, "The Price Mechanism and the Australian Balance of Payments," *Economic Record,* XXXII (1956), 255–56. See also J. E. Meade and E. A. A. Russell, "Wage Rates, the Cost of Living, and the Balance of Payments," *Economic Record,* XXXIII (1957), 23–28.

50. W. B. Reddaway, "The Australian Economy, 1937 and 1965," *Economic Record,* XLI (1965), 523–38.

51. W. B. Reddaway, "An English Economist's View," *Economic Record,* XLII (1966), 13–26.

52. Alicia Murdoch, "Bibliography of Selected Periodical Articles on Australian Economic Subjects Published in English Outside Australia, 1946–62," *Economic Record,* LX (1964), 200–213.

Economia Internazionale. He is surpassed in number of contributions only by J. O. N. Perkins, an Australian academic economist, with twenty-one entries. The articles by non-Australians are principally on highly specialized topics and comparative in focus.

The unmistakable impression one receives from a survey of the postwar economic literature is that despite continued investment and emigration, Britain had lost much of its curiosity about Australia. Businessmen still required commercial data, and prominent economists would occasionally visit the country and offer their reflections, but the old urgent fascination with distinctive Australian institutions and policies had disappeared.[53] Britain's decision to enter the Common Market and her reduction of military commitments east of Suez were manifestations of the conviction that her future lay in Europe rather than with the Empire or Asia. Warm and friendly feelings continued to be held for Australia, but these were far different from the nineteenth-century notions of imperial responsibility and economic complementarity. An added note was the growing suspicion in Britain that Australia was developing a close economic relationship with Japan similar to that which had grown up between Canada and the United States. Postwar trade statistics confirmed the impression that Britain's links with Australia, in relative terms at least, were diminishing ones.

At the level of academic inquiry, interest in Australia also declined after the war. A widespread impression grew from the 1930's onward that in the main all of the dominions were not appreciably more or less developed socially and economically than Britain herself, and therefore they no longer had any special grounds for fascination. Different factor endowments the dominions did have, but their wartime economic practices and postwar policies were similar in general form, if not in every detail, to Britain's own. One senses that the question might have been asked of persons setting out to study Australia in the 1950's and 1960's, "Why spend your time on their central banking, or their farm sup-

53. A discussion of general works on Australian society in the 1960's—esp. Craig McGregor, *Profile of Australia* (London, 1966), J. D. Pringle, *Australian Accent* (London, 1958), and D. Horne, *The Lucky Country* (Ringwood, 1964)—is R. W. Connell, "Images of Australia," *Quadrant*, XII (1968), 9–19.

port problems, when our own are similar and more pressing? And anyway, the Australians now have their own economists!"

Another consideration in the decline in academic interest in Australia was that other countries of the world, in contrast, grew rapidly in interest. The planned economies of the Soviet Union, China, and Eastern Europe provided exciting novelties. The old colonies of Asia and Africa were found to be "underdeveloped" and therefore, presumably, still capable of benefiting from the wisdom of those who had achieved development. Even the United States had new glamour for Britain after the war because of its impressive economic performance. It is indicative, perhaps, that in postwar Britain no centers of social and economic research on old dominions grew up which were comparable to those on Eastern Europe, America, and the Third World.

Some Concluding Observations

This study may suggest certain tentative generalizations about the process whereby one country develops an understanding of another's economy. One rather obvious conclusion is that the amount of attention paid by any interested country is affected by its perception of its need to know about the other. When the observer country believes that its own destiny is closely linked with that of the observed, economically, politically, or culturally, it will bring to bear its analytical forces with exceptional energy and acumen. Moreover, a change in the methods of determining self-interest may be as important as a change in real circumstances in altering the perception of this relationship. In the Australian case the most obvious reasons for self-interest—ties of blood, trade, and investment—were supplemented at different times by anxiety about economic heresy and by the hope of discerning social prophecy in the circumstances of this new land. A decline in British perception of Australia's significance to its own future early in the twentieth century coincided with development of a more relaxed attitude toward that country's development.

A third generalization concerns the power of social theory in affecting international images. Not even the most sophisticated and experienced observers can look at other countries without ordering the material they examine in terms of familiar theoretical structures. They are led naturally to make judgments based on models of performance developed more often than not for the land in which they live. Specific explanatory constructs exist in any advanced country for such aspects of the economy as banking, international trade, and the role of government; as a result, observers have seldom to leave open the question of just what these institutions and policies should be in another country. A most persuasive general paradigm which has been imbedded in Western social thought over the last two centuries pictures a steady upward path of national development. This has several variants, but all have had in common the principle of "progress," meaning expansion of economic aggregates. The single-track, unidirectional development model has the virtue of being consistent with Western political and religious philosophy and, therefore, personally satisfying to many users; it is also simple to comprehend. The model postulates the existence of certain basic driving forces in an economy—the acquisitive motive, voluntary capital accumulation, educational and technological improvement, and population growth; in a healthy economy these forces are thought to keep a nation in forward motion. The model also has a relatively simple standard of achievement in the volume of production of goods and services, which is believed to represent aggregate want satisfaction of the citizens. One of the distinguishing features of the model is that it enables users of it to assign all countries places along the upward track, according to one of several criteria: per capita income, type of production, or stage of institutional development. It also provides a normative standard by which a social and economic system may be judged. That system is good which keeps a nation moving swiftly along the upward track.

Australia during her early years was usually pronounced to be at an early development stage and therefore expected to stick to grazing, farming, and mining. Later in the nineteenth century, ideas changed when it seemed that because of the discovery of gold, rapid urbanization, and an extended franchise, Australia had moved quickly ahead of Britain and now deserved study as a source of prophecy concerning the effects of "advanced" legislation and institutions. In the twentieth century, a contributing factor to the decline of British interest was the belief that Britain had again overtaken Australia on the upward path and that the two were more nearly comparable in development.

One of the most insidious features of the evolution of this simplistic development model is that, paradoxically, it was at the same time based on static theory and supported by appeals to economic history. One conclusion drawn from static market analysis was that optimum economic activity could be achieved with a given body of resources through maintenance of such institutions and policies as free trade, homestead agriculture, and political integration. This conclusion was easily transformed into a prescription for growth. To strengthen the model it was observed at an empirical level that in countries such as the United States and Great Britain adoption of these several policies had been coincident with periods of rapid economic growth. Despite the post hoc ergo propter hoc fallacy involved, these specific cases were taken as adequate proof that in general, "liberal" policies were essential to "natural" upward development. Special political or administrative conditions of other cases were swept away or overlooked, before the persuasiveness of the general model. The ease of using biological analogies to strengthen this economic reasoning only magnified the power of the doctrine.

Such was the fate of Australia's image during much of its history: a hostage to preconceptions about economic growth and paths to achieve it. Powerful minds may, it is true, question inadequate theories and images and eventually reject them for new ones. But such revolutionaries come seldom on the scene, and Australia's wait for improvement was almost a century in length.

A crucial determinant of any British observer's perception and judgment of the Australian economy was his conception not only of how the growth process should proceed but also of what the relationship should be between economic activity and development of a new nation-state. For example, if an observer thought of Australia merely as an external appendage of Great Britain with the single purpose of satisfying British needs, then considerations of Australian growth as a distinct nation simply were not relevant. By this standard the Australian economy performed well when it produced raw materials at minimum cost and absorbed to the largest extent possible British manufactured goods, surplus capital, and redundant population. Even for those British observers who did regard development of a distinct Australian nationality as important in some degree, a tendency to deny any relationship between economic activity and political growth affected their conclusions. The Australian economy was judged by these persons according to its capacity to produce goods and services in maximum quantity at minimum cost, or for its capacity to support markets with the fewest possible restrictions on freedom of action. These observers seldom conceded the possibility that an economic sacrifice in a strict market sense, in the form of a tariff, a program of non-remunerative public works, or a system of wage arbitration, might be worthwhile in a wider political sense for its contribution to social growth or tranquillity. Nor did they appreciate that delays in achieving such "economically desirable" goals as colonial federation might have legitimate explanations in the social and political realm.

In their segregation of matters economic from the wider social context, the British observers examined here had much in common with economists before and since. They reflected the continuing attraction to social scientists of relatively clear and measurable criteria over and above more vague and ill-defined collective social goals, despite the fact that such collective goals may be among the declared and demonstrated objectives of the people they study.

Stated in simple terms, British perception of the Australian economy depended on three interrelated elements: acquisition of data, tools of analysis (which to some extent determined selection of the data itself), and the assumptions which underlay and directed the analysis. The perception was not a clear image projected by the one country and observed and absorbed more or less well by persons in the other. Rather, it must be pictured as the observation of an object by viewers with light coming through a selection of filters which change, move, and vary over time in color, intensity, and shade. An objective of this book has been to gain some understanding of these filters and their evolution.

No attempt has been made in this study to weigh the effects of British attitudes upon flows of trade, people, or investment to Australia. Such a task would be difficult at best. Nevertheless, it is hard to believe that these effects were not appreciable, and that the importance for the nation of foreign attitude formation was not substantial. If this can be assumed, the individuals and institutions which helped to transmit and order information about Australia, and thereby to form foreign attitudes, take on a new significance in Australian history. For example, it may be fair to regard William Pember Reeves, Douglas Copland, and the *Economic Record* as national assets which yielded external economies to their homeland in excess of the returns that accrued to them individually. Similarly, critics such as Fortescue and Fairfield may have imposed important costs on the new nation. In the twentieth-century world of many large and powerful nations examining and attempting to understand smaller and newer ones, the sobering British-Australian experience gives food for thought.

Index